the Other Child Grows Up

Other books by the author:

From Vinland to Mars
The Voyages of Apollo
The Nuclear Power Rebellion
Appointment on the Moon
A Continent for Science
The Other Child

Other Child the

Grows Up

A Moving Account of the Battle and
Triumph over Learning Disabilities

RICHARD S. LEWIS

Times
BOOKS

Library of Congress Cataloging in Publication Data

Lewis, Richard S 1916–
  The other child grows up.

  Continues the author's The other child.
  Includes bibliographical references and index.
  1. Brain-damaged children.   2. Learning disabilities.
3. Brain-damaged children—Education.   I. Title.
RJ496.B7L47 1977   618.9′28′5884   77–79032
ISBN 0–8129–0700–0

In Memory of
ALFRED A. and **MARIE STRAUSS**

CONTENTS

PREFACE   ix

PART ONE: FROM IDIOCY TO LEARNING DISABILITY

1   From Restoration to Rejection: The Nineteenth
    Century   3
2   The Endless Controversy: Heredity vs.
    Environment   32
3   The Brain-Injury Syndrome: The Search for Cause   59
4   The Disabilities Syndrome: Diagnosis by Effect   83

PART TWO: THE YOUNG ADULTS

5   The Alumni: The Cove School Study   113
6   Reunion: The Joliet Report   144
7   An EMH Follow-up: Outcome of a High School
    Program   172

PART THREE: EMANCIPATION

8   Normalization: The De-Institutionalization Trend   195

 9   Mainstreaming: The New Integration   221
10   The Learning-Disabilities Movement   240

                    NOTES   257

                    INDEX   265

PREFACE

In 1951, I wrote a book for parents and laymen about the learning and behavior problems of brain injured children. It was done in collaboration with Laura Lehtinen Rogan, Ph.D., a psychologist, and the late Alfred A. Strauss, M.D., a psychiatrist.

We called the book *The Other Child*. The title referred to a certain "otherness" exhibited by many brain-injured children as a result of neurological dysfunction; an otherness in behavior and in responding to the world that set them apart from the normal child.

In 1951, the concept of brain injury was new in special education. It introduced a neurophysiological approach in dealing with specific learning disabilities.

It offered an explanation of why some children of normal or near normal intelligence could not learn in a conventional classroom. It suggested that such children could make academic progress at a rate consistent with their growth after receiving their primary education in a highly specialized teaching environment. This was one that identified their learning disabilities, devised methods for overcoming them and enabled the handicapped children literally to learn how to learn.

Revised and enlarged in 1960, *The Other Child* has served as a handbook for parents for many years. In the meantime, the generation of children whose problems it described has grown into adult-hood.

As the sequel to *The Other Child*, this book, *The Other Child Grows Up*, tells how some of these children have fared.

Twenty-five years ago, we addressed rather cautiously the question most frequently raised by parents:

What will become of my child?

We ventured a prognosis: Given a program of special teaching that understood and treated his learning disabilities, we said the Other Child could mature as an independent, capable adult.

In most instances, this prognosis has been fulfilled. I believe that it can now be made with confidence.

As I assembled the material for this report, it occurred to me that it would be more meaningful to parents if it were presented in the context of social history. Mental deficiency is as old as human society, but effective efforts to deal with it are relatively recent.

I think it is important for parents to realize that the great advances are recent; that the present climate of optimism has been brought about not only by the advances in treatment but by parents' insistence that they be implemented in the schools. This climate has not long been with us. It has followed more than a century of pessimism and inertia, during which children we consider educable were relegated to the social scrap heap.

Positive attitudes toward correcting learning disabilities in children have prevailed for hardly a generation. The term "learning disabilities" was not adopted until 1963. A quarter of a century ago, when *The Other Child* was first published, the learning-disabled child was treated as "retarded." Specific disabilities often went unheeded. The idea that his problems expressed specific elements of neuromental dysfunction resulting from trauma or infection was not widely accepted; nor was the belief that his problems could be treated successfully in a special environment.

The clinical identification of the brain-injury syndrome and the recognition of neuromental dysfunction as causes of learning disabilities have revolutionized special education. They have led to treatment methods that enable the handicapped to acquire an education and live normal adult lives.

During the early years of this process, several hundred children in

Northern Illinois who were diagnosed, medically, as brain-injured received public and private programs of specialized teaching. The results, as shown by the adult achievements of this group, are impressive. They form the basis of this report.

In America today, there are some two million learning-disabled children. Public education is only beginning to provide adequate programs for them. Some of the best programs are in school districts where parents have been most demanding.

If there is lingering skepticism about the efficacy of treatment for learning disabilities, I hope this report will help resolve it.

What it says is that the Other Child need not remain "Other."

PART I

FROM IDIOCY TO
LEARNING DISABILITY

Chapter 1

From Restoration to Rejection:
The Nineteenth Century

The idea that the abilities of mentally handicapped children can be improved by special education and training is a product of social and intellectual revolutions in the eighteenth century. It is essentially a concomitant of the libertarian, egalitarian philosophy that motivated that period—the Age of Enlightenment.

During the Middle Ages and the Renaissance, severely retarded persons might find refuge in monasteries or convents that would take them in. In feudal society there was room for the moderately or minimally retarded in an illiterate peasantry, provided they were able-bodied. And in that milieu, most of the learning disabilities that can so seriously handicap a child today would hardly show.

The first scientific attempt to train a grossly mentally deficient child was made by an eighteenth century French psychologist, Jean Itard, in 1798. Itard was well known as a teacher of the deaf. One day, officials of the Department of Aveyron in south central France consulted him about a boy who had been found living in a cave in the wilds of the Auverne highlands, a mountainous region. Hunters discovered the boy crawling and scuttling about like an animal and captured him. He had no speech and although he could hear perfectly

3

well, he did not understand anything spoken to him. Like the legendary twins, Romulus and Remus, he had been reared by or among wolves. His behavior was not human; it was more akin to that of a wild animal.

Itard examined the boy with interest. Although the boy's chronological age was estimated at ten, he had the size and weight of a six-year-old. His origin was never determined. Could special training in human society restore his humanity and give him the power of speech? Itard believed it could and he began to train the boy whom he named Victor. Otherwise, the scrawny, feral creature became known as the "Wild Boy of Aveyron."

In trying to teach Victor speech, Itard applied methods that worked with deaf patients, but speech did not develop. Was early socialization the condition for its development? Had Victor been found too late? Or did the boy suffer from a defect called "aphasia," which is lack of or loss of language?

After five years of work with Victor, Itard believed that the experiment had failed. The boy had learned the rudiments of human behavior but he had not learned to speak or to understand anything said to him. Although the experiment had not come out as Itard had hoped, it is the consensus of modern educators and psychologists that the French teacher had scored a breakthrough of historic importance. He had laid down the foundations of special education.

Itard's experiment reflected the social philosophy of Jean-Jacques Rousseau and the French revolution which promulgated the doctrine of human equality—genetic as well as political—among human beings. The spirit of the time had come to reject the idea of hereditary superiority along with the divine right of kings as a royalist hoax to exploit the common people. From this viewpoint, it was an obligation of society to attempt to rectify the inequality of mental deficiency by training and education. Egalitarian philosophy held that this could be done, for in rejecting the concept of hereditary superiority it also rejected hereditary inferiority—not only in social status but in human potential.

Since Itard, social policy toward mental deficiency has swung back and forth between the poles of positive and negative attitudes toward rehabilitation. Educational services for the handicapped have responded to these attitudes; these states of mind have determined the amount of money public school officials would spend to educate retarded children.

The period of positive action, when it was believed that the mentally deficient could be improved by patient teaching, extended well into the nineteenth century. It was inspired by a belief in the role of environment in determining mentality. After the Civil War in the United States, this optimism faded. Mental deficiency acquired the cast of an hereditary affliction that led to a variety of social evils. The belief spread that intelligence, or the lack of it, was fixed by inheritance; that no amount of education or training could affect it significantly. The result of that negative and pessimistic attitude was the decline of special education for mentally handicapped children and the rise of a policy of shutting them away in state institutions.

In the last thirty years, the wheel has turned. A new conception of the influence of the environment on intelligence has overtaken the older view. Since the 1954 U.S. Supreme Court decision against racial segregation, a new social policy has arisen that holds that special education for the handicapped is a right, not simply a privilege.

In general, the philosophy of education for the retarded has responded to social and political movements; to the climate of public opinion. It has responded also to the demands of parents who have gone to the courts and made new law to help their children. But that battle has only just begun.

SEGUIN AND IDIOCY

The heir to Itard's research was Edouard Seguin (1812–1880) who devised a theory of mental deficiency, which he called "idiocy." Some of these terms may seem offensive to parents. The nomenclature reflects the effort of professional people in the nineteenth century to describe the nature of mental deficiency relative to normality. The term "idiot" originally implied a separateness or uniqueness, resulting from lack of development.

Seguin classified all mental handicaps as idiocy. There were two kinds, superficial and profound. In the superficial idiot, only the peripheral nervous system was thought to be impaired. The brain was intact but was prevented from functioning normally by defective "receptors"—that is, the signals it received from the environment were coming through weak and distorted.

It seemed reasonable, therefore, that brain function could be improved by training sensory organs—eyes, ears, nose—that were thought to be impaired so that correct impressions could be transmitted to the brain. Seguin's work antedates by about a century a modern view of perceptual handicap as a cause of learning and behavior problems.

The second type of idiocy Seguin considered was called "profound." It was the result of damage to the brain substance. Even so, Seguin believed that sensory training could be useful also in improving the victim's prospects for a normal life because it would stimulate repair of the damaged tissue.

At an institution called the Bicêtre Lycée in Paris, Seguin developed a training method that emphasized increased precision in vision and hearing. A similar program was created in Switzerland by a Swiss physician, Henry Guggenbuehl, for training retarded children suffering from cretinism, a condition resulting from thyroid gland pathology.

Both scientists were principally concerned with the external causes of mental deficiency. They did not consider that it was primarily a hereditary condition and consequently were not inhibited by such a stringent view in their efforts to find a cure.

ABOLITION AND EDUCATION

The rise of concern about mentally handicapped children in America paralleled the rise of the abolitionist cause in the first half of the nineteenth century. The whole history of mental retardation in America shows that progress in treating it is tied to social reform.

In 1818, a home for the feeble minded was set up in Hartford, Connecticut. During the 1840s, Dorothea Dix (1802–1887) led a crusade to improve the conditions for the insane and severely retarded in public asylums. From her work there evolved the concept of state hospitals and schools for the retarded. These are now being replaced by the "new" trend toward placement of the handicapped inmates in the communities, a practice that existed from colonial times until it was superseded by the development of large state institutions in the early part of the nineteenth century. There are signs today that the wheel is turning again and the system of community placement will once more yield in some states to a new institution concept.

In Massachusetts, Samuel Gridley Howe (1801–1876) organized an institution for retarded children with the help of his wife, Julia Ward Howe, a dedicated abolitionist. Howe, who had received a medical degree from Harvard College in 1824, was fascinated by the work of Seguin in Paris and invited the French psychologist to America.

Seguin came and stayed. He received his M.D. degree from the University of the City of New York (New York University) in 1861. His son, Edward C. Seguin (1843–1898), became a famous neurologist after receiving his medical degree from Columbia University in 1864.

THE RISE OF INSTITUTIONS

Samuel Gridley Howe maintained that the education and training of the handicapped was a public charge. He developed methods for teaching the blind and the deaf. Three of his blind students who seemed to be mentally handicapped also managed to achieve a general education. In recognition of Howe's work, the Massachusetts legislature allocated $2500 annually for the teaching and training of ten "idiotic children."

This experiment was so successful that the legislature continued its support. It became the first school for retarded children in America. Initially called the Massachusetts School for Idiotic and Feeble Minded Youth, the institution was later renamed the Walter E. Fernald School.

In Pennsylvania, a similar school was started in Germantown in 1853. Its object was "the uniform cultivation of the whole being, physically, mentally, morally." It was built to house 150 persons.

During the second quarter of the nineteenth century, efforts to educate the retarded were carried on with high optimism. Physicians and teachers involved in the new work believed that with proper care and training, retarded children could be made "normal" and then released to take their places in society as competent individuals. The motif of the period was that mental deficiency could be cured.

Institutions that provided education and job training for mentally deficient children were built throughout the northeastern and middle atlantic states. And then, at the outbreak of the Civil War, the optimism that had characterized the early days of the institutional movement began to wane.

After fifteen to twenty years of experience, it had become obvious that mental deficiency was not cured by the institutional programs. Many of the superintendents were physicians and they observed that although the patients flourished physically their mental capabilities did not change. It began to appear that mental deficiency was incurable.

By 1880, the schools for the retarded that had been started with high hopes of rehabilitating their patients had become custodial institutions. Another doctrine began to replace the optimistic one of rehabilitation. It was supposed that the retarded could become self-supporting by learning simple farm tasks. Consequently, institutions were located in farming areas, at some distance from cities and towns. State legislatures and commissions accepted the reasoning that the institutions could be self-financing with inmate farm labor if they had enough land. The rule of thumb was one acre per inmate.[1]*

The farm colonies became baronial in extent. In Massachusetts, the farm colony for adults covered several square miles. In New York, a similar facility was built on a strip of land three miles long and one-half mile wide.

Toward the end of the nineteenth century, the farms were becoming overcrowded, but even so, critics noted that the inmates were being overworked to meet production quotas set by the goal of self-support.

Medical care for the inmates was generally poor and indifferent. Education and training were reduced to the minimum. The diet was

* Notes for each chapter begin on page 257.

inadequate and food was bad. The standard budget set maintenance cost at $1 per capita per week.

In the post Civil War years, the high minded goal of rehabilitation was abandoned. Decades of experience had shown institution administrators that mental deficiency was not curable, although many inmates, particularly young adults, were able to return to their communites where they seemed to be able to manage with the help of family and friends.

Disillusionment with the failure of institutions to cure mental deficiency or at least rehabilitate most of the inmates so they could live independently or at home led to the conviction that the best the institutions could do was to provide custodial care. The transition to that attitude was demonstrated by the first annual report of the Board of Commissioners of Public Charities in 1871 on the Training School for the Idiotic and Feeble Minded children for the State of Pennsylvania:

> . . . the present situation is on a fine elevation in the midst of a farm of about 89 acres, and is all that can be desired of and for such an asylum. [The report characterized the inmates in this way:] Idiots and imbeciles are held to be such from the imperfect physical organization of the races. They are such from infantile disease or other accidental causes. They are legitimate objects for the same public provision and Christian charity which in civilized countries are accorded to the insane in every community. . . . Repelled and misunderstood in public and burdensome at home, they are seen to be happy in the institution provided for them.[2]

Of 501 admissions to the Training School in seventeen years, the report said that 111 were epileptics and 54, malformed. It added that 401 were of "scrofulous diathesis," a label implying that those inmates were products of a "morally contaminating environment."

The social effect of the farm colonies was to isolate the mentally handicapped from normal society. Whatever deviations they exhibited before being placed in the institution were confirmed and intensified by the institutional environment which was essentially an abnormal one.

At the end of the nineteenth century, the predominant mode of dealing with the retarded, especially the severely retarded, was to "put them away" in some institution. This practice became widespread among physicians, educators, psychologists and social case workers. And it persisted well into the first half of this century. In fact, several of the young adults whose life experiences I will summarize later in this book recall with grim amusement that institutionalization was recommended for them in childhood by public school personnel when their parents sought to enroll them. One as it turned out was "institutionalized"—by being drafted into the U.S. Army, from which he was discharged honorably with the rank of specialist fifth grade after his two-year hitch.

In the 1880s, the rationale for segregating the mentally deficient was "protective isolation," which safeguarded the retarded person from the vicissitudes of the community and protected the community from him. Because of new theories that were gaining popularity in Europe, mental deficiency was being linked with criminality and "moral degeneracy."

The humanitarian view of segregating the retarded held that it provided an idyllic environment for them. Dr. Isaac Kerlin of the Elwyn School, a private institution for the retarded in Pennsylvania, described the institutions glowingly as "havens in which all shall live contentedly, because they would no longer be misunderstood nor taxed with distractions beyond their mental and moral capacity."

One Dr. J. M. Murdoch, superintendent of the State Inspection for the Feeble Minded in Western Pennsylvania, elaborated on this theme in a paper he gave to the National Conference on Charities and Corrections in 1906. Referring to the Polk State School, he said: "It will be a haven of rest where the feebleminded may find comfort and happiness, coupled with useful employment, protected from the storms of a thoughtless world, unappreciative of the irresponsibility of these defective ones. . . ."[3]

To which sentimental observation he added:

It requires no prophetic vision to predict that the community will be made vastly better by the removal from its midst of this waste material, this by-product which blocks the way towards a higher civilization.

The isolation of the mentally handicapped not only heightened the sense of their "otherness" from the mainstream of society but gave rise to distorted ideas about them as "social deviants." Not only public attitudes but also professional attitudes toward the handicapped had been reversed by 1890. Instead of a victim in need of understanding and help, the image of the retarded became one of menace that threatened the well being of society. Mentally handicapped and/or disturbed children became the bewildered targets of a brutal social policy that treated them as outcasts, and literally cast them out. Unless they could be sheltered at home or on the family farm where they could remain unnoticed, they were subject to being hustled off to state institutions where their only prospect was deterioration and where they would remain until they died or ran away.

The role of special education in reducing the deviation or "otherness" of the mentally handicapped not only was doubted, but rejected. Mental deficiency was equated with depravity, indolence, criminal behavior. In 1902, A. W. Wilmarth, president of the American Association on Mental Deficiency, questioned whether the state had done "a commendable deed" when it brought out the best there is in the "imbecile" and then released him with "his inherent defects in no way removed to marry and perpetuate his kind."[4]

Another president of the AAMD, Alexander Johnson, who was president also of the National Conference of Charities and Corrections, asserted: "We made a mistake in keeping many children in school too long and taking them farther than they would have any need for."[5]

BLOOD WILL TELL

The vindictive social policy that sprang up at the end of the nineteenth century to hassle, defame, incarcerate, isolate and sterilize the mentally handicapped had, as its scientific rationale, a dogma based on studies of the British aristocracy called eugenics.

The founder of the eugenics movements was an English aristocrat, Francis Galton (1822–1911), a cousin of the great Charles Darwin. Because Galton is largely responsible for the doctrine that has given mentally handicapped children a hard time in western society, we ought to review his background and outlook on life.

Galton was a member of the landed gentry near Birmingham. Members of his family boasted clergymen, physicians, military officers and members of Parliament. He thus matured in the full knowledge that he was kin to a number of people who were part of the British establishment that had built a world empire.

He studied medicine at the Birmingham General Hospital and King's College London, but he did not pursue it. His was a restless mind. He took up mathematics at Trinity College, Cambridge, but he failed to get a degree because of a nervous breakdown.

When he recovered, off he went to the Sudan. It was a period when British gentlemen were building a tradition of derring-do by exploring *their* Earth. Galton explored parts of Southwest Africa in 1850 and 1854. He received a gold medal for it from the Royal Geographical Society. He then pursued the study of physics, experimented with electricity and became enamored of meteorology. His research in storm patterns led to the discovery of anti-cyclones.

At the age of fifty, Galton began to study anthropology. He was intensely influenced by Darwin's theory of evolution and the doctrine of survival of fittest. Galton attempted to link mental characteristics to Darwin's ideas. It was obvious to Galton that the fittest in British society were those who ruled the empire. He became intensely interested in promoting the reproduction of those he considered "fit" and restricting that of those he considered "unfit." The unfit were the poor and the mentally handicapped.

Galton then devoted the remainder of his life to proving that heredity is the touchstone of success and survival in human society. In 1869, he published his views in a book, entitled *Hereditary Genius*, in which he contended that eminence tended to run in certain families. He picked 977 eminent men and studied their families. He found that they had many more prominent relatives than the laws of chance would suggest. Galton believed that the results of the study proved that mental ability was purely the product of biological inheritance. Although he conceded that environment played a role, since it provided opportunities for superior children that superior parents had created for them, Galton's main thesis was that mental superiority is inherited in the same fashion as physical traits.

Cousin Charles Darwin was impressed, as Galton hoped he would be, and confessed in a letter to Galton in 1869 that he had been converted to Galton's views, having previously believed that "excepting fools, men did not differ much in intellect, only in zeal and hard work."[6]

Meanwhile, a Belgian statistician and astronomer named Adolphe Quetelet (1796–1874) had completed a project of measuring the height and chest girth of French and Scottish soldiers. He found that the measurements showed the same distribution and followed the same contour on a graph as did plots of runs of luck at the gaming tables and the spread of small shot around a target. Quetelet's conclusion was that variations in human beings followed the same statistical conventions as other phenomena.

The concept of distribution of characteristics impressed Galton. He believed that psychological characteristics would follow the same curve as Quetelet's physical measurements. In this research, Galton pioneered the application of statistics to psychological measurements and his student and disciple, Karl Pearson, further refined and elaborated the statistical method of assessing human capabilities.

In seeking further evidence for the heritability of mental characteristics, Galton invented a battery of tests which he gave to those who paid a fee at an office in London. The battery included physical measurements as well as tests for reaction time, sensory acuity and ability to solve puzzles. He worked out a rudimentary intelligence scale.

Galton's work refuted the egalitarian approach to mental deficiency. It was a period when egalitarian political ideals had succumbed in France to the Napoleonic era and the renascence of royalty. This was a period also of colonial development in Africa and India by Western Europeans. The concept of "natural superiority" was a concomitant of colonialism. Genius though he seemed to be, Galton was also a creature of his time, his class and the world view of his society.

His watchword was "blood will tell." Intelligence, he reiterated, was inborn. "I object to pretensions of natural equality," he wrote in *Hereditary Genius.*

This outlook permeated psychology and education not only in Europe but in America in the last quarter of the nineteenth century.

The doctrine that mental deficiency was a unitary heritable trait, like blue eyes, brown hair or white skin, became rooted in the educational and also in the scientific establishments of the western world.

The adoption of that doctrine in America and its application to public education and treatment of the retarded betrayed the Jeffersonian ideal of equality on which the Declaration of Independence was based. In one of the early drafts, Jefferson wrote: "We hold these truths to be sacred and undeniable: that all men are created equal and independent; that from equal creation they derive rights inherent and inalienable." The final draft changed the wording but not the content of this declaration.[7]

Yet, the theories of an English aristocrat had a profound impact on the thinking of American educational psychologists. It now appeared to the adherents of Galton's views that all men were not created equal; that some who were less intelligent than most did not have the same rights to education, since they were considered incapable of applying it. Galton's ideas rationalized the perpetuation of a caste system, on the theory that social classes were maintained by inherited capabilities. The idea was as ancient as the practice of dynastic eugenics which dated back to the Pharaohs. Galton and his henchman, Pearson, gave it a pseudoscientific cast.

EUGENICS AND STERILIZATION

At the end of the nineteenth century, it became fashionable among intellectual groups in America to discuss eugenics. It was a simplistic exercise based on the observation that like begets like. Eugenics went a step beyond the Darwinian theory of natural selection; it fostered artificial selection whereby humans could be bred, like cattle, to bring forth the characteristics that eugenicists considered desirable; namely those characteristics attributed to the white Anglo-Saxon Protestant (WASP) establishment. In fact, the American Eugenics Association was the offspring of the American Cattle Breeders Association. Its leaders permeated the higher echelons of science, education and government. Their credo was expressed by Walter E. Fernald (1859–1924), superintendent of the Massachusetts School for the Feeble

Evidences of Race Degeneracy

Increase of Degenerative Diseases - - -
- Cancer
- Insanity
- Diseases of Heart and Blood Vessels
- Diseases of Kidneys
- Most Chronic Diseases
- Diabetes

Increase of Defectives
- Idiots
- Imbeciles
- Morons
- Criminals
- Inebriates
- Paupers

Diminishing Individual Longevity

Diminished Birth Rate

Disappearance, Complete or Partial, of Various Bodily Organs - - -
According to Widersheim there are more than two hundred such changes in the structures of the body

Methods of Race Betterment

Simple and Natural Habits of Life.

Out-of-Door Life Day and Night, Fresh-Air Schools, Playgrounds, Out-of-Door Gymnasiums, etc.

Total Abstinence from the Use of Alcohol and Other Drugs.

Eugenic Marriages.

Medical Certificates before Marriage.

Health Inspection of Schools.

Periodical Medical Examinations.

Vigorous Campaign of Education in Health and Eugenics.

Eugenic Registry.

Sterilization or Isolation of Defectives.

The Race Betterment Movement Aims

To Create a New and Superior Race thru EUTHENICS, or Personal and Public Hygiene and EUGENICS, or Race Hygeine.

A thoroughgoing application of PUBLIC AND PERSONAL HYGIENE will save our nation annually:

1,000,000 premature deaths.

2,000,000 lives rendered perpetually useless by sickness.

200,000 infant lives (two-thirds of the baby crop)

The science of EUGENICS intelligently and universally applied would in a few centuries practically

WIPE OUT

Idiocy   Insanity   Imbecility   Epilepsy

and a score of other hereditary disorders, and create a race of HUMAN THOROUGHBREDS such as the world has never seen.

From the *Official Proceeding of the Second National Conference on Race Betterment*, August 4-8, 1915, Battle Creek, Michigan. Published by the Race Betterment Foundation. (Reprinted from *The IQ Controversy*, Block and Dworkin, eds., New York: Pantheon.)

Minded and lecturer on the mental diseases of children at the Harvard Graduate School of Education, who opined that, "It is certain that the feebleminded constitute one of the great social and economic burdens of modern times."*

In this regard, the policy of the eugenics movement was to forestall procreation by the feebleminded by sterilizing them. In 1897, Michigan considered a sterilization law, but it failed to pass the legislature. By 1900, vasectomies were performed at the Indiana State Reformatory. Inmates at the Elwyn School, a private institution for the mentally deficient, were sterilized at this time with the consent of parents or relatives. Indiana passed the first eugenics sterilization law in 1907. It empowered the state to prevent the "procreation of confirmed criminals, idiots, imbeciles and rapists." The law was challenged and declared unconstitutional by the U.S. Supreme Court in 1921, but the practice spread to other states.

In 1909 the State of Washington enacted a punitive sterilization law which was amended to include mentally retarded persons in 1921. By 1928, sterilization statutes covering the retarded, the psychotic and criminals had been enacted in twenty-three states.

Under the influence of the Human Betterment Foundation, which counted prominent psychologists and educators as leading members, the State of California sterilized 6200 persons, according to Clarence J. Karier, Professor of the History of Education at the University of Illinois.[8] The California law, Karier said, was based on race purity as well as criminality. Those who were morally and sexually depraved could be sterilized.

In 1916, Lewis M. Terman of Stanford University, who standardized for American children the intelligence test invented by Alfred Binet in France, argued that:

> all feebleminded are at least potential criminals. That every feebleminded woman is a potential prostitute would hardly be disputed by anyone. Moral judgment like business judgment, social judgment or any other kind of higher thought process is a function of intelligence.[9]

---

* *Survey of Historical Attitudes Toward Mental Retardation* by the Institute of Research and Development in Mental Retardation, Inc., Harrisburg, Pa. 1975.

THE HERITAGE OF MENDEL

What was known about heredity in the first quarter of the twentieth century was discovered by the orderly research of an Austrian priest, Gregor Johann Mendel (1822–1884).

Mendel, one of the great biologists of the nineteenth century, was the son of Silesian peasants. After entering the priesthood, he studied physics and biology in Vienna and then, returning to a monastery, taught science at Brunn. His hobby was gardening. For ten years, he experimented with strains of garden peas (*Pisum sativum*) in the monastery garden. He had to stop his experiments after becoming an abbot, but it gave him pause to think about what he found. His experiments led him to several conclusions about the mechanics of inheritance and he published them in the *Proceedings of the Natural History Society of Brunn* in 1866.

When two varieties of peas were crossed, all the offspring showed the character of one of them while the character of the other was submerged, he noted. Mendel called the character (color, seed shape) that all the offspring exhibited "dominant" and the submerged character "recessive."

Next, he let the cross-bred or hybrid peas fertilize themselves. In the offspring, the recessive character reappeared, but only in one out of four. If the recessive trait was dwarfism, the hybrids would produce one dwarf to three tall plants.

Then, he mated the recessives—the dwarfs. They produced only true dwarfs. That proved that the recessive gene for dwarfism had not been lost when the dwarf and tall plants were mated, but only submerged in the cross fertilization.

Now Mendel had the dominant tall plants fertilize themselves. Only one-third of them bred true to produce pure tallness in subsequent generations. Two-thirds produced a mix of tall and dwarf plants in the ratio of three to one. When self-fertilized, pure tall or pure dwarf would produce only their kinds. But hybrids with the dominant characteristic—tallness—would produce both because they were genetically mixed. The experiments also showed that each pair of dominant-recessive characteristics were propagated independently from every other pair (the law of independent assortment).

Mendel demonstrated for the first time that the material of inheritance is "particulate" in nature, not fluid as previously supposed. The germ plasm is passed from parent to offspring in the form of discrete particles and not as a uniform mixture. The particles or units of heredity came to be known as genes. Each inherited characteristic of every organism, modern genetics now asserts, is the result of the interaction of all its genes.

At the time of its publication, Mendel's work was barely noticed. He died without receiving the recognition it deserved, for when its importance was later realized, it revolutionized biology and formed the basis of genetic science. This finally came about in 1900 when Mendel's laws were rediscovered independently by the Dutch botanist Hugo deVries (1848–1945) and two other investigators. DeVries went on to develop a theory of gene mutation which provided the mechanism that Darwinian theory had lacked to explain evolution. And Hermann J. Muller at Indiana University then illuminated the mechanics of mutation in experiments with the irradiation of fruit flies. By the end of 1940, findings of Mendel, DeVries and Muller had become incorporated in a new definition of living material. Biological organisms were those that could reproduce themselves, mutate and reproduce the mutation. The descent of man could be explained by mutation and natural selection, the processes which account for the rise and fall of all species on Earth.

Like many another scientific development, the rediscovery of Mendel's work at the turn of the century and its popularization were seized upon enthusiastically to support dubious causes. One of them was eugenics, the technique of animal breeding applied to people.

The popularization of Mendelian Law by eugenicists led the layman to believe that you inherit physical characteristics, such as height, eye color, nose shape, and so forth, from your parents in the same way that you inherit their property. But that is not the way it works. What you inherit from your ancestors, all of them, are genes. Most modern geneticists agree that if your environment corresponds exactly to that of your parents, a particular gene will tend to express the same effect in you as it did in them. But if the environment is different, that particular gene may not express itself in you in the same way as it did in your parents or grandparents.

For example: the fruit fly, *Drosophila*, has a mutation affecting the hind part of the body. It causes an abnormally large abdomen when the fly grows in moist surroundings, but when the mutated fly grows in a dry environment, it appears to be normal. In human beings, goiter, an enlargement of the thyroid gland, used to be prevalent around the Great Lakes, especially in Ohio near Lake Erie. The reason was a deficiency of iodine in the soil. But not everyone born and bred in that neighborhood had goiter and fewer men had it than women. Why? The difference was attributed to different endocrine factors that were genetically determined. With iodine as an additive in salt and other products, goiter has become uncommon even in the "goiter belt."

The environmental impact on gene expression has been investigated extensively. Physical measurements of draftees in the two world wars showed an increase in average height and weight of men from World War I to World War II. Similar increases were observed in a number of ethnic groups in a single generation following immigration to America.

Comparisons of Japanese in Hawaii and their relatives in Japan showed differences in physical measurements between children born in Hawaii and those born and reared in the "old country." The average sitting height of the Hawaiian/Japanese was greater than that of their immigrant parents or immediate kin in Japan. Head size changed. There was a decrease in head length and a compensatory increase in head width in the Hawaiians. Hawaiian-born Japanese also had longer and narrower noses.

The environmental aspect of inheritance was summarized in this way by William C. Boyd, Professor of Immunology at Boston University:

> From all this, it could be clear that, in general, no statement about a genetic difference has any scientific meaning unless it includes or implies a specification of the environment in which the gene difference is to manifest itself.[10]

Although gene expression may be influenced by the environment, the preponderant belief of geneticists now is that the function of the gene remains unchanged unless a mutation occurs. The cause of mutation is only surmised. Muller's work showed that mutation in flies could be induced by exposing them to high energy radiation. There is evidence that x-rays and cosmic rays (nuclear particles) cause mutations by altering the chemical structure of the gene. Consequently, genes are not impervious to environmental impact; if they were, evolution may not have happened, for the rise of new species is the product of gene mutation.

Otherwise, genes are regarded as stable. If they are as stable as most geneticists think they are, it is likely that our genetic endowment is much the same as that of our remote human ancestors, physically and mentally if not behaviorally. From this point of view, the development of civilization by some people and not by others is considered as determined by culture, or environment, rather than by some mysterious increase in intelligence. As I will show later, this is a controversial point and one that has far reaching effects on society's treatment of the mentally handicapped from one period to another.

ENTER THE KALLIKAKS

The eugenics movement that lent a pseudoscientific rationale to the rise of racism, sterilization and discrimination in America about twenty years before it took the form of genocide in Nazi Germany received much of its impetus from the Kallikak legend, one of the most curious pieces of research in the history of psychology.

The research is the product of Henry Herbert Goddard (1866–1957), a psychologist. It made a strong contribution to the image of the mentally handicapped child as an uneducable, social liability. Goddard was the director of research at the Training School for Feeble Minded Girls and Boys at Vineland, New Jersey. As a research psychologist, he had traveled widely and was acquainted with Binet in France. He was by all accounts a considerate, kindly and well meaning man who loved children, but his influence was for decades a major obstruction to the development of special education and training for the mentally handicapped.

The Kallikaks were real people, a fact that is sometimes doubted because of the pseudonym that Goddard conferred on them to protect them from public curiosity. Kallikak is a composite of two Greek words, *kalsos*, meaning attractive, and *kakos*, meaning bad.

The family history began with a Revolutionary War trooper whom Goddard named Martin Kallikak. The young soldier had two sets of progeny.

One set was the issue of a sexual encounter with a feebleminded tavern girl. She bore a feebleminded son, Martin Kallikak, Jr. The diagnosis of the tavern girl was based, of course, on hearsay. Goddard diagnosed all of these people on the strength of economic status, mode of living and general behavior as recalled some generations later by descendants, neighbors and friends. The tell-tale data are all there were to go on; structurally, the tell-tales have no more authenticity than legends, but their impact on psychology and education in the early part of the century was important. The data "confirmed" what the eugenicists had been saying all along: that bad seed yields bad seed.

From the feebleminded son, Martin Kallikak, Jr., descended 480 individuals of whom, Goddard said, there was "conclusive proof" that 143 were feebleminded and 46 normal. The rest were not accounted for. Goddard's "conclusive proof" was still hearsay.

After the Revolution, Martin, Sr., married a girl of "good family." From this union, Goddard was able to trace 496 descendants, "nearly all owners of land or proprietors."[11]

The Kallikak clan lived in an undeveloped region of New Jersey known as the "piney woods" or "piney barrens" near the site of Fort Dix. In fact, the construction of Fort Dix when America entered World War I uprooted many of these people and scattered them into the skid rows and slums of Trenton, Camden and Philadelphia.

When Goddard and his two dedicated women researchers found them in 1900, the families, like most of the inhabitants of the piney woods, were living in cabins, shacks, lean-tos and other makeshift shelters, supporting themselves by occasional truck farming and odd jobs.

The central fact that made Goddard's study possible was that for a century and a quarter, six generations, the descendants of Trooper Kallikak and the tavern girl remained in the same area. They did not disperse as so many others did to seek a better life with the westward expansion of the republic. They remained in place, in primitive, backwoods communities semi-isolated from the surging growth of the new nation around them. There was nothing diagnostically significant about that. Thousands of people remained similarly isolated almost as long in Appalachia and, like the Kallikaks, did not become caught up in the mainstream of American life until it came to them, as Fort Dix did to Kallikak land.

Goddard became aware of the existence of these folk in the fall of 1897 when Deborah Kallikak, age eight, was brought to the Training School. A photograph of Deborah as a young adult which Goddard later published reveals a demure young woman with a ribbon in her dark hair, wearing a long white dress. She is seated holding an open book, but she is looking instead toward the photographer with an expression of serene contentment. There is a small cat lying in her lap.

Young Deborah, it turned out, had an interesting family history. Many of her relatives in the piney woods country were drunkards, thieves, prostitutes, idlers or public charges. The situation was a set up for a scientist who conjectured that feeblemindedness was hereditary. The proof seemed to be living in the piney woods and Goddard went after it.

Even though the clan had stayed put for six generations, the task of tracing descendants and getting some idea about their mental competence was a formidable one. Fortunately for the research, the Kallikaks were notorious people; everybody knew them. Also, it was a long-lived family and there was nothing wrong with their memories. Most of the interviewing of family members and neighbors was done by Goddard's assistant, Elizabeth S. Kite. Her records have been praised for their detail and precision by a number of modern researchers who have studied them.

Little Deborah was born out of wedlock in the county poorhouse. After bearing her, her mother married a man who was not her father, soon became pregnant, and could not keep Deborah.

When she arrived at Vineland, Deborah could wash and dress herself. She knew a few letters of the alphabet, but she could not read nor count, probably because no one had made much effort to teach her. The grandmother was "somewhat" deficient and the grandfather was quite deficient and usually drunk, according to Goddard's account. Goddard said:

Our investigation of Deborah's mother and her grandparents showed that the family had been notorious for the number of defectives and delinquents it had produced. This notoriety made it possible to trace them back for six generations.

Deborah's great-great grandfather was Martin, Jr. In addition to the 143 of Martin's descendants whom Goddard diagnosed as feeble-minded, 36 were illegitimate, 33 were "sexually immoral"—mostly prostitutes—24 were confirmed alcoholics, 3 were epileptics, 3 were criminals, 8 kept houses of ill fame and 82 died in infancy.

Goddard and his assistants charted some of the descendants of Martin, Jr., who had married into other families so that he had records of 1040 persons. Of this larger collection, he said, "we found 262 feebleminded and 197 normal, the remaining 581 being still undetermined."[12]

In 1803, Martin, Jr., also known as "Old Horror," married Rhoda Zabeth, a normal person. They had ten children of whom eight survived. The oldest, Millard, was the direct ancestor of Deborah. He married Althea Haight and they had fifteen children.

Another of Martin, Jr.'s sons, Nathan, also known as "Daddy," fathered six children and lived to the age of ninety-three. One of his children was a horse thief. Three others were married and their offspring were merely regarded as "peculiar." A fifth child died. The sixth, a daughter, was feebleminded and sexually immoral, according to the ancestral gossip that Goddard accepted as telltale evidence. This woman married a feebleminded alcoholic and of her six children, two "at least" were feebleminded, said Goddard.

Martin, Jr.'s fourth child was known as "Old Sal." She was feeble-minded and married a feebleminded man. They had three children. One had a feebleminded grandchild and another had three feeble-minded grandchildren. One of them was Deborah's cousin, also enrolled at the Vineland institution.

The sixth child of Martin, Jr., was known in the piney woods as "Old Moll." Goddard determined that she was feebleminded, epileptic and sexually immoral. She had three illegitimate children who were sent to the poorhouse and later placed with neighboring farmers.

In reviewing this genealogy, Goddard perceived the workings of Mendel's laws of inheritance which had recently been rediscovered and publicized. But his data were too inconclusive to draw firm conclusions that human inheritance was identical with that of Mendel's edible peas. Nevertheless, Goddard perceived a great truth in the Kallikak study. He wrote:

> We have here a family of good, English blood of the middle class, respectable for four generations. Then a scion of this family in an unguarded moment steps aside from the path of rectitude and with the help of a feebleminded girl starts a line of mental defectives that is truly appalling.
>
> After this mistake, he returns to the traditions of his family, marries a woman of his own quality and through her carries on a line of respectability, equal to that of his own ancestors.

Goddard found the Kallikaks a "natural experiment." On the good side, he said:

> we find . . . prominent people in all walks of life and nearly all of the 496 descendants owners of land or proprietors. On the bad side, we find paupers, criminals, prostitutes, drunkards and examples of all forms of social pest with which modern society is burdened. From this we concluded that feeblemindedness is largely responsible for these social sores.

THE INTELLIGENCE TESTERS

During the first decade of the twentieth century, a method of testing intelligence with fair objectivity was developed in France by Alfred Binet and Theodore Simon. It was then imported into the United States by Goddard, who used the test at Vineland, and further developed by two other psychologists, Lewis M. Terman of Stanford University and Robert Yerkes at Harvard, into a national institution.

Binet was a school teacher who sought some way to classify the variation in learning abilities that he perceived in children. He decided to set a standard of normal learning ability on the basis of that exhibited by 65 to 75 percent of all the children he could muster of a particular age. Those who exhibited less learning ability than this group would be considered backward.

In order to establish the standard, Binet and Simon invented fifty-four tests that they believed would show intelligence and gave them to two hundred children ranging in age from three to fifteen years. When he found a test that at least 65 percent of an age group could pass, he adopted it as a standard test for the age group.

If a group of children age seven took a particular test and 65 percent passed it, Binet could classify that test as the standard for a seven-year-old with average abilities.

Binet and Simon did not consider the tests which they finally perfected in 1905 as precise measuring instruments. They thought of the tests as a "scale" that would yield a general picture of the learning capabilities of a child in relation to other children of similar socio-economic background. Nor did they claim that the tests would measure specific abilities. The thought that such a device soon would be used to segregate human beings and discriminate against them by race, class or national origin, as was done in America shortly after World War I, would have horrified the French pedants.

The tests known as the Binet-Simon scale were revised in 1908 and again in 1911, when Binet died. The educators had made it clear, they thought, that the purpose of the test was "to measure the useful effects of adaptation and the value of the difficulties overcome. . . ." That was as close as they chose to get to the abstraction called "intelligence."

According to the social anthropologist Ashley Montagu, Binet "was never for a moment under the illusion that he had succeeded in the task of measuring intelligence in the sense that all too many English and American intelligence testers believed."[13]

Binet and Simon had established the concept of "mental age" in relation to chronological age. But the idea of "intelligence quotient" as a numerical designation of intelligence came later.

The term "mental quotient" was put forth in 1912 by a German psychologist, William Stern. It represented the ratio of mental and chronological ages. If the mental age, as determined by test performance, was ten and the child was ten years old, the mental quotient was 1. Terman advanced this idea by calling the ratio the "intelligence quotient," which was exactly the same thing. "IQ" could be established by dividing the mental age by the chronological age and multiplying by 100 for convenience. If a ten-year-old child could pass only those tests which the average seven-year-old could pass, he was deemed to have a mental age of seven and an IQ of 70. He would thus be considered, in the nomenclature of the period in which testing came into vogue in America, as "feebleminded."

Although IQ has persisted as the principal classification tool in education and in military and civilian occupations, it has been widely criticized and disparaged. One reason has been its chronic misuse to establish elitist, racist and segregationist policies. During the eugenics-sterilization craze between 1907 and 1930, it was used to identify the "unfit." It was also applied to restrict immigration from southern and eastern Europe in the 1920s.

Some critics of the intelligence test agree that it does provide an estimate of certain problem solving abilities that depend on the acquisition of knowledge and are important in the culture in which the test was devised. Knowing English proverbs is of little significance to a reindeer-raising Laplander and knowing about the habits of reindeer does little for the school child in Chicago. The tests are so culture bound that subjects from another culture who are required to take them can be expected to do worse than the natives. Are they less intelligent than the natives? That was the opinion of immigration authorities when testing was applied to screen immigrants in the 1920s.

At Vineland, Goddard used the Binet-Simon scale to set up a mental age classification of feeblemindedness. At Stanford, Terman revised the test in 1916 (Stanford-Binet Intelligence Scale) and this instrument is still in use.

In the Stanford revision, Terman invented questions that were based on a presumed progression of difficulty in the performance of certain tasks. One is expected to assume that the ability to perform them represents probable achievement in ascending the ladder of success in life. He designed the tests to match the order of difficulty he believed one would find in various occupations. The subject could then be classified in terms of occupational potential.

As a consequence, IQ scores on Terman's test reflected social class bias, the education historian Clarence J. Karier observed. The revision was in fact based on social class order. On the 1960 Stanford-Binet revision, Karier said, a six-year-old child is asked which is the prettier of two faces. He is shown a conventional, Nordic, Anglo-

Saxon face, with the straight nose, thin lips, rather narrow head. Then he is shown a caricature suggesting nonwhite facial features—broad nose, thick lips. To be correct, the child must select the Nordic type.[14] If he does not perceive that the caricature is a distortion of a "pretty" face, the child is stupid, in the testing view. What if the child is of Black, Amerindian or oriental extraction and does not share the Nordic idea of an attractive physiognomy? Is he still wrong? The tester would say so.

THE "DUMB" DOUGHBOY

When the United States entered World War I, Terman's test was adapted by the Army to classify recruits and draftees. From the adaptation evolved the famous Army "Alpha" and "Beta" tests and these instruments made it possible to conduct the first mass intelligence test in American history. When the results were eventually interpreted in 1919, the conclusion was hysterical. It gave the average American "doughboy" a mental age of fourteen. Cries of outrage greeted this disclosure.

About two million young Americans were given the Army intelligence tests in the World War I period. The results of the testing program were reviewed for the Army by Yerkes of Harvard. It was he who came up with the conclusion that the data showed an average mental age of fourteen. According to the social definitions of mental age at that time, the average doughboy was a moron.

Social scientists cried havoc. How could democracy work in a population with an average mental age of fourteen? If that was the case, of what possible use was it to improve the education and living standards of the "masses"?

Yerkes' analysis was published by the National Academy of Sciences in 1921. In addition to the general conclusions, the data provided the first large-scale evidence that blacks scored lower than whites and that inductees born in Southern and Eastern European countries scored lower than those of Anglo-Saxon or Nordic stock.

Although it was claimed that the tests made allowances for illiteracy (the Beta Test was given to men who couldn't read) and for those for whom English was a second language, the tests were clearly and rather obviously culturally biased—as was the Army General Classification Test in World War II. Native born, white Americans of a middle class economic background and a high school education or better had an advantage. Indeed, the test seemed to be designed for them.

Despite the cultural bias, the test results were treated as though they were a real measure of something called "general intelligence." And they tended to support the notion that this quantity, general intelligence, was an inherited characteristic that varied by race and national origin; that the variation divided mankind very scientifically into superior and inferior populations.

David Wechsler, a test designer whose scales are widely used, argued that any IQ test presupposes the existence of general intelligence. The whole object of specific tasks set up in the test is to measure "something" that will emerge from the totality of the subject's performance and that "something" is supposed to be general intelligence.[15]

In describing the Stanford-Binet intelligence test of 1916, Terman observed that Mexican and American Indian children did poorly on the tests compared with Anglo-Saxon children. Without considering differences in the environments of the Amerindians and Mexicans, he concluded that "their dullness seems to be racial or at least inherent in the family stocks from which they come. . . ."[16]

This view dovetailed with those of Goddard and Yerkes, who ignored the cultural bias of the tests. Anyone reared outside of an Anglo-Saxon or northern European culture and for whom English was a second language stood a fair chance of scoring in the feeble-minded range.

In 1912, Goddard was asked by the Public Health Service to test arriving European immigrants at Ellis Island. He did so and reported in 1913 that 83 percent of the Jews, 80 percent of the Hungarians, 79 percent of the Italians and 87 percent of the Russians were feeble-minded.

This report stirred up the eugenicists. They expressed the fear that unrestricted immigration was diluting the native American intelligence. The World War I assessment of the average fourteen-year-old mental age of the Army inductees confirmed these fears. According to them, the country was becoming more stupid with every boatload of newcomers from southern and eastern Europe.

Yerkes became a member of the National Research Council, a companion organization of the prestigious National Academy of Sciences. He persuaded the Council to create a Committee on the Scientific Problems of Human Migration.

The Committee granted research funds to one Carl Brigham, Assistant Professor of Psychology at Princeton University, for a study of intelligence in the American population. The results of the study were published by the Princeton University Press in 1923 as *A Study of American Intelligence.*

In it, Brigham tried to show that the wave of Anglo-Saxon and Nordic immigration at the turn of the century had brought to America people whose offspring scored higher on the Army tests than more recent arrivals or their offspring from southern and eastern Europe.

Brigham said that there had been a decline in the intelligence of immigrants from 1895 to 1915. He contended it paralleled the diminution of "Nordic blood" in the immigration stream and the increase in "Alpine and Mediterranean blood." He classified Jews as "Alpine slavs."[17]

Brigham became secretary of the College Entrance Examination Board where he devised the Scholastic Aptitude Test (SAT). This test is still taken by American high school students for college entrance. Later, he became secretary of the American Psychological Association.

Terman, Yerkes, Brigham, Charles B. Davenport, H. H. Laughlin and a host of lesser lights in the testing field projected an establishment view of hereditary, ethnic differences in intelligence, which they based on test experience. The view was influential in persuading Congress to pass the Immigration Control Act of 1924. It discriminated against southern and eastern Europeans by establishing a quota system for newcomers based on the census of 1890. The census reflected a predominantly white population of Anglo-Saxon and North European ancestry.

The testers were also influential in shaping the goals of public education and in selling the testing method of classifying people to government bureaus and to industry. Terman had reached conclusions about the occupational implication of IQ scores. He said that an IQ below 70 rarely allowed a person to do more than unskilled labor; that those in range of 70 to 80 could perform only semi-skilled labor; those from 80 to 100, skilled or clerical work and those who scored from 100 to 115, semi-professional work. Those who scored higher than 115 were the only ones intellectually qualified to enter the professions or become business leaders. The view suggested an occupational caste system based on intelligence tests.

The "scientific" basis of such a system was the theory that (1) IQ measured general intelligence and (2) that general intelligence was inherited and unchanging throughout life. If your father was a peasant, it was not likely that you would be anything else; if he was a banker, you could become one, too. Social stratification was genetically determined in the long run and reflected the thing called "innate intelligence."

As Leon J. Kamin, Professor of Psychology at Princeton University, observed, "the genetic interpretation of socioeconomic class differences in test scores, fostered by Terman, Goddard and Yerkes, could clearly serve to legitimatize the existing social order."[18]

Among the strongest advocates of eugenics control was Charles B. Davenport, a student of Galton, who became director of a fledgling biology experiment station at Cold Springs Harbor, Long Island, in 1904. The station was supported by the Carnegie Institution of Washington. Davenport, according to Karier, applied Mendelian law to human heredity and asserted that mental deficiency and certain aspects of self control were Mendelian traits.[19]

Davenport experimented with animal breeding. He became secretary of the Committee on Eugenics of the American (Cattle) Breeders Association. In that office, he generated interest in the study of human heredity. In 1910, he founded the Eugenics Record Office, which functioned in an analogous way to the Holy Office of the Spanish Inquisition in the sixteenth century by ferreting out deviants. In 1918, the Eugenics Record office was absorbed by the Carnegie Institution. Its influence was enhanced with the appointment of several committees of eminent practitioners. On the Committee on Mental Traits sat Yerkes and Edward L. Thorndike, one of the giants in educational psychology in that period. Alexander Graham Bell was appointed to the Committee on Heredity of Deaf Mutism. The Committee on Heredity of the Feeble Minded included Henry H. Goddard. There was also a Committee on Sterilization.

Through these committees, the Eugenics Record Office operated as a central intelligence agency, self-appointed, in identifying genetic subversives, who were those who carried defective germ plasm (as revealed by intelligence tests). The Unholy Office also put forth propaganda urging the states to enact sterilization laws. Laughlin of the Carnegie Institution was a member of the Committee on Sterilization. He asserted that at least 10 percent of the American population carried "bad seed" and called for sterilization to remove this defect from the national genetic pool. He characterized the "bad seeders" as feebleminded, insane, criminalistic, epileptic, inebriate, diseased, blind, deaf, deformed and dependent, including orphans.

Most Americans were hardly aware of the genetic jingoism of the testing and eugenics establishment, but its influence was pervasive in public education policy. Thousands of children who are now adults were victimized by being shunted aside from the mainstream of public education by school administrators who subscribed to these naive views. The ideology of the eugenics movement in America had its analogue in the racism of the Nazi Party in Germany.

In America, the concepts of race superiority and "pure blood" never became the credo of a major political party, but remained to fester in the backwaters of a small group of self-appointed saviors of American civilization who occupied influential niches in prestigious institutions.

At the root of this movement was a belief in heredity that turned out to be hardly more scientific than witchcraft in the light of later advances in the understanding of genetics and a conception of "general intelligence" based on myth.

What was intelligence? Was it merely the thing that intelligence tests tested? How did intelligence relate to mental abilities? And how were these determined?

After World War I, a rising generation of intellectuals began to challenge the conclusions of the testers and their tools. New evidence came to light, pointing to the role of environment in the determination of mental abilities or, at least, in their expression. With it came the promise of a new deal for mentally handicapped children.

But it was only a promise.

Chapter 2

The Endless Controversy: Heredity vs. Environment

Parents of children with learning difficulties frequently exhibit more concern about the child's performance on intelligence tests than about his performance at home or in the classroom. There is a strong predilection, especially among middle-class parents who are college graduates, to accept the IQ score as the index of the child's performance and ability rather than his actual performance on a day to day basis, which they can observe for themselves.

The IQ score has little value for the parents. Until recently, the testing profession has parried and evaded parents' inquiries about the IQs of their offspring, sometimes on the theory that the layman is likely to misinterpret them. Yet, the results are frequently made available to an array of social agencies and also to prospective employers who tend to regard IQ as a quality specification, like the rating of a piece of electronic equipment.

Some years ago, as a reporter in Chicago, I was assigned to write a series of articles on the Family Court of Cook County, essentially a juvenile court. I heard several hundred cases brought before the harried judges on delinquency petitions. In case after case where the young offender was being considered for probation, the pre-sentence investigation included the school record and IQ score. Irrespective of guilt or innocence, the disclosure of a "low IQ" often influenced the placement of the defendant under supervision or in a correctional center. And those with "high IQ" would be remanded to the custody of parents, foster parents or relatives.

In the tradition of the Goddards, the Davenports, the Termans, mental deficiency was equated with delinquency in the Family Court of Cook County in the 1950s.

Parents have told me that one of the main reasons they were concerned about their child's IQ score was that they believed it was a predictor of his success in life. Could he be a doctor? A lawyer? President? The IQ would tell.

Or would it? Despite their deep concern about IQ, parents rarely ask the important questions: What are the tests supposed to measure? Intelligence? What is that?

Although intelligence testing has been in vogue in Europe and America for more than seventy years and represents the most widely used method of classifying human beings since feudalism, there is no consensus among psychologists, psychometricians, statisticians and other experts about what the tests mean and what intelligence is.

Obviously, the tests indicate a form of academic ability. The Scholastic Aptitude Test, which is plainly designed to predict academic performance in college, is mainly an adult version of the Stanford-Binet Intelligence Scale.

How does academic ability affect success in life? In the days of the National Youth Administration, a survey was conducted by a psychologist at the Pennsylvania State College (now a university) to determine what aspect of college activity contributed most to after-college success. Success was defined as an income of $5000 a year. When all the data were compiled, the activity that contributed most to success turned out to be the R.O.T.C.

Alfred Binet, the inventor of the intelligence scale, believed that all he was measuring was a range of capacities or abilities. His student, the Swiss psychologist Jean Piaget, grappled with the concept of intelligence but never succeeded in pinning it down to a formula.

What Piaget called "cogitative" or verbal intelligence was based on "practical" or sensory-motor intelligence and that depended on acquired habits and associations. Piaget thought that certain hereditary factors were involved in intellectual development, but he did not rule out the effects of environment.

He considered heredity in terms of the physiological structure and function of the nervous system and of the sensory organs—the eyes, ears, nose and the mechanisms of taste, touch and balance. We perceive reality in a selective way, he said. We are sensitive only to certain radiations in the electromagnetic spectrum, but not to all. We cannot see ultraviolet or x-rays. Matter that we can perceive has to be of a certain size; we do not see microbes without a microscope. These limitations have influenced the development of our conceptions of the world around us. Until Anton van Leeuwenhoek (1632–1723), the Dutch lens grinder, assembled his first microscope at Delft and peered at a drop of pond water, no one had ever seen amoeba. Leeuwenhoek might not have identified them as living organisms if they had not been wiggling and swimming around.

Piaget considered intelligence as adaptation. He said:

> Life is a continuous creation of increasingly complex forms and a progressive balancing of these forms with the environment. Intelligence, as an instance of biological adaptation, is essentially an organization and its function is to structure the universe, just as the organism structures its immediate environment.[1]

Piaget wondered at the organism's "anticipatory knowledge" of the external environment, as shown by its reflexes and the responses of the organs connected with them. How did it happen that a creature was born knowing something about the world in which it was to live? Did the environment shape the organism, after all? Or did the organism simply evolve into forms that could survive in particular environments as a result of random, unregulated and chance mutations?

"This biological problem is insoluble at present," said Piaget.[2] He was writing in 1952. The problem is still unsolved—this question of heredity versus environment. The extent to which the environment determines the organism has been debated since antiquity. If intelligence represents an adaptation in man, then environment must have had a great deal to do with its evolution.

The debate, though academic, has a direct bearing on the question of special education. For the position on it that the education establishment takes determines how much help parents of mentally disabled children can expect from public sources.

Piaget noted that the "first solution" to the question of environmental determinism was that of Lamarckism in the eighteenth century. Jean Baptiste Pierre Antoine de Monet, Chevalier de Lamarck (1744–1829), was a French naturalist. He was one of the great intellectuals of the Age of Enlightenment. Despite his aristocratic name, Lamarck died in poverty after going blind at the age of eighty-five. During his eventful life, he became the founder of invertebrate paleontology and devised a pre-Darwinian theory of evolution.

Lamarck promulgated the theory that all life forms have arisen by a continuous process of gradual modification of their structure in response to changes in the environment. His theory was based on the premise that acquired characteristics can be inherited; that new traits that an organism develops to cope with the environment are transmitted to offspring. Thus, the organism is fashioned on the outside by the environment.

Darwin opposed this theory. He believed that organisms changed from within, irrespective of the environment. He held that the changes (mutations) appeared by chance, spontaneously. If the change enabled the organism to cope with a particular environment, it survived, and since mutations breed true its descendants survived. If the change did not aid the organism in adapting to the environment, it died and left no descendants. Darwin called this process "survival of the fittest" and it formed the keystone of his theory of evolution.

In considering the ideas of Lamarck and Darwin, Piaget confessed that the theory of spontaneous mutation seemed to be "impregnable to attack." Yet, it did not cover every case. Piaget cited the example of an aquatic mollusc called *Limnaea stagnolis*. Its form was elongated in European and Asian marshes, but short and globular in the lakes of Sweden and Switzerland. Why? Piaget said that the globular form gave the animal an advantage in withstanding waves and winds in the large lakes. If this mutation had been a spontaneous one that by chance fitted the creature to a windy lake environment, why was it confined there? Why did it not exist in quiet marshes?

"One cannot speak of chance mutations or selections after the event to explain such an adaptation," Piaget said. It seemed logical that organisms do undergo adaptation to the environment and pass it on. From this point of view, Piaget reasoned, the organisms and the environment "form an indissoluble entity."

Besides chance mutations, he concluded, there are "adaptational variations simultaneously involving a structuring of the organism and an action of the environment, the two being inseparable."

Applying this principle to the nature of intelligence, Piaget said, ". . . intelligence finds itself in a network of relations between the organism and the environment . . . it is not at all an independent absolute but it is a relationship between the organism and things. . . ."

STATIC INTELLIGENCE

The heredity versus environment controversy was crucial in defining the nature of intelligence. If intelligence were purely a hereditary trait, it could be considered a fixed quantity; it would remain basically unchanged throughout life. On the other hand, if intelligence were determined to any extent by environment, it could change with the environment. It could be increased by education.

The support of special education has depended on which of these views prevails. From the hereditary determinism viewpoint, the case for protracted special education was vulnerable, because the belief was built into that view that little could be done to abate mental deficiency. Conversely, environmental determinism provided the option of special education for the mentally handicapped and left it up to social policy. Those who espoused it took the position that mental deficiency could be treated through education and environmental stimulation with the result that intelligence could be increased.

So long as a definition of intelligence defied a consensus among the savants, there was no way of resolving the controversy except by observation and experiment.

Effective experiments, however, required a considerable portion of a lifetime. While these, which I will describe shortly, were in progress, the predominant view held that whatever intelligence was— and some people cut the semantic knot by defining it as what intelligence tests test—it was heritable as a single trait and immutable for life.

Those with varying levels of intelligence below normal were labeled, as if each label represented some biological entity or subspecies of man. Binet applied certain terms to characterize below-normal mental ages. They were simply technical terms at first, but soon they became social stigmata.

The older child with a mental age of two was called an "idiot." If he exhibited a mental age of seven, he was called an "imbecile." Those with a mental age above seven but less than average were tagged as "moron."

When the mental quotient was invented by Stern in Germany, the idiot was defined as one who scored below 25 on a scale where 100 was normal. The imbecile exhibited an IQ of from 25 to 50 and the moron, from 50 to 75.

These terms lasted for generations and have become common epithets and insults in every European language. It was not until 1959 that the American Association on Mental Deficiency revised its terminology to label those with IQs below 50 as moderately, severely or profoundly retarded.

During the first half of this century, the belief that mental retardation was an inherited, fixed condition was so general that it scarcely needs documentation. It pervaded public education and gave school boards an excuse to sidetrack special classes for slow learners in periods of tight budgets.

Parents of a retarded child were often advised to keep him at home for a year or two until he was "ready" for the first grade. Elementary school authorities in many communities believed that the retarded child simply was developing at a slower rate. That idea was implicit in the term "retarded." The child was slowed down. If he could not do first grade work at six, he might be able to do it at eight. The possibility that the child's learning disability might yield to therapeutic teaching and that barring him from school increased his handicap was often overlooked.

During the late 1940s and the 1950s, parents of children who exhibited serious learning and behavior problems were advised by school authorities as often as not to place the child in a state institution for the retarded. Later, I will describe two cases in which this recommendation was made to parents who rejected it; one in Indian-apolis, Indiana, and the other in Wilmette, Illinois, on Chicago's North Shore. The subjects of these recommendations are now inde-pendent, self-sufficient and well-adjusted adults living in the Chicago area.

Dumping children with learning problems into state institutions was one way school systems could save costs, and it worked until the institutions became hideously overcrowded and the parents rebelled.

Looking back at that period, it seems obvious that teachers and administrators who believed that public education could not benefit retarded children reflected the predominant view in their profession.

Gunnar Dybwad, Professor of Human Development at Brandeis University, has analyzed the problem of the retarded in that period as part of an evolutionary process. Urbanization, industrialization and specialization as well as competition, he said, conspired to reduce tolerance for the retarded and tended to exclude them from socioeco-nomic activity.[3]

By failing to provide for the special needs of the mentally handi-capped, public education guaranteed that such a child would remain dependent as an adult. What could he do? Industrial society was growing too complex for him to compete for jobs. The conventional public education cop-out of manual training prepared some handi-capped children for employment, but not all. The handicaps that kept the mentally deficient out of the professions also barred them from skilled work and from trades, unless they had special training. Where could they get it?

The idea that the mentally handicapped were displaced persons in an industrial society was regarded as natural law a generation ago; today, it has been shown up as nonsense. Hundreds of specialized, repetitive tasks in industry are ideal for mentally handicapped young adults, as I will show in a later chapter. The handicapped become displaced if the education establishment fails to teach them the mini-mal academic skills that an industrial society requires.

The point here is that in the first part of this century, children classed by tests as retarded were kept that way all too often by a philosophy of public education based largely on a disputable concept of the nature of intelligence.

As I have related, the high hopes of idealists like Samuel Gridley

Howe in the early part of the nineteenth century that the mentally handicapped could be restored to a full life had been dashed by institutional experience in the second half of the century.

Added to this disillusionment, as Dybwad has phrased it, was the "negative impetus" of the eugenics scare during the first two decades of the twentieth century which regarded the mentally handicapped as a menace to the well-being of society.

As a consequence, the overall education field reacted negatively, Dybwad said. "They introduced some terminological sleight-of-hand by setting up supposed philosophical and methodological differences between educability and trainability. Mildly retarded children with IQs above 50 were termed "educable" and those called moderately retarded were classed as "trainable." Dybwad added:

"Many responsible education leaders believed that the training was not a public school responsibility but a welfare job."[4]

Children below the trainable level were considered custodial cases. Under pressure from parents, state after state made the education of trainable children a mandated task of the public school, Dybwad said.

"However, the terminology remained and with it the static view-point toward mental retardation on which it was founded," he added. Moreover, he said, "post-school vocational training centers and workshops adopted this labeling, thereby injecting the label of inedu-cability into adulthood."

Generally, that was the situation in public education that confronted parents in the 1940s and 1950s when they sought to enter children with learning disabilities into public schools. They were lucky if the school had a class for the educable mentally handicapped (if the child tested as educable) and if he could be squeezed into it.

These classes often were segregated and socially stigmatized as "dummy rooms." Even more segregrated, more isolated from the mainstream of education were classes for the trainable mentally handicapped. Trainable programs set a limit on what the child was taught, on the theory that his capacity to learn cut off at a point where higher thought processes were called into play. It was generally assumed that the child who had a "trainable intelligence" could not think in abstract terms nor perform tasks that required reasoning.

The term "retarded" is not so much a label as it is a libel, Dybwad said. It is not so much a clinical designation based on compelling evidence as it is a social status, conferred upon children by the education and testing community.

THE MYTHOLOGY OF IQ

If the mentally slow child should not be called retarded, what should he be called? Why should he be called anything? Why not treat his learning problems as specific disabilities without applying a generic label?

But that is not the way it has been in our public schools. It has been conventional for thirty years to classify children with learning disabilities as "retarded" or "educable" or "trainable" and these labels have been written into school codes, so that they have legal significance.

The labels evoke certain conventions that have been designed to deal in a rote way with the educational problem the child presents. Whether they deal with the individual problems of the child is not a primary consideration; what they deal with is a general syndrome of problems. Consequently, whether they work for the child also is beside the point. They work for the school system by dealing with the administrative problem the handicapped child presents to the system.

The label reflects an IQ number that, in turn, defines a certain level of "intelligence." A number of beliefs about IQ and intelligence tests have been characterized as "myths" by two researchers at Harvard University, Christopher Jencks, Professor of Sociology, and Mary Jo Bane, a research associate at the Harvard Center for Educational Policy Research.[5]

The first myth is that the IQ is the best available method of delineating human intelligence. What kinds of intelligence? the researchers ask. The kinds that schools and psychologists value. But, they argue, the tests are not accurate in measuring the kinds of skills required for success in the adult world.

A second myth they cite is that IQ determines economic status. Not so, they say. Other factors are involved, such as motivation. In fact, they said, people who do well on IQ and achievement tests do not perform much better in most jobs than those whose scores are average. Nor do they earn much more than the average.

More than a hundred studies of the relationship between IQ and performance on jobs show that differences in IQ account for less than 10 percent of the variation in actual job performance. So far as income variation is concerned, IQ explains only 12 percent of it; 88 percent of the variation in income is not related to IQ.

For example, the investigators said, results of the Armed Forces Qualification Test given a group of inductees in 1962 showed that blacks who scored the same as the average white score had earned 32 percent less than the average white. Whites of middle-class parents earn more than whites of working-class parents, but only 25 to 35 percent of the difference is traceable to differences in IQ.

A third myth is that IQ is fully determined by inheritance. The researchers contend that although inheritance may account for 45 percent of the variation in IQ scores, environment is a critical factor in actual learning achievement and test performance.

In this connection, the researchers took into consideration the alleged failure of the so-called compensatory education programs, such as "Head Start," that were designed to boost the school performance of culturally deprived, underprivileged children.* These programs expressed the theory that early environment was a powerful factor in learning acuity.

The Harvard investigators assert that the apparent failure of these programs generally to improve IQ scores does not mean that environment is irrelevant, but simply that the special programs did not succeed in altering the environment and its effect.

A fourth myth is that black and poor white children have low scores because they have inferior genetic endowment. The notion that genetic inequality explains economic inequality is also a myth. Like the divine right of kings, such myths help legitimatize the status quo, but they should not be taken seriously, the Harvard team said.

"One of the many difficulties surrounding IQ tests is that no one really knows what intelligence is," said the popular anthropologist Ashley Montagu.[6]

---

* Early conclusions that Head Start had failed to produce expected results have been challenged by later assessments. See Chapter 7.

He conceded that the tests provide a rough estimate of certain problem solving abilities, but the abilities represent trained capacities. "And therefore, experience and learning enter substantially into their development."

Inasmuch as the ability being tested represents the training of a capacity, Montagu said:

> The measurement of the ability can tell us nothing about the original quality of the capacity.
> The genetic capacity may have been considerably altered by the operation of environmental conditions, both prenatal and post-natal, long before its complex elements have been exposed to the more socially complex conditions of the cultural environment.

STUDIES OF TWINS

Valiant efforts have been made to settle the heredity-environment aspects of intelligence and devise some ratio between them by studies of identical twins reared in different environments. The results do not prove the case one way or the other. They bear a remarkable likeness to the results of the exploration of the Moon which was supposed to settle the question of its origin. After the Apollo program ended in 1972, the data could be applied to conflicting theories with equal force. The twin studies data have been interpreted with similar ambivalence.

Four major studies comparing the IQs of monozygote (MZ) twins (from one egg) who were reared separately have shown clearly that the IQs are similar where the environments are similar.[7] Generally, the twin studies show similarity in IQs, but critics of them contend that none has demonstrated that the environments in which the separated twins were reared were substantially different.

The largest number of twin pairs was studied by an English psychologist, Cyril Burt. The IQ correlation between separated twins was .771, or 77 percent. Among twins reared together, the correlation of IQ was .94, or 94 percent.

In a review of the studies, Leon J. Kamin, Professor of Psychology at Princeton University, noted that twins put out for adoption were placed in foster homes on the basis of the educational level of their mothers.[8]

Montagu cited a study by H. H. Newman, F. N. Freeman and K. J. Holzinger that elaborated on the environmental impact on separated twins.[9] The study, made at the University of Chicago in 1937, involved nineteen pairs of separated identical twins. Ratings of physical, social, educational and economic environments in which they were reared were made by a panel of five judges.

In the majority of cases, the differences in environment were low. The data showed a definite tendency to place each member of a twin pair in a similar social, economic and educational setting.

Of the nineteen pairs, eight had the same number of years of schooling and showed an average IQ difference of 1.45 points. Eleven pairs differed in the amount of schooling by an average of five years. Their average IQ difference was 10.4 points. The largest single difference in education between a pair was fourteen years. Their IQ difference was 24 points.

Since all of these are identical twins, Montagu noted, the differences in score cannot be genetic in origin and are therefore the product of varying educational environments. The investigators concluded that differences in education and social environment produce undeniable difference in intelligence, according to Montagu.[10]

A number of scientists who are not psychologists or geneticists have examined the heredity-environment question in intelligence. One is William B. Shockley, Professor of Physics at Stanford University, a 1956 Nobel laureate in physics (with John Bardeen and Walter H. Brattain) for work in developing semiconductors. Shockley is best known in physics, perhaps, for the invention of the junction transistor.

However, he has aroused a considerable amount of controversy with his theories on racial differences in intelligence, on which he has written extensively. Shockley considers intelligence a heritable quantity and appears to reject the idea that environment has any role in determining it.

Another physical scientist who had investigated the mystery of intelligence is David Layzer, Professor of Astronomy at Harvard University. He takes the opposite view. Layzer contends that the hypothesis of genetic difference in intelligence among ethnic groups is "untestable by existing or foreseeable methods. Hence it should not be regarded as a scientific hypothesis but as a metaphysical speculation."[11]

Although the results of twin studies indicate that genetic factors can play an important role in the development of cognitive skills, said Layzer, none of the studies show that environmental differences between separated twins are representative of those between randomly paired children of the same age.[12]

It seems probable that the interpretation of twin studies varies with the preconceptions or biases of the interpreters. Those who are convinced that intelligence is inherited like brown eyes find that the twin studies confirm it. Their opponents find that twin studies confirm the effects of environment.

The middle-of-the-road view is that intelligence refers to the ability of the individual to adapt successfully to his environment; that heredity accounts for from 40 to 80 percent of it and environment from 20 to 60 percent. The compromise was adopted by Piaget, who perceived genetic and environmental forces as interlocking.

Still another view suggests that intelligence, or adaptive capacity, is inherited in the form of a potential for development; that development occurs only insofar as it is stimulated by the environment. Remember the Wild Boy of Aveyron? He lived outside the pale of human environment as a child and neither intelligence nor language developed in the human way.

There is an increasing weight of evidence that certain traits or abilities atrophy if they are not developed at critical periods in the life of an organism. And development does not occur without stimuli from the environment.

Although now believed to be endogenous, that is, operating from within the organism, biological clocks which regulate metabolic activity in the animal and vegetable kingdoms are linked to the environment in a roughly twenty-four-hour cycle. There are countless other expressions of the environmental connection. It is difficult to see how it can be rejected in accounting for differences in intelligence.

Inadvertently, Francis Galton, the apostle of hereditary genius, set the stage for a demonstration of environmental impact. In a letter to the Swiss botanist Alphonse de Candolle in 1884, Galton stated:

It strikes me that the Jews are specialized for a parasitical existence upon other nations and that there is a need of evidence that they are capable of fulfilling the varied duties of a civilized nation by themselves.[13]

Jews were migrating out of pogrom-ridden Eastern Europe to Britain, Canada and the United States in the nineteenth century. Galton's view of them reflected the prejudice of an aristocracy that was itself an essentially parasitic class. Galton apparently overlooked the career of England's greatest nineteenth century statesman, the Earl of Beaconsfield, Benjamin Disraeli.

The son of a literary critic of Jewish origin, Disraeli founded the Conservative Party in Britain, piloted that nation to world empire and made Queen Victoria Empress of India. Despite the fact that Disraeli's father converted to Christianity, the brilliant prime minister was never allowed to forget his Jewish heritage.

But Galton was generalizing about a whole ethnic group, and not concerned merely with any individual. Galton's student, Karl Pearson, reiterated the concerns of his master about Jews in support of agitation in Parliament to restrict Jewish immigration into the United Kingdom. "This alien Jewish population is somewhat inferior physically and mentally to the native population," Pearson averred.

It was fortunate for the British war effort in 1917 that the Galton-Pearson views did not prevail. The Jewish chemist, Chaim Weizmann, gave England the chemical defenses and weapons it needed to counter Germany's poison gas offensive.

In Israel, the Eastern European Jews whose capacity for statecraft Galton questioned led the development of a powerful, democratic state and it survives against incredible pressure from the encircling Arab world. Several modes of child rearing have been in progress in Israel for a generation. The environmental impact on IQ shows up clearly, according to Jerry Hirsch, Professor of Psychology and Zoology at the University of Illinois, Urbana.[14]

Hirsch cited studies showing that children whose parents came from Europe display an average IQ of 105 when brought up in individual homes. But when raised in a kibbutz, where they experience a group nursery environment in addition to living with parents, the children's IQ average is 115.

Children of Middle Eastern Jewish parents reared at home had an average IQ of 85. But those reared in the kibbutz averaged 115, Hirsch said.

ETHNIC DISCRIMINATION

The idea that intelligence responds to environment is not new, but it was submerged in the period between the world wars by the animal husbandry outlook of the eugenics people. Many of them took the same position in the United States concerning Jews and other immigrants from Eastern and Southern Europe as Galton and Pearson had in England. They and the savants of the testing club served as midwives at the birth of the Immigration Act of 1924, which, in effect, repealed the welcome of Emma Lazarus on the Statue of Liberty.* Under the restrictions of this Act, an Italian by the name of Columbus could have been sent back and another Italian named Enrico Fermi could have been barred from reaching the University of Chicago where he directed the construction of the first atomic pile and opened the atomic age.

One of the great anomalies in the whole history of intelligence testing is the jump in national IQ from World War I to World War II. The average World War II inductee did better on the Army General Classification Test, 1941–1946, than the average World War I inductee did on the Army Alpha Test, 1916–1919. The tests are similar enough so that it is reasonable to conclude that the average World War II "GI" would have scored in the 83 percentile of the World War I doughboys.[15]

The gain was probably due to an increase in average education of the GIs and their greater familiarity with the customs and folkways of the country, as well as with the language. A much larger percentage of the doughboys in World War I were foreign born.

A number of studies show that changes in educational opportunity for isolated groups produced marked IQ increases in a school popula-

---

* From her sonnet, "The New Colossus." Its most famous lines are: "Give me your tired, your poor, your huddled masses yearning to breathe free."

tion. Tennessee mountain children averaged 11 points higher in 1940 than mountain children, many of them from the same families, in 1930. In the intervening decade, there was a considerable improvement in education and economic opportunity, thanks in part to the development of the Tennessee Valley Authority.

WALTER LIPPMANN TACKLES THE TESTERS

The testing movement, with its built-in assumption of genetic determinism of intelligence, has been the tool of ethnic discrimination since it was brought to this country by Goddard in the first decade of this century. It was inevitable that many would challenge its ubiquitous influence. One of the first was the New York journalist Walter Lippmann.

A writer on the *New York World*, Lippmann was repelled by the eugenics propaganda that Eastern and Southern European immigrants were inferior in intelligence to those earlier arrivals from the British Isles, Western Europe and Scandinavia. In a series of articles in the *New Republic* magazine in 1922, he attacked the notion that innate intelligence could be measured by intelligence tests and that it varied with national origin.

One of the sensational disclosures in psychology of that period was the "finding" that the average score on the Army Alpha test indicated a mental age of fourteen. This was construed to mean that the average mental age of Americans was fourteen.

The "finding" was actually a conjecture, based on a comparison of the Alpha Test data with the results of intelligence tests given to a group of California school children in 1913–14 by Lewis M. Terman of Stanford.

Lippmann noted in his first article that all the talk about the fourteen-year-old mental age of Americans was based on the testing of eighty-two school children.

"Their success and failure on the day they happened to be tested," he thundered, "have become embalmed and consecrated as the measure of human intelligence!"

The tester, said Lippmann, starts without a clear idea of what intelligence means. He then invents puzzles that will, according to his best guess, test memory, ingenuity, definition and the rest. By a great deal of fitting, Lippmann continued, he gradually works out a series of problems for each age group which 60 percent of the children pass, 20 percent cannot pass and 20 percent of the children one year younger can also pass.

> By this method, he arrives under the Stanford-Binet system at a conclusion of this sort: 60 percent of the children twelve years old should be able to define three out of five words: pity, revenge, charity, envy and justice. According to Professor Terman's instructions, a child passes if he says pity is to feel sorry for someone, but not if he says "to help someone" or "have mercy." A correct definition of justice is "what you get when you go to court." Another answer, "to be honest," is incorrect.

Lippmann went on to assert that the intelligence test fails to measure whatever intelligence is by any objective standard. He said, "It is an instrument for classifying people in a group according to their success in solving problems that Terman believes reveal intelligence."

Lippmann was critical of the use of the tests to delineate "A," "B," or "C" people on a declining scale of intelligence.

> It is not possible, I think, to imagine a more contemptible proceeding than to confront a child with a set of puzzles and after an hour's monkeying with them proclaim to the child or to his parents that here is a "C" individual . . . there is nothing in these tests to warrant a judgment of this kind.

From Stanford, Terman issued a sardonic reply, entitled "The Great Conspiracy" which the *New Republic* published as rebuttal. With the sarcasm of the professional squelching the amateur, Terman maintained

> that all the intelligence testers have done is show that the average representative of genus homo is not a particularly intelligent animal and that some members of the species are stupider than others; that school prodigies are usually brighter than school laggards; that college professors are more intelligent than janitors and that the

offspring of socially, economically and professionally successful parents have better mental endowment, on the average, than the offspring of janitors, hod carriers and switch tenders.

"These," said Terman sarcastically, "are indeed dangerous doctrines, subversive of American democracy."

High IQs, Terman insisted, are "not to be sneezed at." He said that the difference between an IQ of 150 and an IQ of 50 is the difference between the Phi Beta Kappa college graduate at twenty and the twenty-year-old who can hardly do long division. It was obvious that Lippmann had an emotional complex about IQ testing, Terman added.

"Well, I have," Lippmann admitted:

> I hate the impudence of a claim that in fifty minutes you can judge and classify a human being's predestined fitness in life. . . . I hate the pretentiousness of that claim . . . I hate the sense of superiority it creates and the sense of inferiority which it imposes.

Although this exchange settled nothing, it illuminated the issue of intelligence testing for the first time in the mass media of communication, so that thoughtful people who were not psychologists or educators, but who had children going to school, became aware of it.

INTELLIGENCE AND RACE

The heredity versus environment issue becomes superheated in the context of claims that variations exist in racial intelligence. During the Age of Discovery, Europeans came to believe in their innate superiority to peoples they found living in primitive or barbaric states.

Whether a higher culture is the product of a higher intelligence or vice versa remains an unsettled matter, probably because it is not a scientific question. Since the industrial revolution, a general belief has existed in western society that it is superior because of its scientific and technological accomplishments. Proponents of the notion overlook the fact that, until recently, western society was underdeveloped relative to the richer and more sophisticated cultures of India and China. In the New World, Mayan and Incan cultures were the intellectual equal of Western Europe in the fourteenth century, but were less developed technologically.

When George III of England sent an embassy to the Chinese Emperor, Chien Lung, in 1793 proposing trade, the emperor is reported to have replied with royal condescension:

> You, O king, impelled by your humble desire to partake of the benefits of our civilization, have dispatched a mission respectfully bearing our memorial . . . [but] even if your envoy were able to acquire the rudiments of our civilization you could not possibly transplant our manners and customs to your alien soil.[16]

During the last ice age, when sea level was so low that Siberia and Alaska were connected by the Bering land bridge, Asiatic hunters migrated into the Americas. Their descendants ranged in culture from Eskimos and primitive woodland Indians to the high civilizations of Mexico, Guatemala and Peru. What, indeed, can be said about culture and intelligence?

Although anthropologists, geneticists and most psychologists now agree there is no difference in intellectual capacity among the races of man, there is a persistent contention by a small number of scientists that there is racial variation in intelligence, as measured by intelligence tests.

The principal spokesman for this view is Arthur R. Jensen, Professor of Educational Psychology at the University of California, Berkeley. In the winter of 1969, the Harvard Educational Review published Jensen's thesis in an article entitled, "How Much can We Boost IQ and Scholastic Achievement?" Not much, according to Jensen. The article's opening sentence announced: "Compensatory education has been tried and apparently it has failed." It would not reduce racial differences in certain learning abilities because these were hereditary, he argued. Jensen quoted the influential educator, Edward L. Thorndike, as having stated (circa 1905) that, "In the actual race of life, which is not to get ahead but to get ahead of somebody, the chief determining factor is heredity." Thorndike had been the director of the Division of Psychology of the Institute of

Educational Research of Teachers College, Columbia University. Under his supervision, the division produced a monumental study called *The Measurement of Intelligence* in 1925 under a Carnegie Corporation grant. The study reflected the prevailing attitude in educational psychology of the period in such pronunciamentos as "white pupils gain much more than colored pupils."

Jensen asserted that blacks perform more poorly, on the average, on standard intelligence tests than whites do, on the average. The failure of programs of compensatory education especially aimed at helping black children to remove or reduce the difference proves it is hereditary, he said.*

Jensen argued that since IQ was 80 percent determined by heredity, there was no use trying to even out the racial difference in IQ by costly special programs. The thing to do for black children was to capitalize on the skills for which they were adapted by inheritance. These were not the skills that intelligence tests measured.

Although Jensen's conclusions were not new, they aroused a storm of protest since they challenged not only compensatory education theory which had won federal funding support but also the value of desegregation in the schools. Scientifically, they contradicted a widely accepted premise in human genetics that variation in mental abilities is not racial but individual.

Intellectuals, both black and white, and especially geneticists had a field day tearing apart "Jensenism." Jensen himself, mild mannered, patient and as persistent as a steel spring, was branded a "racist" and his efforts to debate the issue before university audiences were frequently drowned out by the booing, catcalling and stomping of outraged students.

A cogent criticism of Jensen's thesis that blacks exhibit a racial deficit in intelligence compared with whites was written by Richard C. Lewontin, a biologist at Harvard.[17] He charged that Jensen's conclusion was "so clearly at variance with the present (1970) egalitarian consensus and so clearly smacks of racist elitism . . . that a very careful analysis is in order."

First, said Lewontin, Jensen erred by confusing the heritability of a

---

* This conclusion was based on a preliminary evaluation of Head Start which was disputed by later surveys.

genetic character within a population with the heritability of the difference between two populations. There is no evidence one way or
another about the genetics of interracial IQ differences, Lewontin
asserted.

Jensen erred again, Lewontin continued, in the conclusion that
compensatory education failed because of the genetic aspect of IQ.
Such an idea arises from "a misapprehension about the fixity of
genetically determined traits," he said. At one time, it was believed
that genetic disorders were incurable, because they were genetic. He
pointed out that inborn errors of metabolism which arise from genetic
disorders are curable if their biochemistry is understood and if certain
products that are lacking as a result of them can be supplied from the
outside.

Jensen contended there was no reason to believe that the IQs of
environmentally deprived children would rise to the IQ level of privileged children if the environment were enriched. Lewontin disputed
that contention. It was a mistake to argue that if the richest environment we can think of does not raise IQ that we have exhausted the
environmental possibilities, he said.

For example, in the seventeenth century, infant mortality rates at
all socioeconomic levels were many times the present rate at our
lowest economic level. In terms of what was then a normal range of
environments, the infant mortality rate at the top of seventeenth century society would have been regarded as the minimum for the whole
society. But changes in sanitation, public health and disease control
that would have seemed incredible to people of the seventeenth century have reduced the infant mortality rate among the poor in America well below that of the rich in seventeenth century society. Lewontin said:

> The argument that compensatory education is hopeless is equiva-
> lent to saying that changing the form of the seventeenth century
> gutter would not have a pronounced effect on public sanitation.
> What compensatory education will be able to accomplish when the
> study of human behavior finally emerges from its prescientific era
> is anyone's guess.

Although the failure of compensatory programs could be blamed
on their inadequacy, as well as on genetics, such programs cannot

counteract negative attitudes toward education in the student's family and peer group or gang.

Jensen answered Lewontin.[18] He cited a national survey by the U.S. Commission on Civil Rights which concluded that compensatory education programs had failed to produce significant improvement in the measured intelligence or the scholastic performance of "disadvantaged" children.

Jensen then sought to clarify his views, contending that Lewontin had misconstrued them. He listed two categories of mental abilities. One was the capacity for abstract reasoning. He called that one intelligence. The other involved associative learning ability and memory. Jensen said:

> These types of ability appear to be distributed differently in various social classes and racial groups. While large racial and social class differences are found for intelligence, there are practically negligible differences among these groups in their associative learning abilities, such as memory span and serial and paired-associative rote learning.

Other types of abilities remained to be discovered. Jensen said research should be directed toward finding out how the particular strengths of each person's pattern of abilities can be brought to bear on school learning and occupational success.

So far as IQ tests went, Jensen pointed out that these had evolved to predict scholastic performance in largely European and North American middle class populations. They measure abilities relative to the curriculum. The curriculum was shaped by the pattern of abilities of the children the schools were intended to serve, he said.

IQ or abstract reasoning ability, Jensen went on, is just one part of the whole spectrum of human mental abilities. It is the part that intelligence tests measure. It is important to our society, he said, but it is obviously not the only set of educationally or occupationally relevant abilities. There are other mental abilities but they have not been adequately measured. Their distribution in the population has not been determined. Their relevance to education has not been explored.

So far as IQ goes, Jensen said, its heritability is about 80 percent. He explained that this estimate was based on tests given to European and North American people. Consequently, it should not be generalized to other populations. Similar heritability studies should be made of minority populations.

However, he said, in the population that has been measured, it has been shown that IQ differs on the average among children from different social class backgrounds. Some of this is attributable to environment and some to genetic differences among social classes. The genetic differences arise, he maintained, largely from the selection in the parent generations for certain patterns of ability. Selective factors in social mobility and assortive mating have resulted in a genetic component in social class intelligence, he said.

Statements by government officials and bureaus denying the genetic component of intelligence were "without scientific merit," he said. He cited the 1966 credo of the U.S. Office of Education that "the talent pool in any one ethnic group is substantially the same as in any other ethnic group" and the 1965 pronouncement of the U.S. Department of Labor that "intelligence potential is distributed among Negro infants in the same proportion and pattern as among Icelanders or Chinese or any other group." But that is not so, Jensen insisted. Such statements "lack any factual basis and must be regarded only as hypotheses," he said.

Lewontin replied: Despite years of research, there is no agreement on what behavioral function is designated by the term intelligence. But Jensen treats it as if it had the same standing in psychology as "energy" or "mass" has in physics.[19]

The foregoing exchange between Jensen and Lewontin appeared in the magazine *Science and Public Affairs, The Bulletin of the Atomic Scientists.* The editor, Eugene Rabinowitch, a biologist of distinction, could not refrain from adding his own comment. So far as the black and white races are concerned, he said:

it is . . . not very likely that the inheritance of one such trait (intelligence) is correlated with that of some other, unrelated trait, be it body height, skin color, color of the eyes or of the hair, unless we deal with a closed, isolated population. . . . In large populations which have gone through much interbreeding as all major human races have . . . there is little probability of predominant association of two entirely independent characteristics. To explore the IQ of

dark skinned children in comparison with that of light skinned ones
has, it seems to me, as much scientific significance as . . . comparing the IQ of red haired children with that of black haired ones.

In an analysis of general intelligence and heritability, Jerry Hirsch,
Professor of Psychology, and Terry R. McGuire of the Interdiscipli-
nary Program of Genetics at the University of Illinois, Urbana, remarked:

> There are undeniable genetic differences between individuals in
> anatomical, physiological and behavioral traits. The genetic differ-
> ences are important in determining how any individual develops in
> a given environment. Observation of development in one environ-
> ment, however, provides no basis for predicting how the same indi-
> vidual might have developed in a different environment. In fact, it
> does not give 100 percent predictability how a replicate (twin) with
> an identical genotype (the genetic endowment) might develop in
> the same environment.[20]

THE GENETIC JUNGLE

For parents of mentally handicapped children, this argument about
predetermined development is of crucial significance. Obviously
where the education establishment believes that a handicapped child
is predestined, by heredity, to be retarded, nothing much will be
attempted by the school system to enhance his intelligence. Jensen's
argument against the efficacy of compensatory education bears specifically on this point. Educators who believe that Jensen is right are
likely to regard special programs that seek to boost the IQs of mentally handicapped pupils as a waste of time and money. Although
Jensen does not apply his racial theories to mental retardation in
general, the implications of his theory about heredity are plain
enough.
   But there are environmental "fixes" for mental deficiency that
refute, specifically, the concept of hereditary predestination.
   In 1934, a Norwegian physician, Dr. Ivan Folling, discovered a
metabolic disease called phenylketonuria. It is a disturbance of

normal body chemistry that almost always results in severe mental deficiency in an otherwise normal child.

Investigation disclosed that phenylketonuria (PKU) is inherited. In that sense, the retardation it causes could be said to be heritable. The genetic aspect is the transmission of a single recessive gene that prevents a normal biochemical activity—the conversion of the amino acid phenylalanine to tyrosine, another amino acid. The failure to make this conversion causes a buildup of phenylalanine in body fluids. In excess, it is toxic and causes neural and brain cell damage.

It is now routine in maternity wards to examine newborn infants for excess phenylalanine in body fluids. When it is found, PKU can be averted and its retardation effect stopped by keeping the infant on a diet free of phenylalanine.

Another inborn error of metabolism is called "galactosemia." It is caused by the lack of a gene and of the enzyme the gene makes that enables the infant to convert galactose sugar in milk to a usable form.[21] Untreated, galactosemia causes damage to the brain, eyes and liver.

The discovery of genetically transmitted metabolic diseases has raised the question of whether all forms of so-called "familial" (hereditary) retardation are a result of metabolic errors as yet undiscovered. We have just begun to learn that physiological causes of mental deficiency can be passed on from one generation to the next by several metabolic disorders. Others not yet known may be discovered in years to come. The prospect exists that the biochemical basis of all forms of retardation may some day be as familiar to us as in PKU today. By contrast, the older notion—which still persists—that mental deficiency is inherited as a unitary character seems to have no discernible scientific foundation.

With the discovery of the chromosome basis of heredity,* geneticists learned that there must be precisely the right number of chromosomes in the fertilized egg for the production of a normal individual.

Most species, including man, are "diploidal." They have two representatives of each chromosome in the fertilized egg. All cells that grow from the egg are diploidal. There are some organisms that are

* The chromosome is the structure in the cell nucleus that contains the genes. Genes are large molecules of deoxyribonucleic acid (DNA).

"triploidal." They have three representatives of a particular chromosome. They are called "trisomic."

In the human species, a trisomic arrangement is abnormal. In 1959, John Hayden Langdon Down, a British pathologist, identified a trisomic disorder that caused severe retardation and a shortened life span in children. He called it "mongolism" because he thought the infants born with the trisomic abnormality looked mongoloid. It was an unfortunate label, but it stuck.

Down's syndrome, the correct term for mongolism, is one of a group of trisomic diseases. They are believed to be caused by the breakage of chromosomes, often the effect of drug abuse. Broken pieces of the chromosomes reattach themselves, but not in the same way as before. The rearrangement interferes with the normal process of sperm and egg formation. A large proportion of children whose parents have rearranged chromosomes have physical abnormalities and mental retardation.[22]

Cytologists—specialists in cell structure—can identify chromosome rearrangement in normal men and women and advise them that they risk having abnormal children. If this is discovered during early pregnancy, cells can be taken from the amniotic fluid of the embryo and grown in a culture. It is then possible to tell whether the chromosome balance is normal. If it is not, it is likely that the child will be damaged and the pregnancy can be terminated.

These are several known hereditary causes of mental deficiency. To the extent that gene damage or chromosome breakage are produced by agencies outside the organism—high energy radiation or chemical poisons (drugs)—the basic cause is environmental.

Still another cause of mental deficiency is trauma—physical injury to the brain. It is much more common than many parents realize and its effects can be devastating to a child who is developed in the womb with a normal potential and who is then damaged by an accident before birth, during birth or during early life after birth.

What kind of accident? Oxygen deprivation during the critical delivery period can cause brain damage. The use of drugs by the mother or an infection in the mother may cause it. The child may suffer a blow on the head in a game or brain damage in an automobile accident.

There are myriad causes of physical brain damage. In many instances, but not all, it can result in learning handicaps that are similar, but not quite the same, as those exhibited by the child who is said to have familial retardation.

Traumatic dementia, or brain injury, is characterized by a group of behavior and learning problems that form a clinical syndrome. Its existence in children and its implications for their development were not fully realized until after World War I.

The clues that led to the identification of the brain-injury syndrome in children were found in military hospitals in England and Germany. Some of the mystifying behavior and mental difficulties in certain children were also exhibited by soldiers who had been shot through the head and survived.

Chapter 3

The Brain-Injury Syndrome:
The Search for Cause

The most powerful organ in nature is the brain. It is the center of energy transformation in the animal kingdom. Through its unique ability to interpret and organize the stimuli that are transmitted to it by the sensory organs, it can create order in the outside world. It has the power to modify and control nature. It can alter the environment to insure its survival.

Functioning on neuroelectric energy that can be measured only in microwatts, the brain is capable of reproducing by means of technology the energy processes of the sun. Yet, this organ is so delicately constructed and so highly organized that any disruption of its physical structure by inflammation or injury may alter, irrevocably, its manner of functioning and change the behavior of the organism.

Human beings may sustain damage to the heart, lungs, kidneys, spleen or the sensory organs and continue to function much as before. But damage to the brain may change the total capacity of the organism. If it comes early in life, it reduces the inborn potential of mental ability. It may cause severe neuromuscular crippling. It may cause also specific problems in learning and behavior.

Until recent times, brain injury was not commonly diagnosed as the cause of mental deficiency although it was often blamed for "peculiar" behavior. There was a jesting folk wisdom that one who exhibited bizarre behavior must have fallen on his head. In this there was likely to be more truth than metaphor.

Although medicine has been aware since antiquity that the center of thought, sensation and emotion lies in the brain, little was known about the way it worked until the rise of modern medicine.

Whether the brain operated as a unit or whether certain functions were carried on by certain parts of the organ intrigued neurologists of the late eighteenth and nineteenth centuries. Curiously, the invention of a pseudoscience called "phrenology" by a German neurologist, Franz Joseph Gall, popularized the idea that brain activities were localized and could be affected by trauma.

Gall published his views in 1808. He maintained that not only sensory faculties but also behavior characteristics were located in parts of the brain. These sites, he announced, could be identified by bumps on the head. Phrenology spread quickly throughout Europe and America. Gall and his disciples claimed to be able to decipher a person's personality by feeling the head. There were bumps of acquisitiveness, of inquisitiveness, of greed and of generosity. The phrenologists claimed they could identify centers of the brain for overeating, for wit, love of family, patriotism and some aspects of criminal behavior. There was even a bump for politics.

Although few scientists took phrenology seriously, it nevertheless stimulated research in the connection between brain structure and perception and thinking. A milestone in this development was the disclosure of evidence in 1861 that stroke damage to one part of the brain left the victim with severe speech difficulty for the rest of his life.[1]

The evidence was presented by Paul Broca, a surgeon, to the Paris Anthropological Society. Broca exhibited the patient's brain. It had suffered a lesion in the left hemisphere, in the posterior third of the inferior frontal convolution. He found similar damage in the brain of another patient who had also lost most of his speech after a stroke. From this evidence, he concluded that speech was localized in the stroke-damaged part of the brain.

Neurologists found they could produce specific muscle spasms in a dog by electric shock to certain parts of the brain. After the Franco-Prussian War ended in 1871, military surgeons operating on soldiers with head wounds also noted that exciting certain parts of the exposed brain produced specific muscle contractions. It appeared that motor (muscle) functions are localized in the frontal lobes of the brain. Auditory functions seem to be concentrated in the temporal lobes and visual functions in the occipital lobes.[2]

With these findings, neurologists were able to identify a group of signs and symptoms (syndrome) in adults called "traumatic dementia," which means loss of mental functioning as a result of injury or trauma. Young adults, such as soldiers, showed a loss of mental ability after they had suffered damage to the brain following serious concussion, skull fracture, bullet wounds or brain disease.

The enormous casualty list of World War I presented thousands of brain-injured soldiers to challenge the new techniques and understandings of neurosurgery. Many of the wounded had been shot through the head and had survived. German and British neurologists who worked with the wounded in hospitals in England and Germany found that after surgical recovery the soldiers had lost some of the skills and abilities they had before being wounded. They also exhibited conspicuous behavior abnormalities, which parents, wives, relatives and friends said had not existed before.

Two leading research neurologists in the new field of brain damage and its effect, who later came to the United States as refugees from Nazi Germany, were Dr. Alfred A. Strauss and Dr. Kurt Goldstein. Both worked with brain-injured patients in German military hospitals after World War I.

The nervous disorders and abnormal behavior of the soldiers could not be explained by arteriosclerosis or senile changes in the brain, Strauss, who specialized in a neuropsychiatry, wrote years later after settling in Wisconsin.[3]

Here a brain had received at the peak of its development circumscribed destruction of nervous tissue from penetration by a bullet or shell. The disturbed functions of speech could be explained by the old localization theory, but the deviations from normal behavior which appeared regardless of the brain area which was injured could be understood only as damage to the brain or to the organism as a whole.

Goldstein and an English neurologist, Dr. Henry Head, collaborated on their studies of brain-wounded soldiers. Goldstein found that the entire visual field of a person would be recast if even a slight

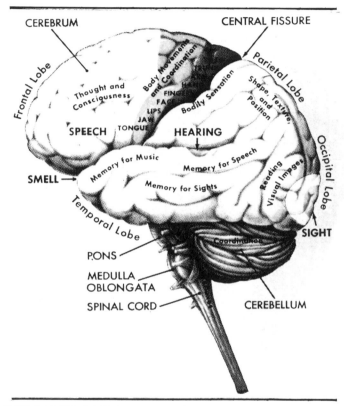

THE PARTS OF THE BRAIN. (Adaptation from *The World Book Encyclopedia,* © 1977 Field Enterprises Educational Corporation, based on diagrams from *Science Problems 3* by Wilbur L. Beauchamp, John C. Mayfield and Joe Young West. ©1957 by Scott, Foresman and Co. Reprinted by permission)

injury was inflicted on the visual area of the brain. The injury forced the brain to adopt another mode of organizing perceptions. Intellectual function was reduced. In fact, the victim's entire level of activity was diminished. He did not attempt as much as he had before. He seemed to lose ambition. He adapted, presumably, to the reduction in functions at a lower energy level.

Even after brain lesions were healed, the patient showed disturbances in general behavior, Goldstein noted. Strauss interpreted them as evidence of a change in the total organization of the individual.[4]

For example: when confronted with a task he could no longer perform, the patient may react with rage, despair, anxiety or extreme depression, with the accompanying body reaction of weeping, Strauss said. Goldstein called this behavior "catastrophic reaction."[5] After such an outburst, he said, the patient becomes unresponsive and fails even in those tasks which he could readily do under other circumstances. The disturbing effect of catastrophic reaction is long enduring, Goldstein said.

This behavior affects interpersonal relationships, Strauss noted.[6] A situation which the normal person would consider as moderately frustrating becomes unendurable for the brain-injured person and may trigger a vehement reaction. If an expected visitor is late in arriving, the patient may become distraught. If the patient has been promised a visit to a movie and the promise cannot be kept, he may become antagonistic toward the person who made the promise. Although this sort of behavior may appear neurotic, Strauss said, the intensity exhibited by the brain-injured person is much greater than the reaction seen in neurosis.

A classic case in the literature of neurology is that of a German infantry soldier referred to as "Schn." He was wounded in the head by shrapnel from a mine explosion June 4, 1916. Following surgery, Schn. was sent to the Hospital for Brain Injury at Frankfurt early in 1917. There, Goldstein and a colleague, Adhemar Gelb, a psychologist, examined him.[7]

Except for headaches, Schn. appeared normal. His intelligence was intact. He had no language disturbance. His visual acuity seemed to be adequate and he was still able to read and write. To all appearances, he had been lucky, but not entirely.

On tests, Schn. exhibited a striking abnormality. He could not identify words and objects when they were flashed briefly on a screen. Nor could he perceive letters or pictures if their contours were partly obscured or if they were crosshatched.

Goldstein and Gelb noticed that Schn. read with slight head, body and hand movements. When prevented from making them, he could not read a word. The physicians then found that Schn. identified words and objects by some conspicuous feature, not by the whole image. A clock was identified by its hands, a pair of dice by dots. If four dots were arranged in a square pattern, he could not "see" the square.

The difficulties exhibited by Schn. revealed a pronounced perceptual handicap which the investigators concluded was the result of brain damage. In normal perception, the individual sees a scene in terms of foreground and background relationships. A figure or objects in the foreground stand out; they can be separated from the background. In a photograph, the foreground figure is the object on which the lens is focused.

Schn. could not distinguish foreground from background. He could not pick out a particular form unless he could relate it to a familiar class of objects by some clue. Without the clue, he often failed to identify the whole object, but would simply stare at disparate parts without being able to see them together.

Goldstein and Gelb concluded that while the patient's visual acuity was adequate, the ability to organize his visual impressions into meaningful forms had been destroyed by the brain lesion. The report on Schn. supported a tenet of Gestalt (form) psychology that the perception of a form is an activity of the brain, in which sensory data from the environment are organized.

After leaving Germany where he had begun his research, Goldstein continued his work on the nature of brain injury in the United States. He was convinced that a major result of brain damage was the loss of "abstract attitude." He defined it as the capacity to assume a mental set voluntarily; to shift from one aspect of a situation to another; to retain simultaneously several aspects of a situation; to break up and isolate the whole into its constituent parts; to abstract common properties, plan ahead and think and behave symbolically.[8]

Both Strauss and Goldstein observed that the brain-injured person deals with elements of experience in a concrete, habitual way, usually the way he has learned in the past. His responses tend to be stereo-typed. His behavior is predictable in the routine aspects of life. The damaged brain, the neurologists concluded, has lost its former flexi-bility. And the person after brain damage was "otherwise" than before the trauma. His "otherness," as Strauss defined the general nature of his behavior, was a conspicuous sign of the brain-injury syndrome.

THE BRAIN-INJURED CHILDREN

Strauss pioneered the application of these findings to techniques of special education. Born in Karlsruhe in 1897, he took a degree as medical doctor in 1922 at the University of Heidelberg. He then specialized in psychiatry and neurology. After five years of training in the specialty, he entered private practice. He was a research associate at the University of Heidelberg Psychiatric Clinic and served as asso-ciate professor of neuropsychiatry there and also as consultant to the Heidelberg school board and the municipal Children's home.

With the rise of Nazism, Strauss and his family left Germany in 1933. He became a visiting professor at the University of Barcelona in Spain. He set up the city's first municipal child guidance clinic and organized a private clinic where he saw patients. In 1937, as a result of turmoil of the civil war in Spain, Strauss and his family emigrated to the United States. He joined the professional staff of the Wayne

Alfred A. Strauss, M.D., 1897–1957

County Training School, an institution for the mentally handicapped, at Northville, Michigan, as resident psychiatrist.

Earlier in his work with brain-injured patients, Strauss had concluded that the condition called "traumatic dementia" also occurred in children and led to mental handicap. Children who exhibited the same symptoms as the brain-injured soldiers and other adults must also have experienced brain injury at some time before, during or after birth.

Like the adults, these children exhibited excessive anger or frustration when confronted with tasks they could not perform. In some respects, their "catastrophic reaction" resembled a normal tantrum, and usually was set off by frustration, but it was much more violent and many of the circumstances that brought it on would not have disturbed the nonbrain-injured child.

Frequently, children exhibiting the brain-injury syndrome were diagnosed as mentally deficient. The schools lumped them with children who were classified as retarded but who did not exhibit brain-injury symptoms. However, in the class for the retarded, the brain-injured child exhibited the same learning difficulties as in the regular class. He was a mystery to the teacher who was unfamiliar with the syndrome. In some cases he appeared bright, eager, alert, but he could not sit still; he could not pay attention; he could not learn.

Although the presence of brain damage may be deduced by experts from the patient's behavior, the syndrome is diagnosed by several techniques. An electroencephalograph that measures brain waves may provide some clues, but its results are not always considered definitive if other symptoms and signs are missing.

Strauss and his associate, Laura E. Lehtinen, a pyschologist, cited four criteria for diagnosing brain injury in children where it was not apparent in gross motor (muscle) damage.[9] First, the child's history showed trauma or inflammatory process before, during or after birth; second, slight neurological signs are evident indicating a brain lesion; third, retardation of intellectual growth is apparent and is unique in the child's family; fourth, perceptual and conceptual disturbances appear on tests as well as in general behavior.

Many newborn infants show that they have experienced trauma at birth. Sometimes there is blood in the spinal fluid. But not all develop the brain-injury syndrome. Strauss and Lehtinen suggested that in many cases the damage was repaired and no evidence of it remained to handicap normal development.

However, if infants with minimal damage are exposed to infectious diseases, even a minor one, during the first few weeks of life, "our clinical experience shows that either the organism is not able to repair the damage or that the injury is aggravated and becomes more severe," Strauss and Lehtinen said. "The combination of trauma and inflammatory process has then proved destructive when either alone might not have been."

DISTRACTION AND DISINHIBITION

Although brain damage had been suspected for centuries as the cause of abnormal behavior, its role in producing learning difficulties in children is a recent discovery. It was a form of mental deficiency that was no more hereditary than a broken leg. It was clearly environmental—imposed from without, or *exogenous*.*

Moreover, it did not carry the onus of "immutability" that characterized familial retardation in the views of leading psychologists and educators. Often, brain-injured children showed neuromotor damage. It ranged from severe crippling, as in the case of cerebral palsy, to mild awkwardness and poor coordination. Although there was a strong tradition in American public school systems of providing for the physically handicapped, it did not extend to the brain-injured child who did not exhibit physical crippling, even though he was damaged in the same organ as the spastic child.

In the brain-injured, the handicap was often invisible. It affected mental activities: perception, concept formation and behavior. Until these effects had been clearly identified in brain-injured adults and their relationship with trauma had been established, the problem of the brain-injured child was not understood. It continued as a persistent mystery to his family and to teachers. In some instances,

*Retardation in children that was attributed to inheritance was called *endogenous*.

although his intelligence was normal, he was not educable by conventional methods or those used for the retarded children who did not exhibit the brain-injury syndrome.

Although Strauss accepted the theory that some brain functions were localized, his observations and those of Goldstein indicated that the impairment of a psychological function was determined by the amount of nerve tissue destroyed in a particular area rather than by a precise locus of damage. Strauss and Goldstein saw evidence that all brain lesions, wherever located, resulted in similar kinds of disordered behavior. This suggested that wherever the lesion occurred, the whole brain was affected, not only the part that sustained the injury.

In their description of the brain-injury syndrome, Strauss and Lehtinen advanced the idea that behavior was affected also by a disruption of the coordination of the "new" brain and the "old" brain.[10] The "old" brain is the primitive part of the organ. It is believed to have evolved first. It regulates all those strong feelings—fear, rage—that are involved in survival. It governs gestures and expressive movements. The "new" brain is the seat of reason, of higher mental process. It elevates man from the rest of the animal kingdom.

However, in theory, the old brain constantly influences the activity of the new brain, which in turn restrains the impulses of the more primitive part of the organ. The authority of the new brain over behavior develops as the normal child grows older. Sudden outbursts of laughter, weeping, aggressiveness, anger, restlessness and fear are repressed. Control by the new brain makes socialization and cooperation possible. It modulates the "raw passions," as the movie blurbs would say.

If this inhibiting effect is weakened by trauma that disrupts the connections between the old and new brains, the old brain acts unchecked. The brakes are off. Excessive emotional reaction and hyperactivity follow.[11]

The brain-injury hypothesis offered an explanation for some of the changes in behavior of adults who sustained head injuries or stroke. The patient had difficulty paying attention to anything; his attention wandered. He did not appear able to concentrate. He could not control violent outbursts. He would complain that he couldn't keep track of things. Everything seemed to change in a bewildering fashion. Because of these fluctuations, he would find it necessary to keep all of his possessions in a rigid order, where he could keep track of them. His room had to be arranged in a certain way all the time. The table had to be set the same way for dinner. Any change disturbed him. Strauss and Lehtinen noted that this person was quick to notice when something was missing or out of order. They observed that these patients often called attention to some oversight in dress or unusual ornament. They commented:

> Such meticulosity is puzzling unless the observer is aware of the mental instability and emotional lability (changeability) which the person who has become brain-injured in adulthood constantly experiences.[12]

Another abnormality shown by brain-injured soldiers was extreme distractibility. There were two forms. In one, the patient would become riveted to some minor, irrelevant detail of a scene, to the exclusion of everything else. Goldstein noted that when an examiner flashed a light in the patient's eyes, the patient responded by turning his head and moving his eyes to follow the light wherever the examiner moved it.

Strauss and Lehtinen said that this compulsive response took several forms. Often, it appeared as a fixation on some article of clothing that no one else noticed, or paid little attention to.

In a group situation, such as a classroom, this form of distraction would appear to normal persons as deliberate inattention to the teacher. But it was involuntary. The patient had been snared by a detail.

A second aspect of distractibility gives the appearance of a short span of attention. Goddard regarded it as a symptom of feeblemindedness. The individual seems to be unable to pay attention to anything very long. He shifts his attention from one thing to another. A brain-injured war casualty being interviewed by a psychologist or social worker turns away to look at someone passing by the door. With a nonbrain-injured soldier, this kind of distraction would seem normal enough if the passerby was an attractive nurse. But with the brain-injured patient, the stimulus could be anybody or anything; the nature of it is irrelevant. For this patient, all the stimuli in his field of view seen to have equal power to capture his attention.

In any situation, the normal person is aware of a variety of stimuli, but he can focus on the one that seems important at the time and relegate the others to the background of his awareness. The brain-injured person is unable to do this. For him, there is no main event.

Goldstein theorized that this form of distractibility is a fluctuation in figure-ground perception. Instead of the figure standing out against its background, the situation might appear to be reversed to the brain-injured: the background appears to be important and the foreground figure becomes irrelevant.

Strauss and Goldstein held that both the fixation of attention and its opposite, the constant shifting of attention, are aspects of impaired figure-ground perception.[13]

PERCEPTION

A basic cause of learning difficulty in the brain-injured child is the disruption of the neuromental process of perception. This is the process by which the brain is linked to the environment. We perceive the world around us through the senses of sight, hearing, touch, taste, smell and balance. If all our senses were blocked off, we would lose contact with the world around us. Experiments have shown that sensory deprivation has a profound effect on the brain. Mental processes quickly deteriorate and the personality becomes disorganized. Cut off from the world, one actually does lose one's mind.

Although the process of perception is instantaneous, there are two aspects of it: the detection of the physical stimuli by the sense organs and their interpretation by the brain. Interpretation is a mental process in which experience is involved. Detection of the stimuli and their transmission by the nerves may be considered a physical process.

All interpretation of environmental data seems to occur in the context of experience and culture. The ancestral savage regarded a lightning stroke as a manifestation of any angry deity; that was the interpretation of his culture. His civilized descendants regard it as electrical phenomena in nature. That is the interpretation of their culture. Perception is culturally conditioned.

To the experienced motorist, the flashing of the turn signal on the car ahead forecasts its change of direction; to a small child it may be meaningless. Much of the generation gap results in the different ways parent and child perceive the same aspects of environment. To the child, the puppy in the pet store window is an exciting prospect; but to the mother it may be a potential nuisance.

At Disney World, a child was screaming at the top of his lungs that he wanted to have "fun." No matter where his parents took him, he kept on screaming. It was obvious that the parents had promised him that he would have "fun" at the amusement part. Unfortunately, his experiences had not prepared him for the kind of "fun" purveyed by the amusement park, so he wasn't having any.

Although perception can be described as a two-step process, it seems to function as a unity in spite of the semantic difference between sensation and interpretation. What do our sensory organs sense? They react to natural forces: electromagnetic radiation, gravity, mechanical force and chemical elements. What we see is a narrow band in the electromagnetic spectrum, the visible light band. It is our physiological window to the universe. It is a small one compared with the wide range of electromagnetic energy emitted by our sun and other stars. At wavelengths too short for our eyes to register are ultraviolet rays; at wavelengths too long for us to see are infrared waves, although we can sense them as heat. At the short end of the wavelength scale are the gamma waves emitted by the decay of radioactive isotopes; at the longest are the radio waves which we can sense only when they are converted into sound. Most of the electromagnetic phenomena in the universe are detectable only by instruments which translate energies we cannot sense into energy forms we can sense. Biologically, we sense only a small part of the energy processes going on around us.

Sound waves are sensed by the tympanum and associated structures in the ears and transmitted to the brain by the auditory nerves. The hearing "system" allows us to detect vibrations in the atmosphere in the range of 20 to 20,000 cycles a second.

We sense heat and cold by means of nerves in the skin. Cutaneous (skin) sensation allows us to "feel" texture, hardness, softness, wetness, dryness through peripheral nerves—the sense of touch. Taste buds in the mouth and olefactory receptors in the nose react to chemical stimuli, mainly gas molecules. We sense gravitational force by means of balance organs of the inner ear that tell us which way is down—toward the center of the Earth. We sense this force also as weight, the resistance of mass to gravity. When astronauts fly in orbit around the earth, or travel to the Moon, they are in free fall and there is no resistance to their mass. They are then "weightless" and do not sense gravity. In this condition, another "sense"—the kinesthetic sense—provides orientation. It enables them to keep track of the parts of their bodies, to know where a hand is in relation to a foot. During the early days of manned space flight, psychologists feared that disorientation caused by the loss of gravity sensing would have serious pathological effects. But it didn't have much effect at all, probably because the astronauts had developed a new set of experiences as the result of training that enabled them to interpret the strange, new sensations of orbital flight as normal for the space environment. The Skylab missions in which nine men experienced orbital free fall a total of 171 days demonstrated that perceptual training plus lots of exercise enables man to adapt to that novel environment.

Perception goes beyond sensation. It organizes information from the environment so that the organism can use it. By interpreting some volatile, chemical compound as scent, the predatory animal detects its prey. Hearing a laugh tells us something about the emotional state of the person emitting it. A scream may signal distress. A red light at an intersection means stop.

The sensory organs of the brain-injured person may be functioning normally, but if the brain is not, the percept becomes inadequate. This disability is not so serious if it occurs in the adult after basic learning experiences are completed. Despite the handicap, the adult has a matrix of experiences that enables him to straighten out the aberrations caused by the injury.

But the child who has suffered brain damage early in life, before he has acquired experiences and learning, has a massive problem before him. He does not perceive the world around him in the normal way. He does not see the whole as a unity along with all of its parts and the relationships between them. He does not always separate the figure in the foreground from the background. In normal perception, as Strauss and Lehtinen have described it, "every activity whether it is reading, listening to music, driving a car or playing golf is always performed against a background of varying visual, auditory, kinesthetic and cutaneous perception."[14] The brain-injured child's confusion between background and foreground makes this separation uncertain. One result is that he is easily distracted.

The child's confusion in foreground–background arrangements extends across the whole range of sensory data. It affects his ability to perceive correctly social modes of organization and conduct. At an early age, he is unable to perceive the structure of a game. Consequently, he often does not play very long or very successfully with other children. He may not be able to tell what is expected of him in a game of tag; he is likely to perform some irrelevant activity that disrupts the game. When he is hiding in a game of hide and go seek, he may pop out of his hiding place at the wrong time, or call out, or laugh, and give himself away. If he is one of the seekers, he may run off in any direction, unable to perceive the goal of the game.

As children's games become more highly organized, he becomes less able to figure them out. He sees the parts, but not the whole, and when he responds to the parts, and not to the whole, he breaks up the game. If his difficulty is understood and tolerated, he can be taught how to play the game, and then he will perform more adequately. That is not likely to happen in the average neighborhood. And so he becomes isolated and rejected, and you see him on the periphery of a game, jumping up and down when the other children do, crying out or laughing when they do, but not a part of the game, alone and usually unwanted.

Allied to perceptual handicap is an aspect of behavior called "perseveration." It means perseverance without purpose. It generally appears as meaningless repetition of some activity. After hammering the peg into the peg board, the brain-injured child may continue to hammer away after the peg is thoroughly seated.

Perseveration is often shown after the child successfully completes a task. He seems to be unable to break away and start something new. Like that form of distraction in which he fixes on some irrelevant detail, the child appears to be transfixed by an activity that once he starts he cannot stop.

Confronted by a new task, the perseverative child is likely to repeat the old one. After drawing a picture of a car, he is asked to draw a house. The house has wheels on it. Teachers have found that the perseverative bond can be broken if some intermediate and unrelated activity is introduced to interrupt the perseverative activity.[15]

CONCEPT FORMATION

Some children suffer mental retardation as a result of brain injury and some escape it, Strauss and Lehtinen found. Nevertheless, the thinking disorders of both retarded and nonretarded brain-injured are similar, they said.[16] Although the intellectual potential is more severely reduced in the retarded group, the physiological basis of the handicap is the same.

Disorders in concept formation, or thinking, are the result of disorders in perception. If the child does not perceive the world around him adequately, he cannot think about it adequately. His ability to form concepts is based on the process of abstracting, or taking away, certain details of his perceptions and organizing and reorganizing them into patterns of thought.

The ability to perform this organizing task is considerably diminished in many brain-injured children, whether their intelligence is normal or below. It can be enhanced by a program of education that enables the child to strengthen his perceptual ability, but if special help is not provided, he must struggle to interpret reality as he sees it—and frequently that is not the way others see it.

The mind, which may be considered a product of the brain's electrochemical activity, functions in a timeless continuum. Past, present and future form a unity. With our organic time machines, we can rove through the past and project the future, to the limits of our experience. One of the important mental activities is retrospection, the process of reviewing past experience in terms of present events and future expectations. In retrospect, we reorganize some of our past notions or percepts; we modify them with present percepts. In looking back on an event or an experience, we often change our view of it. We see something in it that we did not see before; an angle of a business deal that escaped us at the time suddenly pops up as we "think it over." Or some detail of an experience that we considered irrelevant at the time suddenly becomes important—in the light of a later experience or bit of information, or in the light of an earlier one that is recalled.

Do brain-injured children think things over? They certainly do, but the recollections they talk about often show a certain degree of misconstruction. Parents of brain-injured children have observed that retrospective thinking improves in adulthood; it becomes less deviated and closer to actuality (as the parents may remember it). What has happened? Possibly this is the result of overlays of experience. Possibly the individual has been able to rearrange his earlier percepts when he brings them "up" into recall in the light of later experience.

Where experience is misconstrued because of faulty perception, the misconstruction is not so brittle that it cannot be remodeled. It can be corrected by parents, teachers or friends who bother to reinterpret a past experience for the brain-injured.

One of the principal sources of "static" in the brain-injured person's neuromental activity is preoccupation with detail, often irrelevant detail. In a test comparing conceptual ability in brain-injured, mentally retarded children and nonbrain-injured children, Strauss and a colleague, Heinz Werner, found that the brain-injured grouped objects by some unessential detail while the nonbrain-injured grouped them by general appearance or function.[17]

One of the difficulties the brain-injured child reveals early is in generalizing, which is a process of abstract thinking or concept formation. Generalizing is a way of organizing an array of things or experiences by perceiving a common denominator. Inability to do this represents a severe learning handicap.

Generalizing requires the individual to discern similarities in things and experiences that have many dissimilarities, and to separate the similarities from the dissimilarities. It is a method of classifying disparate things and of organizing them into meaningful and manageable patterns.

The child with the perceptual handicap has a considerable degree of difficulty in this kind of sorting. His organization may be faulty, so the generalizing he does is faulty.

In creating a generalization, such as reaching a conclusion about the behavior of certain breeds of dogs or the performance of certain makes of automobiles, we wrap up a variety of details in a mental package. Then we retain the package, often losing the details. This is a way of incorporating a large variety of experiences and of handling them as classes or patterns. The brain-injured child may not package experience in this way. As a result, he remembers details. Often, he exhibits a truly remarkable memory. He can recall the street address of the place where he lived many years before, long after his parents or brothers and sisters may have forgotten it. He recalls old telephone numbers and similar trivia. In some respects, this specificity of memory compensates for the difficulty in generalizing; in others, it is a handicap, burdening "Mr. Memory" with a mass of irrelevant clutter.

Although the foregoing discussion of perception and concept formation suggests a sequence, it is probable that both functions are stages in a single process of cognition—the process of knowing. We seem to recognize this intuitively. We say, "I see," when we mean, "I understand." We "get the picture" or "put it together."

In attempting to "see" the world as others see it, the brain-injured person's perceptual handicap causes a chain reaction in cognition. Confusion of figure-ground relationships interferes with his organization of perceptual experience. Since abstract thinking is based on perceptual reference, it, too, becomes aberrated. Irrespective of his intelligence—if that means his ability to think in abstract terms—the perceptual distortion serves to distort the whole cognitive process.

Thus, the brain-injured child of normal intelligence potential gives the impression of a "retarded" child. If he does not receive an education program that is specific to his handicap, he may not reach his potential. He may, instead, remain retarded in learning and behavior.

What can be done for him? Twenty-five years ago, I ventured a prediction that the brain-injured child of normal or near normal intelligence could reach his potential and become a self-sufficient adult if he received special teaching that took his handicap into account.[18] Now, it is no longer necessary to predict. As I will demonstrate in another chapter, the proof is alive, employed and in most cases doing very well.

I know—as do other parents of my generation—that brain-injured children who are educable can be "normalized" to the extent of achieving independence and self-sufficiency. But there is a condition. They must have early special education so that they can learn how to learn in the conventional school situation.

The reason they require special teaching at an early age is that although they may have the same experiences as normal children, they cannot utilize them as the normal child can because of the handicap. The result is that the average run of experiences that make the normal child ready to start school do not always promote the same degree of learning readiness in the brain-injured or "Other" Child.

The Other Child must then be made ready by a program that deals with his handicap. What the special teaching program does is show him how to deal with it, how to work around it and how to rectify his perpetual experiences so that they make the same sense to him as to others. The special program teaches him how to learn and how to become a school pupil. This is so basic that it hardly applies to the nonbrain-injured child. Without it, however, the Other Child faces failure, frustration and ultimately rejection in the classroom.

A generation ago it was a common practice, as I have mentioned earlier, to keep the unready child out of school a year or two, on the theory that he would somehow grow into readiness. The Other Child who is kept out of school for this reason is simply being denied an education.

Like the normal child of average intelligence, the brain-injured child of average intelligence is ready to learn to read at age six. But he does not learn to read until his perceptual handicap is addressed by a program that helps him overcome it. Before long, the Other Child who could not learn to read in the regular program has learned in the special program.

Many educators agree that there are optimum periods in human development for certain types of learning. Reading should begin at age six. By age eight, the ability to reason is developing and subjects that require it can be taught. These optimum periods exist for the Other Child, too. In their survey of general intelligence and heritability, McGuire and Hirsch (University of Illinois) maintained that the concept of predetermined development is being replaced by that of critical or optimal periods—that is, stages of behavioral development where both the opportunity to learn and the nature of what may be learned are especially important.[19]

HYPERACTIVITY

One of the most conspicuous symptoms of brain injury in children is hyperactivity, or superactivity. Children who are not brain-injured exhibit it also and a number of causes have been hypothesized, from food additives to emotional insecurity. In the brain-injured child, hyperactivity appears to be part of the syndrome.

In many ways, hyperactivity is an exaggeration of the activity of the excited normal child. Strauss and Lehtinen observed that it resulted from at least two factors: poor integration of the child's central nervous system and a tendency to accumulate excess energy because of a less than normal expenditure of energy in neuromental processes.[20]

Anyone who has experienced the manic jumpiness of a hyperactive child can compare it to the sudden explosion of a horde of children suddenly released from school by the sound of the bell at the end of the day. Energy that has been pent up all afternoon finds release; the volcano erupts.

The normal child appears to be better able to control this buildup than the brain-injured child. Consequently, he contains it until an appropriate release time. The brain-injured child cannot do this. He releases his excess energy in response to a variety of triggers, some of them emotional, others emanating from the environment.

Hyperactivity has commanded increasing attention among pediatricians and neurologists. Some recommend drugs to control it. In most of the cases I will describe, hyperactivity among brain-injured children was significantly reduced by the teaching program itself. The program kept the child occupied, busy and gave him a feeling of accomplishment. In certain respects, especially in providing relief from distractions, it reduced his anxiety. Hyperactivity diminished in school and also, for the most part, at home.

As the Other Child grows up, hyperactivity fades in most cases simply as a result of maturation. Presumably growth improves the integration of the central nervous system. In late adolescence and young adulthood, bouts of hyperactivity may appear, usually as a result of some exciting situation or of anticipation. But as maturity proceeds, I have seen once-hyperactive children whose continual jumpiness drove their parents up the wall become calm, sedate, deliberative and thoroughly relaxed where their life-styles did not exert undue pressure on them. So there is hope for the six-year-old jumping bean. Eventually, he will quiet down—in most cases. There are exceptions. Drugging the hyperactive child may reduce the hyperactivity but it also reduces his responses. It is the lack of controlled responses that causes energy to accumulate—action-specific energy, as Strauss defined it—until it is dissipated in hyperactivity.[21]

BEHAVIOR

The conspicuous behavior problems of the brain-injured child are signs of lack of integration and disorganization in the central nervous system. They are, as I have described them, catastrophic reaction (tantrum), hyperactivity, perseveration, distractibility and meticulosity. Not all brain-injured children show all these signs and children who exhibit some of them are not necessarily brain-injured.

What parents often see in the behavior of the brain-injured child is a distortion, exaggeration or excess of normal child behavior. It has the aspect of uncontrollability, of brakes off, of wildness. But often these behaviors are so close to those of normal children that parents become confused, especially when the child is young. They ask themselves: Is he really "different"? Do they imagine it? At length, the ambiguity about the child's behavior merges into a conviction that something is wrong. Then it's time to seek professional help.

In the brain-injured child, catastrophic reaction is closer to a temporary nervous breakdown than to the normal child's tantrum. It is a collapse. There is less anger in it than anguish. The child really suffers while he is weeping or shrieking or kicking his feet and thrusting his arms. He requires comforting, not scolding, not threats, not punishment, and certainly not isolation. Yet, how many children exhibiting this sign of neurological disorder have been mercilessly beaten by uncomprehending adults who later plead that they were just trying to teach him to control himself?

As in the case of hyperactivity, catastrophic reaction decreases in frequency and intensity with maturation. After the beginning of adolescence, it may take on the character of a lashing out at something or someone—or it may suddenly disappear. However, this change is not invariable. When catastrophic reaction persists in infantile form well into adolescence, professional help is needed.

Distractibility, often thought of as "limited span of attention," has been associated traditionally with mental deficiency. It may be the first sign to the elementary school teacher that the child has learning problems. This condition is treatable if it is viewed as hyperattentiveness rather than lack of attentiveness. The child is attending to everything at once and has been drawn by irrelevant stimuli away from the focus of attention. In the classroom, he turns his head away from the teacher and looks out of the window at a truck passing by. Unlike the normal child who can also be distracted, but is capable of swinging back to the main focus—the teacher—the brain-injured child does not swing back; presumably, his perceptual disorganization gives the irrelevant detail the same power to attract his attention as the teacher.

From this point of view, it is possible to reduce distractibility by reducing the distractions. Windows can be covered or made translucent so that the child cannot see what is going on outside. In the special class, children who are beginning school may be separated from classmates by a screen or a partition for a time. By reducing distracting stimuli, the teacher can help the child attend to the presentation. Before long, as the distractible child is no longer pulled this way and that, he learns what the primary focus is. His "span of attention" is then increased.

Perseveration often persists well into adolescence, although if the child is made aware of it, he will try to control it. In the older child, it may reflect an unwillingness to shift from one activity to another, rather than an involuntary fixation on a particular action.

In the older child, perseveration may appear as a stereotyped response to a number of different situations where the stereotype is not appropriate. The child who has learned that it is proper to shake hands when meeting someone may persist in shaking hands in casual encounters where it is not appropriate or with passersby on the street or passengers on a bus or train. He does not distinguish among gradations of greeting, from handshaking or hugging to a casual wave. When it is apparent that these gradations confuse him, they can be explained to him so that he can acquire clues to appropriate behavior.

Most brain-injured children have been struggling since infancy to conform to the world around them; most have a drive toward conformity which eludes them. It is easier to conform, and more acceptable—and acceptance is a great goal for this child. Showing him how to win acceptance goes a long way toward reducing bizarre behavior which may not be willful, even though it may appear to be.

Another aspect of perseveration is the constant repetition of a word or phrase. Normal children may do this, too, but the brain-injured child continues it for a longer period.

An adolescent girl in a family where tennis was a major activity became transfixed by the word *doubles*. She repeated it for months. The repetition in or out of the context of her activity seemed to work as a pacifier. It also might have represented a form of reassurance that she had been included in a group activity. The tactual sensation of the tongue and lips in forming the word appeared to please her.

There were a number of explanations for this particular perseveration, not the least of which was emotional gratification. For many people, tennis is more than a game; it is a social activity that confers status on the players, irrespective of their skill. In order to play tennis, one must have a partner, and to have a partner, one must be socially desirable or acceptable. Tennis becomes a symbol of physical and social achievement, a source of pride and accomplishment.

The intensity of hyperactivity and catastrophic reaction in brain-injured children suggests a lack of control over thalamic activity. The thalamus is one of the largest ganglion centers in the central nervous system. It is located below the main part of the "new" brain and is considered part of the "old" brain. Its function is thought to be to promote survival in the wild state by preparing the organism to meet stress and danger. It generates fear or rage. With the evolution of the "new" brain, man learned to control the activity of the thalamus and thus mastered to some extent impulsive behavior and emotional outbursts.

Strauss and Lehtinen observed that when the subcortical neurons of the thalamus are "released for action, they discharge precipitately and intensely."[22]

They cited the observations of Walter B. Cannon, a neurophysiologist who modernized older theories of emotions in 1915 by pointing out their physiological origin in the thalamus. Cannon said:

> These powerful impulses originating in a region of the brain not associated with cognitive consciousness and arousing, therefore, in an obscure and unrelated manner the strong feelings of emotional excitement, explain the sense of being seized, possessed, of being controlled by an outside force, and made to act without weighing the consequences.[23]

Strauss and Lehtinen commented:

> Everyone who has observed brain-injured children in their states of hyperactivity . . . can readily accept the statement that their reactions are extraordinarily intense and disinhibited and that they are released without control.[24]

They added that anatomical findings have shown that lesions from birth injury or early trauma are most frequently found in the region of the thalamus.

Insofar as the release of thalamic energy in the generation of strong emotions is controlled by higher mental processes, the enhancement of these processes in the brain-injured child tends to decrease catastrophic reaction, hyperactivity and distractibility, they said.

For the brain-injured child, special education tailored to his needs is therapy. By reducing the perceptual and conceptual disturbances of brain-injured children, special education programs have succeeded in reducing their behavioral disorders.

They make it possible for the child with the brain-injury syndrome to become independent and to contribute to society.

Chapter 4

The Disabilities Syndrome: Diagnosis by Effect

The identification of the brain-injury syndrome exerted a powerful influence in reinstating a positive attitude toward mental deficiency. It offered a medically detectable cause. It suggested a program of treatment that could reduce the effects of the handicap and enhance performance. Among educators, it revived the intuitive optimism that inspired efforts to rehabilitate the mentally handicapped before the Civil War.

Beyond that, it had the effect of mobilizing parents to demand that school boards treat mentally handicapped children as youngsters in need of special help rather than as juvenile mendicants. New evidence in the 1940s and 1950s that school performance could be improved by special teaching methods, such as those developed for brain-injured children, gave substance to these demands. Parents' organizations all over the country began to criticize limited educational programs for the mentally handicapped. They retained experts who reported that the programs were inadequate, humiliating. They hired lawyers to demand an accounting in the federal and state courts from school boards that provided only inadequate "dummy room" classes as some form of largesse, like township poor relief in the great depression.

The elucidation of the brain-injury syndrome by Alfred A. Strauss, Kurt Goldstein, Heinz Werner, Newell C. Kephart and others offered an explanation for the presence of the mentally handicapped child in families of normal intelligence. The explanation relieved many parents of guilt, fear and anxiety about the transmission of "bad genes" through the family tree. The notion that mental deficiency was passed on from generation to generation as a unitary, genetic character began to crumble. Geneticists had found a multiplicity of factors in the heritability of traits. Genetic and environmental factors were inextricably interlaced.

In education, a new generation of elementary school teachers began to specialize in programs for the mentally handicapped. Still, the expansion of special education was slow and spotty and, in general, the education establishment was slow in responding to the demands of parents. But once parents realized that the failure to provide special teaching was itself a handicapping condition for their children, they increased the pressure. They challenged school boards, lobbied in state legislatures, appealed to Congress and went to court.

Their struggle was implemented by the U.S. Supreme Court decision in 1954 against segregation. From then on, it was a part of the civil rights movement. With the establishment of the doctrine that education for every child was a right, and not a privilege to be granted or withheld by a local board, official indifference toward special education no longer had to be tolerated. Advanced school systems began to revise stereotyped teaching programs for retarded children.

One of the centers of development of special education was a state institution, the Wayne County Training School at Northville, Michigan. For a time, such pioneers as Strauss, Kephart, Werner and Lehtinen formed a cadre of staff physicians and psychologists.

Their approach to mental deficiency was based on two principles, both new and untested in the context of educational psychology. The first was that when retardation appeared to be the result of brain injury, the teaching program should be specialized to deal with the specific effects of the brain-injury syndrome. The second principle was that intelligence as measured by tested IQ was not fixed, as many educators had believed, but could be raised by education and training.

These ideas imparted a new mood of optimism that further encouraged parents to seek better programs for their children. Moreover, researchers were reporting experiments that suggested the possibility that favorable biochemical changes could be induced in brain cells through the environment and would improve brain functioning.

A recent example is the report that protein metabolism in brain tissue can be influenced by acquiring new behavior patterns.[1] Using goldfish as subjects, a team of investigators found that not only was there an increase in the incorporation of amino acids, the building blocks of living cells, by the brain, but certain proteins were modified by training. Conversely, long-term memories, the investigators reported, could be inhibited by reducing protein synthesis.

Evidence accumulated in the laboratory and in the school room indicated that early education and environmental stimulation enhanced the abilities of retarded children. But in the first half of this century, such programs were rare. Special education was based on the surmise that if a child could not progress at an average rate, the rate had to be slowed down. The programs were generally the conventional ones slowed down. Few reflected any effort to ascertain the child's specific disabilities. Classes tended to be large, often overcrowded. They were frequently disrupted by behavior problems that were not solvable in that environment. The classes were often added long after the school was built. Consequently, many were held in isolated basement rooms or annexes. Teachers were harassed, overworked and also overwrought. Often, they did not get a lunch hour, but were required to remain with their charges at lunch time.

A former teacher in such a class recalled:

In the 1960s, I accepted my first teaching position, a special education class in a basement room next door to the furnace. Of the thirteen "educable mentally retarded" children assigned to work with me, most were simply nonreaders from poor families. One child had been banished because she posed a behavior problem to her fourth grade teacher.[2]

This situation was a common one. Here and there a special class teacher struggled against apathy and indifference to seek a better deal for her children. As one of the best I have known commented, *"You had to find out how the child learned and then teach him that way."* There were many unsung heroes and heroines struggling alone to improve teaching programs, often without parent or supervisory support. And there were many also who simply went along with the system. Even in big city school systems where special classes for the mentally handicapped were provided, and teachers with special training for them were recruited, there was a tendency to place the new, inexperienced teacher in the classes with the most difficult learning problems, allowing the veterans to move on to less demanding assignments. The Chicago school administration routinely assigned the least experienced and youngest teachers to the "worst" schools—those in underprivileged neighborhoods with the largest number of learning and behavior problems.

In a survey for the Chicago Board of Education, Robert J. Havighurst, Professor of Education at the University of Chicago, stated:

> It is clear that the more mature of the regularly assigned teachers have clustered in the high status and main line schools which have 26 percent of the elementary school enrollment. On the other hand, 93 percent of the substitute teachers are in common man and inner city schools and overwhelmingly in the latter type school.[3]

In the period from the great depression to the end of World War II, the public school situation for brain-injured children who exhibited specific learning disabilities was generally deplorable. The experience of one family may illustrate the problem that hundreds faced.

During the decade of the 1940s, the largest generation of children ever born in North America flooded the maternity wards. In the family whose experience I cite, the first child was a boy, born in 1942. There was a birth complication. Labor was protracted. The infant had to be delivered by caesarean section. The maternity ward was so overcrowded that mothers recuperating from childbirth were parked in their hospital beds in the halls awaiting ward space. Gastrointestinal infection swept through the hospitals that autumn, taking its toll of newborns. This child, however, seemed to escape it.

The baby appeared to be a normal, healthy, eight-pound boy and was named Victor. Before he reached his first birthday, the father was called into military service, served two-and-one-half years overseas and returned at the end of 1945. It was after the reunited family settled down in its own home and the father returned to his prewar employment that the parents became aware that the child exhibited unusual behavior difficulties.

Victor was going on four. He was talking, but not as much as other children of the same age. In games, he often withdrew to the edge of the group and performed purposeless movements that seemed to simulate the activities of the others. At his fourth birthday party, he disrupted the games the parents tried to organize and squabbled with his guests.

For several months, he attended a nursery school, but eventually he was withdrawn by the parents when it became evident that he could not fit into a preschool program. When the other children were quiet during story telling, Victor would become restless, call out, or get up from his chair and run around the room. He was unable to color with crayons between lines. He could not keep track of his clothing. He made no social progress in nursery school.

The parents sought private psychiatric help. For them, as for many others, as they later learned, the rounds seemed endless. After tests administered by a state agency and by a private psychiatrist specializing in children, Victor was diagnosed as having severe emotional problems which, the psychiatrist surmised, resulted from the absence of the father in military service. The parents were assured that there were "any number of cases like that" in the families of returned war veterans. Instead of a "lost generation" of veterans, the war was producing a "lost generation" of children.

But the parents didn't buy it. They continued their rounds. Victor was "seen" by a school psychologist who counseled the parents to keep him at home until he was a little older. The public school system of this midwestern city had special education classes. The father visited one of them. It was, typically, in the basement of an older elementary school building, behind the big coal furnace. In the mornings when the furnace was stoked to heat the first and second floor classrooms, the heat in the "dummy room" was hardly bearable and the children were given a recess in the hall. There were forty-four pupils in the room ranging in age from seven to nine. "Thank heaven, we have no more chairs," the teacher explained. "So we can't take any more children." The waiting list was two years long.

The parents enrolled Victor in a private school which espoused the principle of "progressive" education. There Victor's behavior was tolerated, but he did not learn to read or write. The parents continued their quest for some explanation of his problems. A diagnosis of neurosis was too vague and uncertain to indicate a course of action. Institutionalization was suggested by a state agency, but only as a last resort.

The baffling aspect of the child's behavior was its variability. At times, he seemed to react like the average child of his age. At other times, he expressed bizarre, infantile behavior. Confronted with a toy that required manipulative skill, he would speedily become frustrated and break the toy or throw it away. Once he began an activity, such as hammering pegs into a peg board, he could not stop. It was the year when *The Little Engine That Could* became popular. Victor played the record over and over until it wore out.

At last, the parents were referred by a friend to a Vienna-trained psychiatrist who was aware of the theories of Kurt Goldstein, Heinz Werner and Alfred Strauss. After a series of tests, the psychiatrist diagnosed brain injury.

What could be done? Dr. Alfred A. Strauss, his wife, Marie, and a Wayne County colleague, Laura E. Lehtinen, had opened a residential school for brain-injured children at Racine, Wisconsin, with the financial support of a group of Wisconsin industrialists and businessmen. At the age of seven and one-half, Victor was enrolled in the Cove Schools. And then his education began.

THE BOUNCING IQS

In addition to the elucidation of the brain-injury syndrome as a cause of treatable learning disabilities, evidence that IQ can be increased by environmental stimulation helped break down resistance to special education.

The evidence was collected carefully in a series of experiments and studies made forty years ago by Harold M. Skeels, H. B. Dye, Marie

Skodak Crissey and others. The most elaborate of the surveys involved twenty-five orphans under three years of age in an Iowa orphanage. In a monograph relating the results, Skeels noted that in the
early 1930s when the subjects were infants,

> the prevailing concept of intelligence held by psychologists, social
> workers and educators was that intelligence is a fixed, individual
> characteristic. It was believed to be related to parental genetic
> traits that were inferred from the parents' occupational and educa-
> tional achievements; to show little fluctuation from early childhood
> to maturity and to be relatively uninfluenced by the impact of the
> environment.[4]

In the light of that thinking, Skeels said, the IQ was deemed to be a
stable predictor of future development, along with the status of the
parents. The object of the experiment was to provide data about the
effects of poverty and deprivation on the child's ability to learn.

Of the twenty-five orphans, twenty were born out of wedlock and
five were separated from parents because of neglect and abuse.
Ethnically, all were white, North European. The orphanage was an
ancient, barnlike structure that had been an army barracks during the
Civil War. It was overcrowded and understaffed—par for state institutions of that day and this. Skeels, who worked at the orphanage,
recalled that the diet, sanitation, general care and "the basic philosophy of operation" were all substandard. He described the institution
as follows:

> Care of the children by adults was limited to feeding, dressing and
> toilet training. The children had few toys to play with. At age two,
> the children were moved from the infant wards and placed in cot-
> tages that had been erected about 1860. These were overcrowded
> with up to thirty-five children in each, under the supervision of one
> matron. She was aided by three or four teenage girls who were both
> untrained and unwilling. None of the children had any personal
> possessions beyond a toothbrush.

At age six, each child started school in the institution. Skeels said
that few children whose elementary education was confined to the
orphanage were able to cope with a public junior high school.

The twenty-five orphans comprising the experiment were divided into two groups while in infancy. One was called the "Experimental" group. It was composed of thirteen children, ten girls and three boys. They were transferred from the orphanage to the Glenwood State School, an institution for retarded children. Although all had been diagnosed as retarded by tests for preschool children, none exhibited any gross physical handicap.

The second group of eight boys and four girls was designated as the "Contrast" or control group. These children had a higher average intelligence than the Experimental group and remained in the orphanage.

The purpose of shifting the thirteen Experimental group children out of the orphanage to the Glenwood School was to place them in an environment where they would receive more attention and training than the orphanage provided. The mean age of this group was 19.4 months and the mean IQ, 64.3. It ranged from 35 to 89. Because of apparent mental retardation, nearly all were unsuitable for adoption. In one case, the child could hardly hold up its head and had little body activity. In another, the child was unsteady at twelve months when sitting up without support. She could not pull herself to a standing position nor did she creep. A third case rocked back and forth incessantly. Three were classified at the orphanage as "imbeciles." In modern terms, they would have been labeled as "trainable."

The thirteen orphans were placed in wards with older, brighter inmate girls who, along with the attendants, became emotionally attached to them. With little else to do, the older girl inmates spent a good deal of time playing with the children. The attendants, a group of motherly women, were given time to train them.

The thirteen received constant attention as part of the experimental design. They were given toys. They went on outings. They were encouraged to play outdoors on swings, slides and in sandboxes. They were given tricycles to ride. As soon as they could walk, they were started in kindergarten, the younger ones for only half the morning, the older ones for the entire morning. They were trained in group singing in the chapel fifteen minutes every day. As they grew older, they attended special school programs, movies, dances and Sunday services in the chapel.

In this "enriched" environmental regimen, the relationship of each child to adults was virtually one to one. The period of each child's exposure to it varied from 5.7 to 52.1 months. As soon as the child showed normal mental development on tests, the experimental period was considered completed. The child was then placed in an adoptive home or returned to the orphanage.

Results

Children in the Experimental group showed a gain in IQ from 7 to 58 points, Skeels said. They were given the Stanford-Binet (1916) and the Kuhlmann Revision (1922) tests. Three children gained 45 points or more and all but two gained more than 15 points.

The three who had been labeled as "imbeciles" in the orphanage gained 45, 49 and 58 points respectively.

Skeels said:

> A close bond of love and affection between a child and one or two adults who assumed a personal parental role appears to be a dynamic factor of great importance.

Nine of the thirteen Experimental group children had such a relationship. Those who experienced it, said Skeels, "made greater gains than those who were limited to more general interactions."

The nine children who experienced closer ties to adults gained 17 to 58 points, with an average of 33.8. Four who had less intense personal relationships gained 7 to 20 points, an average of 14. Two children who had been housed in a ward with eight to twelve other children and older girls of lower mental level showed poor progress, until they were placed individually in wards with the brighter girls who gave them more personal attention. After six months in the new surroundings, they showed marked gains in intelligence.

Of the thirteen children in the Experimental group, eleven were adopted after the experiment period ended. One remained in the orphanage until adulthood. One was returned to the institution for the retarded.

Two-and-one-half years after the experiment ended, both groups were retested. The mean IQ of the Experimental group had risen to 95.9 points, a gain of 31.6 points from the initial mean IQ of 64.3. Among the eleven children who were adopted, the mean IQ was 101.4—normal.

The Contrast Group

The twelve children of the original twenty-five who remained in the orphanage were designated as the Contrast group. Their ages ranged from 11.9 to 21.8 months, a mean of 16.6 months. Their mean IQ was 86.7, with ten IQs ranging from 81 to 103 and two from 50 to 71. There was no evidence of neurological abnormality. Nine members of the group were considered to have normal intelligence.

Although the Contrast group initially exhibited higher average intelligence than the Experimental group, the children came from similar low-level economic and social backgrounds as the children in the Experimental group. Mothers of Contrast group children had an average of 7.3 years of schooling. Nine of the mothers were tested. Only two exhibited IQs above 70. One was 79, the other, 84. In the Experimental group, the mean schooling of mothers was 7.8 years and the mean IQ of five of them was 70.4. One was normal with an IQ of 100 and one was labeled as "feebleminded."

There were little data on the fathers. Paternity was doubtful in many cases. In each group, ten children were born out of wedlock. Two of the fathers of Experimental group children had completed the eighth grade; one had attended high school and one had completed high school. One was a traveling salesman, one a printer and one a farm hand.

In the Contrast group, one father had completed high school, two, the eighth grade, and one, the sixth grade. Three were day laborers, two, farm hands, one worked on a railroad section gang, one was a tenant farmer and one was in a Civilian Conservation Corps camp.

How did the children in the Contrast group who remained in the orphanage fare? Skeels characterized their environment as lacking in stimulation. They did not receive the care, attention and affection that the Experimental group children received.

Over a period of two years, Experimental group children showed a marked increase in the rate of mental growth, whereas children in the Contrast group showed progressive mental retardation, Skeels reported. While the experiment group gained an average of 31.6 IQ points, the Contrast group showed an average loss of 26.12 points.

Twenty Years Later

Twenty years after the experiment ended, a followup study was made by Skeels. It required a good deal of detective work to find these people, but Skeels and his associates located them, interviewed them, tested them and their children and came up with findings that, combined with the earlier results, reversed the old notion of a fixed IQ.

The research took eighteen months, from October 1961 to March 1963. Of the original twenty-five, all but one reached adulthood. One in the Contrast group had died.

All thirteen of the Experimental group were found to be self-supporting. As young children, in the orphanage, they had been labeled as retarded. As adults, they were normal. One boy and one girl had spent time in a state correctional institution, but none had exhibited persistent antisocial or delinquent behavior, economic dependency or the need for psychiatric or welfare agency support.

Eight of the ten girls were married. Occupationally, six were housewives, including one who had been a licensed practical nurse. Another was a nursing instructor, one worked in a gift shop, one was in domestic service and one was a waitress. Of the three males, one was an Army staff sergeant, one, a real estate salesman and one, a vocational counselor.

Among the eleven surviving members of the Contrast group, only one was married and one was divorced—both males. Four remained as inmates of institutions. Three were dishwashers. One was a "floater," one worked part time in a cafeteria, one was an assistant to the gardener at a state institution and one was a typesetter (printer).

The printer was the most successful member of the Contrast group. At the outset of the experiment period, he had shown an IQ of 87. It then dropped to 67 on the final test of the period. On the followup study twenty years later, it had risen to 89.

Although the Contrast group was generally higher in intelligence at the outset of the experiment, its mean IQ not only dropped, but its members did poorly in life compared with the Experimental group—except for the printer. As an infant, he had suffered hearing loss after a mastoid operation. Because of the hearing loss, he was sent to a residential school for the deaf where he completed high school. At the school, the cottage matron took an interest in him because he was the youngest child in the cottage and had no family. He was invited to visit her home quite frequently and also the home of her married daughter. Essentially, he was the only member of the Contrast group who was rescued from orphanage life. That seems to explain his success.

Economically, the Experimental group fared much better than the Contrast group. In 1959, the median income of Experimental group males fourteen years old and older was $4224 a year, slightly above the Iowa median of $4182. In the Contrast group for males of fourteen or above, the median income was $1200. The top earner was the printer, who earned $6720 in 1963 setting type.

In education, members of the Experimental group completed a mean of 11.7 grades. Four had one or more years of college including one who received a bachelor of arts degree. The Contrast group completed a mean of 3.95 grades. Only the printer completed high school.

The difference in offspring between the two groups is remarkable. Nine members of the Experimental group had a total of twenty-eight children, eighteen boys and ten girls. A total of twenty-five children were tested by the Stanford-Binet and Wechsler intelligence scales. Three who were less than two years were given the Cattell Infant Intelligence Scale. These are standard tests widely used.

The mean IQ of the twenty-eight children was 103.9, with a range from 86 to 125. The children who were in school were all doing passing work. None showed any indication of neurological or other abnormality. Skeels described them as attractive and physically well developed.

In the Contrast group, as indicated earlier, only two males had married and one of them was divorced at the time of the followup study. The divorced member had a male child. At 6.6 years of age, the boy scored 66 on the Stanford-Binet (Form L-M). He showed evidence of brain injury.

The other male member of the Contrast group who married was the printer. He had four children. All were physically well developed, attractive and nicely adjusted, Skeels reported. The oldest, a boy 5 years and 11 months old, showed an IQ of 107. A girl, 4½, scored 117. The third child, 2½, scored 119 and a 9-month-old infant scored 103 on the Cattell test.

None of the four girls in the Contrast group married. Two were sterilized in late adolescence before being placed in jobs in the community.

The Iowa experiment is more than a condemnation of orphanage life, although it is certainly that, too. It had a profound influence in persuading state mental health and public welfare officials to move children out of institutions and into foster homes. In summarizing the findings, Skeels pointed out that the main difference between the two groups was the amount of environmental stimulation and the intensity of the relations between the children and "mother surrogates."

Soon after the two groups were separated, their patterns of development diverged, and the divergence continued into adulthood. Whereas all members of the Experimental group became self-supporting, four members of the Contrast group remained as wards of institutions in adulthood—one in a mental hospital and the other three in facilities for retarded adults. Skeels noted that the overall cost to the State of Iowa for members of the Contrast group was five times that of the Experimental group. Skeels said:

> It can be postulated that if the children in the Contrast group had been placed in suitable, adoptive homes or given some appropriate equivalent in early infancy, most or all of them would have achieved within the normal range of development, as did the Experimental subjects.
>
> It seems obvious that . . . there are still countless infants born with sound biological constitutions and potentialities for development well within the normal range who will become mentally retarded and noncontributing members of society unless appropriate intervention occurs.

This indictment of institutional life was seconded later in a paper by Laird Heal of the Department of Special Education, University of Illinois.

Heal cited two studies that found a substantial decline in IQ during the first five years of institutionalization. It was conspicuous for individuals who had normal or enriched family lives before they were shunted off into an institution. He noted: "The IQ drop was greatest for those subjects to whom the institution represented the greatest negative contrast from their prior existence." The studies were done by Edward Zigler of Yale University and his associates in 1963 and 1970. Heal added:

> We have known from the work of Skeels and Dye in 1939 that common institutional rearing practices have a devastating effect on intellectual and emotional development. Nevertheless, these institutional practices have persisted.[5]

THE CASE FOR INTERVENTION

In the light of this evidence, why do state governments passively permit their institutions to promote mental retardation? In the State of Illinois efforts toward institutional reform have failed so consistently that the Department of Mental Health has shifted part of its case load of retarded persons to private shelter care facilities in communities. This policy follows a recent trend toward "normalization" that enables some inmates to escape institutional life.

More evidence that IQs of retarded children rise when they are exposed to appropriate educational stimulation was assembled in a 1958 study in Illinois. It was directed by Samuel A. Kirk, then head of the Institute of Exceptional Children at the University of Illinois. Kirk's study was narrower in scope than the Iowa studies of Skeels, Skodak and Dye. It was designed to test only the effect of early special education and did not involve a change of habitat.

The Illinois experiment involved eighty-one retarded children. An Experimental group of forty-three was given a special program of preschool education. A Contrast group of thirty-eight was not. Both groups were then tested before and after the period of the preschool program and again after each had spent one year in the first grade.

Although there was no change of habitat, each group was sub-divided by residence. In the Experimental group of forty-three children, twenty-eight lived in a community—Urbana-Champaign, Illinois. The twenty-eight constituted the "Community Experimental" group. Fifteen children lived in a state institution for retarded children at Lincoln, Illinois. They were the "Institution Experimental" group.

The Contrast group was similarly divided, with twenty-six children living in the community and twelve at another state institution for the retarded at Dixon, Illinois.

Kirk hoped the experiment would show whether the stimulus of a preschool program affected the IQ of retarded children and whether the effect differed by residence.

All eighty-one children ranged in age from three to six years when the experiment period started. Their IQ scores ranged from 45 to 80. A few were followed up for five years.

On the whole, Kirk reported, the Experimental groups which were exposed to preschool education showed a definite increase in mental growth while the Contrast groups did not. In fact, the Contrast sub-group of institutional children showed a decline in IQ during the period that the Experiment groups received preschool training.[6]

At the outset, the study classified IQs on the following scale:

Those with IQs of 45 to 54 were questionably educable; 55 to 64, low educable; 55 to 74, high educable; 75 to 84, borderline; 85 to 94, low average; 95 plus, average and beyond. These definitions were called levels.

Of the forty-three children who received preschool education in the community and in the institution, thirty exhibited accelerated mental growth and retained it through the first grade. They increased their classification one to three levels. The average increase in IQ scores was about 10 points.

In the Experimental group, differences in the gains of children in the community and of those in the institution were not marked. Both subgroups showed gains during the preschool period, and both re-tained them.

The Contrast group story was different. The twenty-six children in the Community Contrast group retained the IQs they had exhibited at the outset of the study over the preschool period, but the twelve children in the Institution Contrast group who also were excluded from the preschool program dropped in IQ during that period.

The difference between the Community and Institution Contrast groups became even more marked after the preschool period. After a year in the first grade, the Community Contrast group showed a gain in IQ, but the Institution Group did not after a year in the institution school.

Kirk attributed the gain in the first grade by the Community Contrast group to associations with normal children. Before entering school, he surmised, the retarded children in this group had been largely excluded from contact with normal children. For these retarded children, the environment changed for the better when they entered the first grade in a public school.

Kirk accounted for the failure of the Institution Contrast group to show IQ gains after the first grade by the fact that the institution classroom environment was "not sufficiently stimulating to change the rate of growth."

> The Community Contrast children attended a first grade or a special class at the age of six for a full day. In addition, such children tend to intermingle with average children in the community after the school day.
>
> The institution children, on the other hand, attended an institution school for a half-day period. The rest of the time consisted of association with lower grade, mentally retarded patients.

Kirk also found differences in mental growth between brain-injured children whom he referred to as "organically retarded" and nonbrain-injured retarded children.

There were fourteen "organic" children in the two Experimental subgroups. Only seven showed increased rate of mental growth. Of the twenty-nine who were not diagnosed as brain-injured, twenty-three made progress of one or more levels in the educability classification system.

Kirk conceded that the difference in progress between the brain-injured and nonbrain-injured children who attended the preschool program might be accounted for by the teaching program. Another type of program that provided tutoring for special psychological disabilities might have yielded better results in the brain-injured group, he surmised.

PARENTS REVOLT

Once the stationary IQ notion was disproved, public agencies no longer had any excuse for failing to provide effective, special education for mentally handicapped children. The paralyzing grip of the eugenics movement was broken. Its credibility faded away like that of witchcraft. Parents were liberated from the crushing burden of guilt that had inhibited them from asserting the right of a handicapped child to an education at public expense. They no longer had to fear the "sins of the fathers" syndrome that had frightened them into accepting the injustice of public denial of educational opportunity to their children. Nor were they required to tolerate the fraudulent practices of state institutions that gave lip service to rehabilitation and treated charges like animals. Mental retardation in a child was no longer to be taken as a reflection of some defect or early misconduct of the parents.

Much of the mystery about mental deficiency had been resolved by the identification of the brain-injury syndrome and of disorders in metabolism. The impact of the environment was becoming clearer. Trauma, inflammation or drug or radiation damage to genetic material could inflict retardation on an otherwise normal individual. Environment could be therapeutic. It could accelerate or depress the rate of mental development within genetically or organically determined limits. It could make or it could break the handicapped child.

A new optimism toward mental retardation appeared at the end of the 1950s and beginning of the 1960s. The President of the United States, John F. Kennedy, had a retarded older sister who was living in an institution and members of that wealthy and talented family were leaders in public campaigns for better understanding of the plight of retarded persons.

"Retarded Persons Can Be Helped" became the new slogan of the National Association for Retarded Children and Adults. More than ever before the problem of mental deficiency came out into open discussion. It was an aspect of the social revolution that was beginning in America during that period, and, perhaps, represented one of the greatest advances in the understanding of human beings of the twentieth century.

Organizations of parents sprang up all over the United States to promote the welfare of retarded children. They founded special classes, often in church recreation or Sunday school rooms. They created sheltered workshops for older retarded children for whom no other community services existed.

At the outset, parent organizations were motivated in setting up these facilities by the belief that severely handicapped children could be trained to become less dependent and possibly self-sufficient. In many instances, that dream was not realized. In this respect, the optimism of the parents' organizations paralleled that of the public institution movement in the first half of the nineteenth century. And as the children grew older, still requiring a sheltered and supervised life experience, the parents' organizations became subject to similar disillusionment.

But unlike the institution superintendents, they could not give up. Their children still required care—which many state institutions did not provide at a satisfactory level. Gradually, the parental schools and workshops assumed a permanent character. The more successful of them developed into private agencies in their own right, supported by charities or by state agencies.

Workshops where severely retarded adults could be trained to perform many industrial tasks began to evolve into small manufacturing plants and piecework factories.

This development, which I will describe in more detail in a later chapter, has pulled thousands of severely retarded adults out of a vegetative, institutional existence and put them to work at a modest pay scale.

During the quarter century from 1950 to 1975, national organizations of parents grew, modeled on the older National Association for Retarded Children and Adults. One of the most influential in education was the international Association for Children with Learning Disabilities (ACLD), an amalgamation of state and local parents' groups. This organization was the outgrowth of a movement I will describe later.

In 1966, in response to these movements, the U.S. Office of Education set up a Bureau for the Handicapped. It budded into several leafy stems, including one that specialized in learning disabilities.

However, many of the significant actions in requiring public education to provide for the mentally handicapped were taken by parents and their organizations. In 1971, as a result of a suit brought against the Commonwealth of Pennsylvania, a U.S. District Court ordered the state to provide education at public expense for all retarded children. Plaintiff was the Pennsylvania Association for Retarded Children. In 1972, the federal court in the District of Columbia issued a similar order to the public schools in Washington to provide educational services to the mentally handicapped. The court order specified that lack of funds could not be used as an excuse not to comply. By 1975, suits pleading for similar relief were pending in state and federal courts in twenty-five other states. In New York state, a class action suit in behalf of brain-injured children led to an order by the State Education Commissioner that all school districts provide "adequate and appropriate" education.

What is "adequate and appropriate" education? Definitions vary. What is adequate for the nonbrain-injured child may not be for the brain-injured child. The question that confronts parents is straightforward. What is adequate in terms of their child's learning disabilities?

As Kirk pointed out in the Illinois study, perhaps the "organic" brain-injured children might have made better IQ gains than the experiment showed if they had been given a preschool and also a first grade program that was tailored to ease their specific disabilities. But that was not done. They received the same education program as the nonbrain-injured retarded children. As the results showed, they did not do as well.

The failure to provide specifically for the learning disabilities of the brain-injured child is analogous to failing to provide for the blind or deaf child. In either case, the child is excluded from receiving the education that American society should guarantee all children. The brain-injured child, it will be remembered, suffers from an inward blindness and deafness that prevents him from perceiving the world in the normal way.

What kind of a program, then, does the brain-injured child require? I can summarize the approach prescribed by Strauss and Lehtinen.[7]

> The size of the class is kept small—no more than twelve children. The classroom should be spacious enough so that the children can be seated at desks well apart from each other. Decorations are minimal, if any. Bulletin boards, pictures, exhibits and knick-knacks are avoided. A plain room and a plainly dressed teacher are less conducive to distractibility. If some children exhibit distractibility, it may be reduced further by partly or fully screening the child from others with a portable partition, or by turning the desk toward the wall. This should not be done in a punitive way. It is a therapeutic measure that relieves the child from the bombardment of stimuli that are distracting him.

Under these conditions, Strauss and Lehtinen reported that loud talking, running in the room and attacks on other children diminish and sometimes stop altogether in several days. The formerly unmanageable child becomes tractable. I have observed this and so have a number of other parents and special education teachers. The results sometimes seem magical.

With the decrease in "static" from his surroundings, the brain-injured child will often feel relieved. He will exhibit more responsiveness to the teaching program. As he *learns how to learn*, he is able to direct his energy into purposeful rather than purposeless activity. His control of his behavior becomes firmer; hyperactivity and distractibility diminish.

One of the priority goals of the special class is to deal with the child's perceptual handicap—or help him deal with it. Among the techniques designed to accomplish this is one which helped a number of perceptually handicapped children who are now adults:

> If the child cannot color within lines, his perception of the area to be colored can be strengthened by marking it off with heavy, black crayon or by placing a cardboard frame around the area to be colored. The heavy black lines reinforce visual perception; the cardboard frame provides a boundary the pupil can feel, adding the perceptual modality of touch to reinforce the visual percept. In one situation, when the cardboard frame was removed from the paper,

the child perceived the square he had colored red for the first time. "It sticks out, it sticks out," he cried. He was now able to perceive the square as a discrete figure.[8]

In counting, the child is handicapped by his perceptual problem of separating or sequencing the objects to be counted, and also by the disinhibition that drives him through an activity with such abandon that he skips over objects or combines them. Normally, the number of objects we can count at a glance is limited. Four objects usually can be perceived as a number without counting them. In Roman numerology, the number 4 was represented by four vertical strokes or by IV. Five was perceived more readily if a diagonal line was drawn through the four strokes and was represented by the letter V. Beyond that, the number was not represented graphically, but symbolically.

While the normal individual may have trouble perceiving a number of objects greater than four without counting them, the brain-injured may have the same trouble perceiving more than one or two. Counting is difficult for him because of his problem in arranging objects in space. The perceptually handicapped child has the same problem, approximately, in counting small numbers as the nonbrain-injured person has with large numbers of objects. Try counting the number of stars you can see on a starry night, or the number of beans in a jar, or the number of people in a football stadium. That may give you some idea of the problem the brain-injured person has with numbers that the nonbrain-injured can manage.

In learning the meaning of a number, the child first must be able to link it to a perceptual quantity. He must perceive the scheme that the number represents; if it is a large number, he must be able to think of it, abstractly, as a multiple of small numbers with perceptual references.

Techniques of teaching the brain-injured child are endlessly varied. Many teachers devise their own, often intuitively, for each child may present a different array of difficulties. That is, of course, the reason a rigid program is worthless for many children.

DYSLEXIA

The brain-injured child's reading problems are another manifestation of his perceptual and behavior problems. Reading disability is expressed by difficulty in learning new words, faulty identification of familiar words, confusion of similar words and phrases and the omission of words, phrases and sentences when reading a text.

Disturbances in auditory perception may complicate the process of learning to read, and, of course, the perception of letters is a visual perceptual ability. Many children can already perceive letters and identify whole words by their configuration before they enter the first grade, but most brain-injured children have not acquired this readiness because of their perceptual instabilities.

Insofar as reading and writing are visual forms of oral language, the letter forms must be identified with the sounds they stand for. If the child's perception of the letter form is faulty, he may not be able to link it with the phoneme (speech sound) it represents. Similarly, if his perception of certain phonemes is uncertain, it will affect his auditory comprehension.

In the light of these problems, it seems obvious that the child with a perceptual handicap requires a teaching regimen that may begin at a much lower level than one for the normal child. I do not see how this can be done in regular classes or in special classes for the educable mentally handicapped. Until the brain-injured child has mastered a basic reading skill, he simply does not learn.

Reading disability, however, is more specific than the syndrome of brain injury I have discussed. It may be exhibited by children who do not manifest any other signs of the syndrome, by children of normal or superior intelligence. The condition is called *dyslexia* (nonreading). Several research studies, including one by Helmer R. Myklebust and Doris Johnson at Northwestern University, have indicated the existence of a familial component in dyslexia. Two other investigators, Herman R. Goldberg and Gilbert B. Schiffman, reached that conclusion in a joint study. They said: "In summary, there are some reasons for believing that reading disability can be genetically determined. Familial groupings of cases do exist. The observation of reading difficulties in twins, especially identical twins, is strongly suggestive of a genetic origin." Goldberg and Schiffman noted that dyslexia was not an insuperable barrier to achievement. Among prominent dyslexics they listed Winston Churchill, Thomas Edison, Albert Einstein, Paul Ehrlich, George Patton, Auguste Rodin and Woodrow Wilson.[9]

It is generally supposed that in learning to read, children pass through stages that recapitulate the evolution of symbolic writing. They start with pictures, the most primitive form of visual language communication. Later, they recognize words whose configurations they perceive as pictures. The perceptually capable child does this quite early. He may be unusually proficient at identifying such patterns as makes of automobiles.

The perceptually handicapped child may show some of this adeptness, particularly in identifying cars. But he does it differently. Instead of the whole form, or *gestalt*, he picks a fragment of the image—a hood ornament or shape of the tail light. If a similar feature appears on several different makes, he cannot distinguish among them.

As the child grows, he perceives, or is taught to perceive, the written word not only as a picture but as an assortment of phonemes. Emphasis on phonetics or "phonics" in reading has been recommended for perceptually handicapped children because it enables them to "sound out" a word, reinforcing the visual percept.

Persons with dyslexia may not be able to connect the letter symbol with its phoneme. The central nervous system functions like a radio without a speaker: it receives the electromagnetic signals but it does not convert them into sound. The connection is missing or damaged. Or the dyslexic has trouble identifying the letter form and difficulty in shifting from one letter to the next.

In the 1920s, when interest in dyslexia became widespread, the disability was called "word blindness,"* but more recent thinking would consider it a form of perceptual confusion. One of the pioneer investigators of dyslexia was Samuel T. Orton, head of the Department of Psychiatry in the State University of Iowa Medical School and Director of the State Psychopathic Hospital, Iowa City. His studies of the "word blind" children in Iowa City led him to conclude

* The term was first used by Dr. James Hinshelwood, a Scottish physician.

that the problem was in the brain, not the eyes, and was not emotional, as some psychologists had speculated.

Orton proposed that the left hemisphere of the brain, which is thought to control language functions, had failed to gain normal ascendancy over the right hemisphere, which presumably does not do much in language. Consequently, the child became confused in directionality: he might try to read backwards, from right to left, instead of from left to right; he might reverse the normal order of letters. Or he might not be able to decode them at all.

It was Orton's conjecture that normal reading and writing does not develop until hemispheric dominance is established. If it is not, confusing memory images of the nondominant hemisphere may interfere with perception and thinking. Orton called this condition *Strephosymbolia*, or twisted (strepho) symbol.[10]

THE CONCEPT OF DISABILITY

In describing education for the brain-injured child, Strauss, Lehtinen and Kephart established that such a child was disabled. This was a concept much more acceptable to parents and teachers than the umbrella term of retardation, with its derogatory connotation.

The concept of learning disability was derived from the discovery of the brain-injury syndrome. Educationally, a child with a perceptual disability was a child with a learning disability. A brain-injured child might have several specific learning disabilities.

The term learning disability was more specific from the viewpoint of performance. It was what the child demonstrated. Whether the cause was brain injury or not might be hypothetical. Parents and teachers preferred the term learning disability to the more frightening one of brain damage, and after 1963, when learning disability came into use as a classification, it supplanted brain injury.

Strauss and Kephart had applied the term brain injury in a clinical sense. It referred to a group of functional disorders. Neurological signs were not always observed in the children who exhibited other evidence of the syndrome. Electroencephalograms often failed to show any abnormality in children whose behavior followed the pattern of the brain-injured syndrome. Strauss and Kephart said:

> We select a group of individuals who behave in a certain fashion. The vast majority of these individuals display definite signs of brain injury. About the few remaining we do not know one way or the other. It would seem that we are justified in assuming that the factor which is causative in the vast majority is causative in the few remaining, especially in view of the fact that the common neurological examination is known not to be infallible.[11]

Not all psychologists agreed with that assumption. It was criticized as a "logical error" by Charles R. Strothers, a psychologist of the University of Washington and a prominent member of several national committees in special education.[12]

He asserted that it led educators into the error of devising programs based on the common characteristics of brain injury that did not suit all children who exhibited learning disabilities. "It is now clear that children with learning disabilities are a very heterogeneous group," he said.

The question of whether all children with learning disabilities could be classified as brain-injured disturbed experts. It has not been resolved. Some psychologists and educators did not believe that the question of brain injury was relevant to the problem. They felt that if the child exhibited a learning disability, it was not necessary to know the etiology of it in order to treat it.

From this point of view, the brain-injury syndrome could be pigeonholed as a clinical hypothesis; a diagnosis of learning disability did not necessarily have to assume brain injury. Gradually, toward the end of the 1960s, the term brain-injury syndrome was displaced in special education by learning disability. And many parents of young children with specific learning disabilities are not aware today that the term derived from a harsher antecedent.

By 1969, the National Advisory Committee for the Handicapped had accepted a definition of learning disability as a disorder of language and thinking and as a substitute for such terms as dyslexia, aphasia (loss of language), brain injury and perceptual handicap. The term excluded children who were retarded as a result of hereditary or severe environmental deficits. It excluded children with severe emotional disturbances, too.

In 1972, the professional advisory committee of the Association for Children with Learning Disabilities proposed that children who have sensory, motor, intellectual or emotional problems or who are environmentally disadvantaged should be covered by the term learning disabilities if they exhibit learning problems. Learning disabilities thus became an umbrella for the large group of children who test higher than retarded but who do not learn.

Illinois added to its School Code, in 1972, a section covering children with specific learning disabilities. The learning-disabled were defined as children between the ages of three and twenty-one with a disorder in one or more basic psychological processes involved in understanding or in using language, which disorder may manifest itself in imperfect ability to listen, think, speak, write, spell or do mathematical calculations.

The Illinois statute went on to say that such disorders include such conditions as perceptual handicaps, brain injury, minimal brain dysfunction (another term for brain injury), dyslexia and developmental aphasia. In 1973, the Code was amended to provide for state support of children attending private special education facilities that were deemed necessary where the state did not provide them. The local school district had to pay the tuition, but the state reimbursed it. This provision also applied to private summer programs for learning-disabled children.

However, the definition of learning disability in the Illinois code excluded children with learning problems which are primarily the result of visual, hearing or motor handicaps, of mental retardation, emotional disturbance or environmental disadvantage.

A similar definition appeared in the Federal Register of February 20, 1975, in reference to U.S. Public Law 91-230, the federal Education of the Handicapped Act. Approved in 1970, the law provides for model demonstration centers for the improvement of educational services to children with specific learning disabilities. The program was started in the 1971 fiscal year with an appropriation of $1 million. By the 1974 fiscal year, funding had increased to $3.25 million.

One of the striking aspects of both federal and state definitions of learning disability is that both exclude retarded children who also are

disabled in learning. From an administrative viewpoint, children classified as retarded by IQ tests are provided for in other sections of the
Illinois School Code and by other federal legislation.

The legal distinction implies that two different categories of mentally handicapped children exist; one that is classified as retarded and
the other, as disabled.

One assumption behind this distinction is that the child with learning disabilities is not retarded in the familial sense. He is a normal
child who has somehow been disabled.

That is also the assumption in brain injury. The child began life
with a normal potential. Somewhere along the line, it was disrupted
by accident or disease and he was disabled.

I will discuss the ambiguity of this situation in more detail later. At
the moment, I want to call attention to the fact that it is one of the
unresolved questions in this whole field. It is a symptom of the chaos
that pervades the field.

PART II

THE YOUNG ADULTS

Chapter 5

The Alumni:
The Cove School Study

In this book, as in my earlier one, I have referred to the child with learning disabilities as the Other Child. The term was employed by Alfred A. Strauss to describe one of the striking characteristics of the child whom he called brain-injured. This child was "otherwise" than his brothers and sisters or than children in the neighborhood. His behavior was different. His responses were often unusual. He could not learn in the way that others could, although he appeared to be of normal or near normal intelligence. He was an enigma to his parents and teachers.

The first question that parents of the Other Child ask are: What will become of him? How will he get on in life? What can we do? What can we expect?

Thirty years ago, when the syndrome that accounted for this form of "otherness" was identified in children, there were no answers. All that could be predicted was that if the child received an education that dealt with his specific learning disabilities, he had a better chance of developing into an independent, self-supporting adult than if he did not.

In fact, many parents and teachers observed, without such a program the child could not learn much at all; in many cases he was destined to be illiterate in adulthood, a serious handicap for adults in

modern society. In that case, the probability was high that he would
be dependent for survival on his family or on public welfare.

How would he fare if he did not receive the type of education his
handicaps required? After thirty years, there are answers. In this and
following chapters, I will present some of the data.

In summary, the outlook is optimistic. Followups of four groups of
children who received special education for learning disabilities show
that as adults the majority achieved in the normal range of income,
occupational success and social adjustment.

Although all of these persons exhibited learning disabilities as children, they were classified in other terms. Some were labeled as brain-
injured, perceptually handicapped or as victims of minimal cerebral
dysfunction. These terms referred to impaired neuromental functioning that may or may not have been ascertained to be the result of
trauma or inflammation of the brain. Another group of children was
simply labeled retarded, educable mentally handicapped, or educable
mentally retarded.

These two groups are still considered in terms of separate classifications by state and federal statutes and by most educators. Those
classified as retarded are generally thought to exhibit "familial" or
hereditary retardation in the outmoded eugenics sense. While the
genetic aspect of the classification is dubious at best, the label is
applied to the child who exhibits an IQ below 70.

The group classified as brain-injured, perceptually handicapped or
suffering minimal cerebral dysfunction is generally considered to exhibit an IQ above 70. Minimal cerebral dysfunction in members of
this group is not considered hereditary, although one type of cerebral
dysfunction—dyslexia—appears to be hereditary.

Since the mid-1960s, the older labels of brain injury, perceptual
handicap and cerebral dysfunction have been superseded by the less
frightening and blander term of learning disability.

Both groups—those thought of as having familial retardation and
those considered to have been disabled in learning ability by some
trauma, inflammation or undetermined cause—certainly exhibit
learning disabilities. The fact that each is treated differently from
legal and administrative points of view is one of the unresolved
anomalies in special education.

Children whose IQs are in the range legally defined as educable mentally handicapped (or retarded) often exhibit specific learning disabilities. They may exhibit the brain-injury syndrome. And if they are put into a special class for the educable mentally handicapped that does not also treat their specific learning disabilities, they are exposed to the same frustrations and failures as learning-disabled children with normal IQs who are placed in regular classes.

It would be simpler and more humane to scrap the old "retarded" label and treat all children with learning disabilities as children with *learning disabilities.*

THE COVE SCHOOL STUDY

A landmark study of learning disabled children as adults was made by psychologists Laura Lehtinen Rogan and Lenore Dumas Hartman in 1975–76.[1]* It covered ninety-one adults between the ages of twenty-one and thirty-nine who had received an average of three years of early remedial education between the ages of six and thirteen at the Cove School during the years 1947 to 1967. The group was composed of sixty-six males and twenty-five females.

Some of the subjects had attended both the residential unit at Racine, Wisconsin, and the day school at Evanston, Illinois. Others attended only one of the units. Following the death of Alfred A. Strauss, the founder, in 1957, the residential school was closed. However, the day school in Evanston has been continued and enlarged and is a leading center for the remediation of learning disabilities in the United States.

The early Cove School program not only was remedial, but therapeutic. Considering the disabilities of most of the children whose parents brought them to Cove in desperation, the results are remarkable and dramatic.

These were children who could not learn in a conventional public school classroom. As in the case I described in a previous chapter,

* Laura Lehtinen Rogan, Ph.D., is Director of the Cove School, Evanston, Illinois, and Lenore Dumas Hartman, M.S., is a practicing psychologist in Evanston.

parents could not find adequate public school facilities for children with the learning and behavior handicaps these children showed. Some of them in other circumstances would have been relegated to state institutions for the mentally retarded—and for several this is precisely what had been recommended by inexperienced "counselors" in elementary schools and in public agencies. As children, these adults had exhibited behavioral anomalies typical of the brain-injury syndrome: hyperactivity, catastrophic reaction, distractibility and perceptual aberration.

Ten to twenty years later, the Rogan-Hartman survey found that most of them had become independent, self-supporting and reasonably well-adjusted adults. The mean IQ had gained 10 points. As children, the group's mean IQ was dull normal, scores ranging from less than 80 to 130. As adults, the mean IQ was in the average range; more scored above average and fewer below.

Sixty percent were fully employed, with salaries ranging from $5000 to $15,000 plus. The median income was $7500. Another 13 percent were in college in undergraduate and graduate study. Nine percent worked part time or were between jobs at the time they were interviewed. Five percent were marginally employable and 9 percent, consisting of the most severely handicapped, were in sheltered workshops or life-care facilities.

Of the ninety-one alumni who returned questionnaires, sixty-four (70 percent) had been graduated from high school. Of the sixty-four completing high school, thirty-five (56 percent) had been graduated from or were still attending colleges at the time of the study. Four had received master's degrees, two were in master's programs and one was in a doctoral program.

A remarkable aspect of this educational progress is that when these men and women entered the Cove Schools in the twenty-year period from 1947 to 1967 their learning and behavior problems were so severe that they could not succeed in a conventional public or private school. All came from white, middle-class and upper-middle-class families.

Etiology

What was the etiology or origin of the disabilities these ninety-one adults exhibited as children? Less than one-half of them had been given electroencephalograms as children. In all cases, however, a physician had diagnosed minimal brain damage.

More than half (55 percent) had physical or developmental handicaps in addition to learning disabilities. Speech problems were present in 28 percent; language problems in 19 percent;[2] mild cerebral palsy in 13 percent; seizures in 9 percent; visual problems such as congenital cataract, detached retina or optic nerve atrophy in 8 percent; hearing loss in 7 percent, and cleft palate, spina bifida and other physical abnormalities in 6 percent.

In the early diagnostic reports, 64 percent or fifty-eight children had emotional problems. Nearly one-third exhibited poor behavior control. Seventeen exhibited feelings of low self-esteem.

The etiology of the brain injury was not determined in thirty-three of the children. It was traced to difficult delivery in twenty-two, accident or illness in fifteen, premature birth in seven, pregnancy complication in the mother in six, cyanosis in two, arrested hydrocephalus in two* and other causes such as caesarean section, jaundice or infection in the mother in four.

Most of the group (80 percent) entered the residential or the day school between the ages of seven and ten. Most (70 percent) left at ages eleven to twelve (the mean was twelve years, one month).

Intelligence Test Results

The principal tests from which childhood and adult scores could be compared were the Wechsler Intelligence Scale for Children (WISC) and the Wechsler Adult Intelligence Scale (WAIS). There were three

---

* Hydrocephalus refers to an abnormal increase in spinal fluid in the head. If not arrested, it causes enlargement of the skull, especially the forehead, and brain atrophy.

scores in each: verbal, performance and the combination of both, called full scale. Unless otherwise designated, the scores I give are full scale.

The investigating team of Rogan and Hartman noted that there were sometimes wide discrepancies between the verbal and performance scores. As children, some of the subjects could talk a "good line" but couldn't perform very well. And some could perform better than they could communicate verbally.

Persons working with learning-disabled students have noticed that those with higher verbal than performance scores learn to read without extraordinary difficulty but have much trouble with numerical and spatial concepts, the investigators commented.

Of the ninety-one subjects who were located and whose families responded to questionnaires, one who was planning to participate in the study was killed in a traffic accident. Seventy-five were interviewed and seventy-two were given the adult intelligence test. There were some who were too busy or indifferent to bother with the study; there were some who feared that being iden'ified as learning-disabled or as brain-injured might reflect on their social or occupational status; there were some who simply did not want to be reminded of their childhood problems.

A total of eighty-eight subjects had been given the Wechsler test for children and seventy-two took the adult test. The adult scores were higher for the verbal and performance tests than the childhood scores. From childhood to adulthood, the verbal test scores rose from a mean of 91 to a mean of 102; performance scores rose from a mean of 87 to 93; the full scale IQ average jumped from 88 to 98. The first full scale mean represents dull normal and the second, average.

	As Children	As Adults
Verbal IQ	91	102
Performance IQ	87	93
Full Scale IQ	88	98

On the verbal scale, three adults scored 130 and above and ten scored in the IQ range of 120–129. As children, none of the group had scored above 115.

Since eighty-eight took the Weschler test as children and only seventy-two were tested as adults, it may be clearer to describe the gains in terms of percentages.

Eighteen percent scored above 120 as adults on the verbal scale. None had as children.

Another 19 percent scored in the range of 110 to 119. They were high average. But only 12 percent scored in that range as children.

At the lower end of the scale, 45 percent had scored below 90 as children; this was reduced to 25 percent among the adults. None scored below 69 as adults although 2 percent, or two persons, had as children.

On the Wechsler performance scale, 22 percent of the adults scored 110 or above. Only 11 percent had as children.

As children, 37 percent scored below 80 on performance, but only 20 percent scored below 80 as adults.

On the full scale, taking verbal and performance abilities together, 24 percent scored 110 or better as adults. Only 7 percent did as children. As adults, 11 percent scored less than 80, but 30 percent scored less than 80 as children.

Of the seventy-two adults tested, sixty-four scored 80 or higher on the full range Wechsler scale. The mean IQ scores of those sixty-four were 105 verbal, 97 performance and 101 full scale.

This is how the two groups compared by mean IQs:

The survey team noted a suggestion by a colleague that improved performance on an intelligence test may reflect accrued academic skill and knowledge rather than an increase in intellectual ability.

Whatever the tests reflect—and it is surmised to be intelligence—there was an increase among the alumni in the capacities the tests were designed to measure. These are among the capacities that are believed to promote success in modern American society.

Employment

Of the ninety-one alumni whose families returned questionnaires, sixty were employed, four were job hunting, fourteen were students or trainees and thirteen were either marginally employable or too handicapped to work outside of a sheltered workshop or life-care facility.

Of the employed, fifty-two had full-time jobs at an annual income ranging from $5000 to over $15,000. Two had regular part-time jobs; one had a part-time job but was seeking full-time work; one worked part time as a short order cook; one did seasonal work in landscaping in summer and as a member of a ski patrol in winter. Three worked in organizations where part of their income was earned and part subsidized by their parents.

The employed adults were forty-seven males and thirteen females. One-third (twenty) were in clerical jobs (twelve men and eight women). Fourteen were classified as unskilled workers (twelve men and two women); eight were in various professions (seven men and one woman); five were in sales (three men and two women); four were in managerial positions (all men); four were in service occupations (two men and two women); three in military service (all men) and two were craftsmen (men).

The eight employed in professions were an accountant, commodities broker, electronic technician, photographer, research technician, children's music teacher, psychological diagnostician in private practice and an urban planner. The psychological diagnostician was part owner of a successful testing service for learning-disabled children.

The four members of the managerial group were an executive secretary at a camp for the handicapped, a food store manager, a manager of the sports and toy department in a retail store and a retail special projects analyst.

The large clerical group included file clerks, travel agent, receptionist-secretary, mail clerk, stock room clerk, post office mail clerk and sorter, messenger, jewelry tagger, mail order house clerk and an advertising clerk and copy runner.

The sales group were in retail art supplies, insurance, therapeutic equipment, advertising and a home candy and cookie retail business.

The craftsmen were a printer and an electrician's helper. Service jobs included an assistant cook at a boarding school, short order cook, maintenance man, aide in a home for elderly men and the landscaper-ski patroller. The three in the armed services were in the Army, Navy and Marine Corps.

The fourteen unskilled workers included a city sanitation worker, a machine operator at a printing firm, assembly line workers, packagers, supermarket baggers, farm and ranch hands, a janitor and a factory laborer.

Among the full-time employed, 4 percent earned more than $15,000 a year and 24 percent, more than $10,000.

Of the seventy-five alumni who were interviewed, twenty-six were still dependent upon parents, relatives or community services. This group included nine students, six unemployed, eight in a sheltered workshop, a recently divorced housewife with two children, two working only part time, two receiving income from a trust and two receiving social security income for disability.

The marital status of eighty-two alumni, sixty-two males and twenty females, was: fourteen married one to eight years, all males, and two divorced, both females. Thus 16 or 19 percent of the eighty-two surveyed on marital status had been married. One of the women was divorced after less than one year and the other, after ten years.

Five of the married males were fathers. Two had one child, two had two children and one had three. The woman divorced after ten years had two children.

Living Arrangements

Of ninety alumni returning the questionnaire, forty-seven lived away from the parental home, including the fourteen married males who lived with their wives in their own dwellings. The other forty-three lived at home, including six college students, or in supervised situations.

In addition to the fourteen married men, a total of fifteen alumni (ten men and five women) lived alone in their own apartments and eight more (six men and two women) shared an apartment with one or more roommates. Four (three men and one woman) living apart from parents were college students. Two men and one woman lived near their parents, but not in the same quarters.

Of those living with parents, six (two men and four women) did so as a matter of convenience; twelve (ten men and two women) by choice; five (four men and one woman) were planning to move out and become independent; twelve (nine men and three women) lived at home by financial or functional necessity; five (four men and one woman) lived in supervised quarters and three (one man and two women) in a life-care institution.

Of the fourteen married men, eleven worked full time, one worked part time, one was unemployed and one was a student. The part-time worker had been put on temporarily by the postal service and was looking for full-time employment. The unemployed man had just lost a managerial job he had held for five years and was hunting another one. The student had returned to graduate school to study anthropology after successful employment as a salesman.

Educationally, thirteen had completed high school (three in a curriculum adjusted for learning disabilities) and one had dropped out. Of the thirteen, six had gone on to complete a college education. Their occupations ranged from professional to unskilled. The high school dropout was working as a manager.

The other thirty-three who were living independently included four college students in dormitories. The twenty-nine others had about the same employment and educational attainments as the married group. Most—twenty-three—were working full time in professional, clerical and unskilled employment. Three were students who lived independently but were not in dormitories. One was in military service, one was a homemaker (the divorced mother) and two were unemployed.

Among this group of independent singles, one was a visually handicapped young woman who established herself, despite congenital cataracts, in a music career. She was teaching music to children in an Episcopalian religious order. Another young woman in this group lived in her own apartment on the campus of a treatment center for emotionally disturbed children where she worked.

Two in the group were living near their parents—and needed to be near them. One had a severe language handicap (aphasia), hearing loss and vision problems. The other, a young woman, needed her father's help to manage money.

Thus, in one fashion or another, more than half of the alumni (52 percent) were living apart from parents, and only a few were intermittently dependent on them. The other 48 percent, or forty-three alumni, were not living independently, but that does not mean that they could not in all cases.

A total of thirty-five were residing with parents, five were living in supervised situations and three were in life-care institutions.

Of those living with parents, eleven, including six men and five women, were doing so temporarily for convenience and/or working toward independence. Another twelve, including ten men and two women, were living at home by choice. In one instance, for example, a young man lived at home to save money; in another, a young man was employed in the same place as his father and the two often went to work together. Nine men and three women said they lived at home by necessity. In this group, six had attended classes for the educable mentally handicapped in high school, four had received special education for the multiply-handicapped, one completed high school in a program adjusted for learning disabilities and one was a college undergraduate. Four were employed full time, employment of one was subsidized by parents, one was a student, four worked in sheltered workshops and two were unemployed.

Among the twelve living at home by choice, nine were employed, one was a student and two were unemployed.

Social case workers and other professionals working with the learning disabled tend to regard independent living as a sign of adult achievement. Some social service agencies encourage young adults to "spread their wings" and "leave the nest."

However, I have observed that it has been financially and emotionally less stressful for some of the subjects to live at home than alone or with a roommate. These were young men who seemed perfectly capable of conducting their own affairs whether they lived independently or not. They contributed to the upkeep of the family home. Essentially, they continued in adulthood a life-style formed in late adolescence. It suited them and other members of the family.

Unless death or retirement of the parents makes it necessary to break up the home, I do not believe it is essential or even especially desirable for many of these single young adults to live alone if they are compatible with other family members. I do not accept the theory of a number of professionals that independent living is the sine qua non of adult achievement in a group of handicapped adults. This is a recent innovation that departs from the culture of most ethnic groups in America.

In their report on the adults who continued to live at home, Rogan and Hartman noted that many of them had fewer friends and social activities than those living away from home. Some tended to confine their social relationships to work and the family circle. They indicated little need for outside social contact.

"Others perceived themselves as shy and socially isolated outside their contacts at work and within the family," the psychologists said. "They expressed wishes for more friends but were not able to take positive steps toward developing new relationships."

Although competent as adults, the stay-at-homes that I have observed find emotional satisfaction and relief from stress in remaining with the family where circumstances are compatible. In some instances, they may become the chief sustainer of the family in later years. Does this limit their activities? I think not.

They take part in the same bowling team or bridge club activities as they would if living alone. Otherwise, some of them tend to be "loners"—partly as a result of childhood rejection experiences, partly as the result of lack of game skills and partly because social activity is often stressful, uncertain and uncomfortable. They are inclined not to be gregarious.

Can gregariousness and socialization be forced by independent living? I have not seen any evidence that they can. Moving out of the nest does not result in a burst of social activity. It more often deepens loneliness. The highly vaunted life-style of the free spirit, the adventurous "single" is not for them. Not that they can't handle it; they simply don't want it. They are not free spirits. They are tied to conventional living by a lifelong disability for which they have learned to compensate but from which they do not escape.

What happens to the stay-at-homes when the parents die? Would not independent living beforehand prepare them for that eventuality? There is no doubt that it would make the adjustment easier, but the emotional impact would not be greatly reduced. Whether the young adult is living at home or on the other side of town, the family connection is an important reinforcement. When it is broken, he suffers a loss that requires a much greater adjustment than meeting the financial and housekeeping demands of independent living.

I favor independent living where it is highly motivated or necessary. Where it is not, I suggest that the theory of pushing people out of the nest so that they can fly by themselves is mainly for the birds.

The Cove School investigators found that five of those living at home wanted greater independence. Three of them had been in psychotherapy as adolescents and as adults. They continued seeing a therapist occasionally as they felt the need. The three had completed high school. Two were employed in clerical jobs and one in an unskilled job. Their emotional problems were seen by the investigators as a limiting factor toward independent living. A fourth subject, a young woman employed part time as a cook, wanted to live away from her family, but could not afford it. A fifth subject was in a workshop training program where part of the design was to promote independent living.

Of the twelve subjects who continued to live with parents out of necessity, four were marginally employable and one was a college student, as noted earlier. The student was a young woman. Her judgment in practical matters was regarded by her parents as unreliable and her emotional and social development was below par for a young adult despite her academic ability. One young man was physically and visually handicapped by slowly developing neural tumors. He conducted a parent-subsidized candy and cookie business from home. Two of the subjects were unemployed and four were in sheltered workshops, as mentioned earlier. This group was composed of persons with physical problems involving speech, hearing and muscular coordination as well as vision that would have made independent living difficult, if not out of the question. The investigators commented:

> It was possible to project that in time several members of this group could live comfortably in a supervised situation. . . . For others, their own family or a surrogate family would remain as a permanent need. . . .

Parents had arranged for four other subjects to live away from home under supervision. Two were living in group homes supervised by a social worker who involved the residents in housekeeping and management. One was living with a family on a farm where he worked as a hired hand. A fourth lived in a rooming house in the community where he attended a sheltered workshop. The landlady provided some supervision. He was helped by a social worker and regularly saw a psychotherapist. He visited his family in a nearby town on weekends. One young woman lived in a dormitory connected with a workshop where she was being trained to work with deaf children.

The Interviews

The seventy-five alumni who were interviewed by the investigators consisted of fifty-six men and nineteen women.[3] The preponderance of males reflects the makeup of the learning-disabilities population, the investigators said.

In this group, forty-nine were employed. Their satisfaction with their jobs seemed to depend on how well they got along with fellow workers as well as how much they were paid. Thirty-nine were satisfied with their jobs, seven were not and three were not sure whether they liked their work or not.

Conspicuous features of their work were the social contacts and work-related recreation, such as bowling or softball, it provided. Twelve of the subjects said they had no friends whatever and twenty-eight said they had no close friends. Thirty said they did date.

Of the seventy-five, most—fifty-one—could drive an automobile and thirty-eight owned one. One member of the group who lived at home habitually paid cash for a new car, but felt it was advisable to establish credit by securing an oil company credit card. Another who bought an automobile through a finance company submitted the contract to an attorney before he signed it. In spite of perceptual problems that interfered with learning in childhood, members of this group whom I observed were notably free of traffic accidents and violations. One young man who began driving following a high school drivers' education course maintained a traffic-violation-free and accident-free driving record for fifteen years. He had exhibited perceptual handicap as a child but it did not affect his ability to drive safely.

Those who did not take vacations with their families tended to travel on group tours, where transportation and hotel accommodations would be arranged for them. The range of hobbies was quite wide. It included coin collecting, miniature railroad trains, antique cars, Civil War history, classical music, grand opera and archeology.

Rogan and Hartman, who conducted the interviews, said that "the data are rich in feelings and attitudes about learning problems, counseling and therapeutic experiences and skills not yet mastered." They added:

> The less successful subjects are still concerned about their inability to be competent in basic skill areas such as reading, spelling, math and writing. A few complain about "poor memory." Those who have successfully completed college expressed concerns about lack of self-confidence, ability to take pressure. . . . A number of the subjects who have had problems of being "clumsy" or "awkward" would like to improve their dexterity, perception and physical abilities. A few of the college graduates berated a lack of technical skill which prevented them from doing basic maintenance on their automobiles.

The interviewers said it was noteworthy that seventy of the seventy-five interviewees reported no involvement with criminal or delinquent acts and were not in the "drug scene." There was one instance of repeated traffic violations that the investigators believed to be caused by impulsiveness (a general cause of traffic mishaps among adolescents and young adults).

> Factors related to this low incidence of antisocial acts may include the high socioeconomic level of this population, the relative social isolation reported by many subjects and the therapeutic supports provided during adolescence.

Of the seventy-five, only twenty reported having had no counseling or therapy during their childhood and adolescence. Eighteen others said they were continuing in treatment for emotional problems as adults. The rest had therapy for varying periods during childhood or adolescence and some of them consulted a therapist occasionally as adults.

It appeared to the investigators that a key to overcoming physical and perceptual handicaps was intellectual ability. "Those who are able intellectually do attain college level functioning, and some go beyond to attain professional or managerial status," the investigators commented.

The Personality Inventory

Aside from these general impressions, the investigators gave sixty-seven alumni a personality test called the Minnesota Multiphasic Personality Inventory (MMPI). Results for five subjects were discarded as invalid. For the remaining sixty-two, including forty-six men and sixteen women, certain characteristics emerged. But whether they also applied to the "very broad spectrum" now covered by learning disabilities "is an open question," the investigators said.

They interpreted the test results as indicating that some subjects demonstrate sociability and competency "via the safe avenue of engaging in a great deal of activity in social and achievement-oriented areas of living."

Although they try to be likable and successful people, they find it difficult to achieve this in a "psychologically meaningful way."

The investigators explained: Many tasks tend to be undertaken as a defense against poor performances and inadequate resolutions of personal problems.

The subjects avoid admitting failure by rationalizing in this way: "If I had the opportunity to apply myself fully to this one task, then I would have been able to show you what capabilities I really have."

This strikes me as a rationalization that is not uncommon among nonhandicapped people who do not reach self-imposed or parent-imposed goals.

However, the investigators added: "In effect, these subjects may be characterized by a poverty of close, interpersonal relationships. The subjects prefer to be involved in doing many things simultaneously, which may suggest an absence of well-planned, goal directed behavior."

The Minnesota tests indicated that the subjects find social relationships trying, the investigators said.

On the one hand, they want and need people and on the other, the subjects lack confidence that people can like and respect them. In effect, to become known is to become vulnerable.

As protection, the subjects may periodically retreat into themselves or solitary activities to get away from people and to recover from their interpersonal wounds. To be involved in social relationships is to submit to the dangerous possibility of attacks upon the personality; try as they may, they cannot render themselves immune to the possible attacks of others.

Further, the subjects find it difficult to tolerate tensions. These are released by impulsively "doing things." Sometimes, action enables the subject to escape from himself; at other times it helps to discharge tension.

The subjects tend to vacillate between despondent and euphoric feelings. They tend to react to others in terms of moods. They may be disappointed or elated. Others' responses have the power to hurt them or elate them. They want supportive or dependent relationships. However, the investigators said:

Despondency and depression lurk just beneath the surface, even when the subjects appear elated, apparently happy or satisfied. Being with people may make them feel temporarily happy. However, the quality of the interpersonal relations and inner feelings of emptiness and insecurity make the subjects feel like "their show won't make Broadway."

In summary, the personality inventory shows that the subjects are sensitive and easily hurt. Their daydreams may be of the suffering hero type. They are tense and anxious much of the time.

At times, they feel the need to build a wall between themselves and others, and to support the wall by nursing hurts and assigning blame to others. The investigators interpreted test reactions in terms of a model where the subject feels that fate dealt him a poor hand and that he is suffering, being hurt and in pain.

Those are some of the inner feelings. Outwardly, they do not show, and not all of the subjects confess them. One young man I have observed has achieved a specialized professional career and is determined to outdo his father in making money. Another I have observed is aware of his perceptual and thinking difficulties, seems to accept them and never makes excuses for failure. A third young man shrugs off his problems and is content to live at home, work in a non-demanding but steady job at good pay and participate in limited social activity. Essentially, these three are competent, practical men. One is married; the other two are single. My opinion is that they enjoy life. They have something else in common. In each case, institutionalization was recommended by a professional evaluator when the subject was six years old. Had this recommendation been followed, I am sure they could not have achieved the social usefulness and financial independence they now have.

The Case for Special Education

One of the landmark aspects of the Cove School survey is the indisputable case it makes for specialized education. The case is so clear that the failure of a school board to provide for such handicapped children as these subjects is hard to excuse.

All ninety-one subjects whose families returned questionnaires were enrolled in the Cove School program after they failed to make progress in or tolerate conventional public or private school environments. It was only after an average of three years in the program that they were able to progress in regular public and private school classes or in public or private school classes for the educable mentally handicapped.

Twenty-six of them entered kindergarten at the usual age of five, but were eventually withdrawn either from the kindergarten or from a primary grade when learning problems became overwhelmingly frustrating. These children were then enrolled in Cove, in some cases as a last resort.

Another thirty-seven also entered kindergarten at the usual age. School authorities tried to keep them in conventional classes by having them repeat a grade. But that did not work and the special program at Cove provided the only apparent alternative.

A group of eight children entered kindergarten one year late. The parents had become aware of a developmental problem. But they

were not sure what it was. They followed a recommendation to
"give" the child another year at home in which "to mature." That
remedy did not work either.

Nine subjects were enrolled in kindergarten and then withdrawn,
six did not attend kindergarten, four went to a special school kindergarten and one was tutored at home.

The investigators noted that the early school experiences of three-
fourths of the subjects were sufficiently tolerable so that teachers
continued to work with them through kindergarten and in some cases
into the primary grades before withdrawal. For the most part, behavior and learning problems of this group appeared to be mild to
moderate. The investigators said:

> The fact that so many children could have a kindergarten experi-
> ence with nonhandicapped children may also be a commentary on
> the flexibility of the kindergarten curriculum and the sensitivity of
> the kindergarten teachers.

One-fourth of the subjects, however, either had no kindergarten
experience or an unhappy one. Nine were withdrawn after a few
weeks and seven who did not attend kindergarten came directly to the
Cove School after nursery school, home tutoring or a temporary stay
in their local school. One subject came from a residential school for
retarded children. Two others spent a year in a special preschool
facility for emotionally disturbed children. One cerebral palsied child
attended kindergarten with other physically handicapped children.

Most of the children who were withdrawn, usually at the suggestion of the school, exhibited hyperactivity to such an extent that they
could not be tolerated in the room. Those who were not sent to
kindergarten were considered by parents, teachers or both as too
immature or "otherwise" in their development to cope with kindergarten.

What happened to the ninety-one subjects after they were dismissed from Cove as ready for a conventional school setting?

Fifty-five were enrolled in regular graded (fifty-one) or residential
(four) schools. Of this number two needed special help in the graded
school. Twenty-one entered special education classes in regular grade
schools, nine in self-contained classes for learning problems and

twelve in a class for the educable mentally handicapped. The remaining fifteen received programs of special education in private residential (eleven) or day (four) schools.

Of the fifty-five who returned to regular public or private schools, eleven were placed at the grade level expected for their age; thirty-five were placed in a grade a year below that expected for their age; seven were placed two years below age level and two were placed in nongraded residential programs on an age group basis.

Forty-four of the fifty-five continued to make progress until high school. So did the thirty-six who entered special education classes.

Of those who did not do well in their first placement after Cove School, three were moved to small private day or residential schools for more individual attention, one was placed in a class for the educable mentally handicapped and two were placed in a class for emotionally disturbed children.

Only six of the ninety-one subjects did not attend high school. One had severe reading and spelling problems which persisted despite years of intensive, remedial effort; two had multiple physical and intellectual problems and remained in a special class at junior high school level until age eighteen and three went into life-care institutions.

Of the eighty-five who attended high school, fifty-three went into regular graded day or residential high schools. Eight of them required special help in the regular graded high school. Another fifteen were placed in classes for the educable mentally handicapped in a regular graded high school. Another fourteen attended private day and residential schools providing special education. Of the three remaining, one took a high school correspondence course, one attended adult night high school and one received technical training in a residential facility.

Sixty-four were graduated from high school either in a regular program (forty-eight) or an adjusted program (sixteen). Twelve earned high school certificates from an educable mentally handicapped program and one from a program for the hearing impaired. One had not completed high school at the time of the survey and seven dropped out.

At the time of the interviews, twenty-three had completed college as follows: three completed junior college, sixteen had four years of college and, as noted earlier, four achieved master's degrees. Twelve more were college students at the time of the interviews and eight more did not complete college.

The college graduates majored in accounting, engineering, biology, education, economics, history, public relations, music, fine arts, biochemistry, urban studies, library science, education, recreational therapy and anthropology.

Among the eight who did not complete college were three young women. One transferred to an art school and another to a secretarial school. A third was killed in a traffic accident in her sophomore year.

Nine subjects completed technical courses or trade school training in art, electrical work, cooking, key punch, printing and industrial machine operations.

Viewing the general aspect of the alumni they surveyed, Rogan and Hartman remarked:

> The group as a whole gave the pleasant impression of being highly personable, affable and attractive young people. They did not stand out in a crowd, as in a restaurant, unless there was an obvious physical handicap. The majority presented themselves as compassionate, sensitive young people, reality oriented, goal directed and responsible.

BILLY COULDN'T READ

One of the ninety-one alumni was Billy. When he was seven years old, Mrs. W, his first grade teacher, told his mother that Billy was not educable. He could not learn to read. Nevertheless, the teacher passed Billy on to the second grade. Maybe something could be done with him there. At least he was out of her hair. The teacher believed that social promotion was important.

Billy was born September 3, 1947. He was a ten-months baby and required forceps delivery. He weighed eight pounds ten ounces. A bouncing baby boy, the doctor said. He stood, walked and talked normally, the mother recalled.

He was the first born in an upper-middle-class family on Chicago's North Shore, which has some of the finest educational facilities in the world. Within a radius of a few miles are Northwestern University, National Teachers College, Evanston Township High School and New Trier East and West High Schools. These are among the "top" high schools in North America. About 85 percent of their students are prepared for college. Parents are aggressive and insistent in their demands for quality education in the primary grades as well as in the premium high schools. Largely because of these good schools, which have escaped the overcrowding, violence and bureaucratic indifference of Chicago's public school system, property values are high. Many a family has fled Chicago to the North Shore so "my children can get the kind of education I got when I was a kid."

This is the environment in which Billy entered a private kindergarten and then the first grade in a public school. At age seven, he was personable, a good baseball player and described as having good sports tolerance and social adjustment by the director of a summer program he attended.

The Mother's Day Card he made at school showed that he could color between the lines—something perceptually handicapped children have difficulty learning to do.

But Billy couldn't learn to read. Placement in an institution was recommended at the school; it seemed obvious that he could learn little in a regular public school class.

The mother rejected institutionalization and began the long trek that many parents have had to take in search of a school where Billy could learn. A diagnosis of minimal brain dysfunction was indicated by an electroencephalogram Billy was given. Further testing showed he was specifically handicapped by dyslexia, the inability to read. In other respects, his intelligence was above average.

Billy was the model of the child with a specific learning disability that the public schools in one of the richest suburbias on earth did not understand and could not handle. Fortunately for Billy and his family, there was a small, private day school in Evanston where Billy's disability was understood and could be treated—the Cove School. His mother enrolled him there as soon as she could.

After two years, Billy was ready to reenter a regular class in a graded public school. His fifth grade report card said: "He is doing the work of the grade satisfactorily. He seems to have matured considerably in his attitudes. He has advanced academically."

After the sixth grade, Billy attended first one junior high school and then another. His grades were generally low. He failed language arts and physical education, but he scored "good" in industrial arts, music and fine art.

Junior high school in many communities is a rough experience for any handicapped child and many parents wish it could be avoided. Billy did not have an easy time. For children with the brain-injury syndrome, adolescence is a critical period. Biochemical changes are taking place that may either reduce or increase deviation.[4]

In junior high, Billy was a grade behind his age group and this discrepancy, which concerned him, continued in high school. A younger brother was in the same grade as Billy. Although the younger brother was aware that Billy was getting special attention and tutoring, he expressed no hostility, the mother recalled. In some families where an older child is handicapped and receives the lion's share of attention, a younger child will react as though he is being rejected. Emotional problems are sometimes generated that are difficult to resolve.

After a year in high school, Billy was sent to boys' preparatory school where he completed his high school education. He then took a business administration and liberal arts course in college. Before graduation, he married a young school teacher. At the time I interviewed Billy, they had a three-and-a-half-year-old daughter. The mother worked part time to meet expenses. They rented a house but were planning to buy.

I found Billy at age twenty-eight to be a confident, highly verbal young man, enthusiastic about his work as a commodities broker and analyst. We met at his office on LaSalle Street, Chicago. The phone kept ringing so frequently that we were not able to talk until we went out to lunch.

Billy looked prosperous in a gray suit, striped tie, polished shoes, every inch the up-and-coming LaSalle Street broker. He is tall, well set up, with eager good looks, and an outgoing manner. I had known Billy as a child and looked for some residues of hyperactivity, perseveration or awkwardness; there were none.

"You know," he said, "if you have any loose money, you ought to buy coffee futures."

I asked why. Coffee then didn't seem to be doing anything.

"It's going up this fall and winter," he said.

"Really?"

"You better believe it."

That was the spring of 1976. By fall, Billy's forecast was dramatically realized as the retail price of coffee began to escalate.

Billy charmed the restaurant hostess into getting us a table at the rear, where I could set up my tape recorder inconspicuously.

"My brother looks a lot like my dad and I look a lot like my mother," Billy said. "When you're in the family, it's kind of hard to visualize the difference yourself, because you're, well, you have to be objective instead of subjective.

"I don't recall very much of my very early years. Only a few isolated instances and most of those are associated with pain. I got hit on the head by a wooden brick—by my little brother."

Billy remembered that the family moved out of Chicago and lived in the suburbs, near the Chicago and Northwestern Railroad tracks. I asked whether he had been fascinated by trains.

"All little boys are," he said. "I threw a rock at one and got arrested . . . they had me there for an hour and bawled me out. I think I had to pay $25 over several months. Nobody was hurt. I was aiming at the wheels but I wasn't a good enough shot. Like an idiot I was right across the street from the police station."

Billy said that he had no recollection of going to kindergarten. But he remembers going to school in the first grade.

"I don't have any bad memories from that time period," he said thoughtfully. "I think it was a rather good experience, although I'm fairly sure that was the beginning of the discovery of my handicap."

I asked what he thought it was.

Supposedly, according to all the professionals at the time, I had brain damage. It was in the area of perception. I have dyslexia. You know what dyslexia is? I switch letters when I'm reading, like "ae" to "ea" or things like this.

Sometimes I find it myself and correct it immediately. In my business, that is definitely bad news. I've had to overcome that, and I have. But I am still a slow reader. I even tried to take the Evelyn Wood [reading acceleration] course but I just gave up on it. I found it to be some help but frankly I didn't want to draw attention by reading with my fingers. You run your fingers across the page with Evelyn Wood's reading method.

Basically, I'm a little bit on the lazy side unless I want to do something, and then I do it.

I recalled to Billy a report from a camp he attended when he was eleven years old. It said: "Very rebellious at first and had to be pushed into doing his share of the work but later he got into the swing of things." His mother had shown it to me. He said:

Probably true. If I don't want to do something, I'll procrastinate, put it off and then I won't get it done. But I have enough ambition of my own to get up and go.

So far as the dyslexia is concerned, a lot of well-known people have dyslexia.

I can't spell too well, either, but I have a secretary who can.

I believe that the Cove School did improve my reading ability, but probably not as much as I would have liked.

I asked Billy if he now enjoyed reading.

I really don't read enough to know. I haven't read a book for pleasure in years. I watch television, two to four hours a day—the news for an hour-and-a-half because it's important to me, and a show or two.

I hate the damn police and detective shows—they're juvenile. They brainwash people into doing what they're doing nowadays. How many crimes have we had that are identical to the ones in these programs?

We reviewed Billy's education. I asked him how old he was when he entered the Cove School.

"You're pressing me," he said, seriously. "I'm really not sure."

I asked if there were some episodes he did not want to recall.

"I know for a fact that people block out bad memories," he said. "I don't worry about that. I remember that I liked to draw and paint. I did a little watercolor of an underwater scene, with some seaweed and a couple of fishes and so on."

There was a silence as we ate. Billy frowned and said:

I do remember sitting at my desk in the sixth grade and thinking to myself: I'm going to junior high school. Next thing is high school. Next thing is college. How am I going to end up? What kind of future am I going to have?

That is a very distinct and profound memory that sticks with me to this day. I was concerned. I said to myself: Look, man, I don't know what the hell I want to do. There were millions of occupations. To choose among them and to come up with the right one is beyond the scope of the sixth grader. I just remember thinking about it, I was truly concerned, but not necessarily worried. I'm an optimist. If something isn't right at the moment, I'm not too worried about it; I believe things work out in time.

Billy asked me if I remembered seeing a photograph of his wife and little girl on his desk. His wife's background was different than his, Billy said.

He recalled that his family was well-to-do, lived in a big house on the North Shore; it was so big that the first day he got lost on the third floor.

"Some day, I'm going to own a house like that," he said. I asked why.

I think the answer is I want to do as well as my Dad has done. Not only will I do as well; I'll do better. He's got his work and so do I. He's got a terrible ego. And so do I. And I inherited that from him.

Billy talked further about the influence of parents on children. "They shape the kids' attitudes, opinions, judgments and so on," he said. "Incredible! They literally program their kids. The poor program the poor; the rich, the rich."

Billy noted that the poor seemed to get poorer and the rich, richer. The consequence of this process would be explosive. That was something to be very concerned about, he said.

Billy recalled his days at the preparatory school, which he described as "outstanding for education, but absolutely horrible for discipline."

It was a military school. I had to wear a uniform all the time. It was the Old Boy–New Boy system. Run around the track at 3 A.M. nude in a foot of snow. I went through all that. Getting smacked with a coat hanger. I don't think it hurt me; it may even have helped in a way I don't yet realize.

He had a nice social life there "in terms of the town girls." But he did not get along as well as he wanted "with the people that I wanted to get along with."

There were some close friends, "but I never got along with the cliques; you know how you want to be in with the social cliques." He explained:

> They wouldn't accept me, probably because I was a little bit differ-
> ent. I would make dumb comments, not relevant to the situation. I
> couldn't quite be as sharp, cool or as socially acceptable; I didn't
> quite fit the pattern. This happened to me also in junior high school
> and in high school. There was a group I was involved in to a slight
> extent, but they wouldn't invite me to their parties.
>
> I still remember the names of these people [in high school] be-
> cause I looked up to them . . . they were the kind of people I would
> have liked to have been like. They were very popular in high
> school; always considered likely to succeed. But most of them
> haven't; they're not doctors or lawyers or brokers.

We talked about this a while. Billy said he now perceived these boys whom he had looked up to in high school and in prep school as rather ordinary. It was a measure of his own growth.

The time was nearing 2 P.M. and Billy excused himself to go back to the office. He was immersed in his work in which his expertise was recognized. Occasionally he appeared on a public service television program called *Ask the Expert*.

He reached for the check, but I took it.

"I have a rich publisher," I said (hopefully).

"Okay," said Billy. "I yield to seniority. You said you knew me as a kid, but I really don't remember you."

"I remember you," I said. "You haven't changed a bit!"

He grinned, towering over me. We shook hands.

"Thanks for the lunch," Billy said. "Take my advice about coffee futures."

I didn't, but I wish I had.

VIC

When Vic was little, his father used to walk with him to the drugstore before bedtime and buy him a milkshake. The purpose was to put some weight on this thin, tense, hyperactive six-year-old, who was much given to the type of tantrum called "catastrophic reaction."

Victor is the child I referred to in an earlier chapter, who was diagnosed by a psychiatrist as emotionally upset because his father had been away in the service for two-and-a-half years. His behavior was so unpredictable that he could not remain successfully in a kindergarten with a sympathetic and patient teacher.

Like Billy, Vic was a fairly large baby, weighing about eight-and-a-half pounds at birth. He was delivered by caesarean section in an overcrowded hospital. He escaped the gastrointestinal epidemic that was sweeping through hospitals in the fall of 1942 when he was born, but he did not escape brain injury.

Like Billy's family, Vic's rejected a recommendation that he be sent to a state institution for the retarded. The parents eventually received a diagnosis of brain damage, were referred to the Cove Schools at Racine, Wisconsin, and sent Vic to the residential school there when he was just past seven years old. It was the hardest decision the parents had ever made, but they believed there was no alternative. As they look back now, they are sure there wasn't.

It was the dictum of Alfred A. Strauss, the founder and director of the Cove Schools, that the brain-injured child held the highest priority in the family. The parents believed it, but gradually they became aware that the concentration of concern and of special arrangements on Vic had an adverse effect on his younger brother, who felt some sense of rejection.

I have seen this process work in other situations. In one where an older sister was brain damaged, a younger sister developed emotional problems which did not abate until the older girl was placed in a residential school. In dealing with the handicapped child, parents must be mindful of the feelings of the nonhandicapped sibling who does not understand why the other one is getting so much attention.

In all, Vic spent two-and-a-half years at the residential school, coming home on holidays and during summer vacations. One summer his parents sent him to a camp. He came home after two weeks looking healthy, but quite withdrawn. Apparently, he had undergone severe hazing at the camp from other boys, but members of the camp staff did not believe that he had suffered unduly. He remembered the experience mainly as a long, pleasant train ride up through Wisconsin.

Following his residential schooling, Vic was able to live at home, but he still was not ready for public school. He was now ten years old. His parents sent him to the day class which the Cove School had opened in Evanston, Illinois.

Slowly, Vic's independence grew. For a time, his mother drove him to school in the family car. Then at the suggestion of the school director he was shown how to take the bus. As a young child, his play activity was limited and often frustrating, but as he grew older he was able to socialize with a few schoolmates.

After a brief period with training wheels, Vic learned to ride a bicycle. From the Day School, Vic was transferred to a special class for the educable mentally handicapped in a regular junior high school as he approached his thirteenth birthday. Compared with the sheltered, orderly environment of the Cove School, in which he had received all of his education up to that point, the junior high school seemed to him to be a three-ring circus.

The parents found it replete with discipline problems. Unable to cope with aggressive behavior of other youths, Vic was victimized by extortion and often bullied. Sometimes, he came home crying, but for reasons the parents could not fathom he gradually adopted a pattern of keeping these incidents to himself. He seemed reluctant to tell about them.

After a year, he was transferred to a junior high school nearer his home, and placed in a special class for the educable mentally handicapped where a sensitive, experienced and dedicated woman teacher took an interest in him.

Vic was graduated from the junior high school in the special program and entered high school in a similar program. Its director, too, was a remarkable woman with an intuitive grasp of the problems Vic exhibited. She piloted his learning experiences through high school. During his senior year, he entered a work experience program which was designed to prepare students who would not go on to college to get and hold jobs.

Vic was graduated at age eighteen in 1961 at the high school commencement in the special program. He went to work immediately for a printing firm and there he remained until he was drafted for military service in 1964.

His parents notified his draft board that Vic had been diagnosed as brain-injured, but the board passed the decision about his physical and mental qualifications for military service on to the Army. He passed the physical examination at the induction center, and scored average on the battery of tests inductees were given.

His parents asked him what he wanted to do.

"Nothing," Vic said. "I'll take my chances like everybody else."

At the conclusion of Vic's basic training, he was considered for a medical discharge as a result of inability to pass several physical tests and meet minimum requirements for manipulative skills. His training sergeant, who had been training men in the armored command since World War II, telephoned the parents long distance and advised them of Vic's dilemma. For many trainees, there would have been no problem; it was an easy and honorable way out. But Vic didn't want out. More than anything else, he wanted to succeed and the discharge meant failure.

Vic met his parents at a hotel near the training center on a week-end pass. He was certain he wanted to stay in service if he could. The father, a World War II veteran, then wrote a letter to a member of the staff of the U.S. Army Surgeon General explaining Vic's disability. The letter pointed out that Vic had certain skills that could be utilized in a noncombatant area. It suggested that the recommendation to discharge him be reconsidered in the light of manpower policy that called for putting disabled soldiers to work in noncombatant jobs. The response of the Surgeon-General's Office was amazingly prompt. Vic was immediately ordered to clerk-typist school and after three months of special training was sent to Korea where he served as an ammunition clerk at an ordnance unit near Seoul. The only problem he encountered there was in keeping his weight down. He was promoted from private to specialist 5th grade and honorably discharged when his two-year hitch ended.

Vic then returned to his old job at the printing plant, but not long thereafter, the plant was closed and he found himself unemployed for the first time since high school. Jobs were scarce in that period of oncoming recession. Vic was willing to try anything.

Fortunately, he was living at home, had received a substantial amount of severance pay, along with the others who were laid off, and was collecting unemployment compensation. Every day he went out to look for work, to be interviewed, to fill out applications. He met nothing but failure. He bore it patiently and remained optimistic.

Then, suddenly, one of his applications paid off. He was hired as a mailroom clerk at a large manufacturing concern. At the time he appeared at the Cove School for the followup study, he had been employed at the concern for ten years and was in the highest salary bracket of the Cove School alumni. He was then thirty-three years old, single, living at home. He had built up a substantial savings account and company stock holdings.

At this writing, Vic does not exhibit any vestige of childhood hyperactivity, perseveration, catastrophic reaction or perceptual difficulty. His full scale IQ on the Wechsler Adult Intelligence Scale is average, although the performance score is lower than the verbal one.

Like Billy, Vic is a fully competent, dependable and very congenial adult.

There are statistical answers to the parental question: What will become of my child? And there are human answers. We need both; we need to know the learning-disabled as children and adults. It is only then that we can perceive the full role of special education in enabling these children to realize their potential as human beings. Anything short of that is a waste.

It was Dr. Strauss's belief that "if we devise a program of living and education which takes into account the disabilities of brain injury, we can bring these children more nearly into normal focus, so that their 'otherness' becomes indiscernible."[5]

Although he did not live to see it, this has been accomplished by the program he and his associates devised thirty years ago.

And yet, I must repeat his qualification:

"There are, however, some children who do not and cannot respond to any program we know of. They continue to remain 'other.' "[6]

Chapter 6

Reunion:
The Joliet Report

Twenty years after classes for brain-injured children were started as an experiment at the Cunningham Public School in Joliet, Illinois, Charlotte E. Larson, the teacher who pioneered them, was the guest of some of her former students and their parents at a farewell tea. She was retiring.

It was a happy occasion for Miss Larson. It reunited most of the students she had taught in the special classes between 1954 and 1959. When they came to her special class, most were struggling and misunderstood in regular classes. After one to three years, they were ready to cope with a conventional program.

Even after they went to high school, she never lost touch with most of them. There were exchanges of cards at Christmas time. Now, at the tea, she was surrounded by an attractive, enthusiastic group of young adults. It was one of the most rewarding reunions Charlotte Larson could imagine.

The classes at Cunningham were an offshoot of the Cove Schools program, where Miss Larson had received training in special education after years of experience as an elementary school teacher in Downstate Illinois.

They were started in 1951 as an experiment in special education by Ray Graham, a popular, well known and highly respected director of special education in the state Office of Public Instruction. Initially, it was designed for brain-injured children in the educable mentally handicapped range of intelligence test scores. In 1954, Miss Larson started a second class for brain-injured, perceptually handicapped children of normal or potentially normal intelligence.

These classes were continued as self-contained units until 1959 when they were superseded by an "itinerant" teaching program that provided only auxiliary services. Perceptually handicapped children were placed in conventional classrooms and received auxiliary help, as it was determined they required it, from an "itinerant" teacher who was trained to work with learning problems.

The philosophy behind the change was later labeled as "mainstreaming." It was based on a theory that children classified as brain-injured, perceptually handicapped, or suffering from minimal cerebral dysfunction or learning disabilities would benefit in social and intellectual development by their contact with nonhandicapped children in the conventional classroom. Their learning disabilities could then be treated in supplementary sessions with the itinerant teacher one or more hours a week. Miss Larson later supervised that program.

Like the Cove School experience, the Joliet experiment showed that brain-injured children could be placed successfully in conventional public school classes after a year or more in the special class. Some of them—not all, but some—required the special class as the sine qua non of acquiring an education. Itinerant help was not enough. By substituting it for the special class, school districts in some cases forced parents to turn to private facilities that could prepare the child for the public school.

The Joliet experiment followed the Cove School design in arranging the classroom as a therapeutic environment.

Windows were painted over so that they would be translucent but not transparent—a device to reduce distractibility. Desks were separated by screens, so that each child could work without being distracted by his neighbors.

The class size was small. Miss Larson never had more than ten children at a time, and frequently fewer.

Before the first class was opened in 1951, Miss Larson, Dr. Graham and school officials invited parents to a meeting and explained the experiment plan. It was a wise move because it allayed some apprehension that the children were being used as guinea pigs. It also served to explain why some of the children would be screened off from others.

About two years after the class started, I visited it and talked to some of the parents. Those I interviewed were delighted. Most said they had noted a definite decrease in their child's hyperactivity and improvement in his behavior.

I was impressed particularly by the orderly aspect of the classroom itself. Compared with others that were festooned with pictures, cut-outs and miscellaneous exhibits, Miss Larson's room was bare and functional.

Some of these children had been acute behavior problems in regular classes. Some habitually called out, waved their arms, punched their neighbor, threw paper balls or got up and ran around the room.

After a short time in this class, they had settled down. They were learning how to learn. After a year or more, they would go into regular classes. And they did.

ROGER

It was not hard to locate some of Miss Larson's former students. Most of them had been present at the farewell tea and were still living either with parents or independently in the Joliet area.

"When I first got your letter," said Roger, "I thought you were going out after a doctorate or master's degree, or something like that. Didn't think we were important enough to be in a book. I was in Miss Larson's class for five years."

At the time I saw Roger, he was twenty-eight years old, a tall, lean young man with capable, work-hardened hands and an easy, relaxed manner. He was intrigued by the fact that I was interested in his problems as a child. He was newly married and lived with his wife in a one-bedroom unit in a low rent, multi-family housing development in the rolling hills of Will County, beyond the congestion of Joliet. He worked full time at a garage and his wife was also employed.

Roger was the second of four children. At the age of twenty-two months, he had been suddenly paralyzed by an apparent stroke. He recovered, but the condition was never fully diagnosed until at age three years he began to have seizures. A physician diagnosed epilepsy.

Despite medication, the seizures increased in frequency and intensity. When he was four years old, his family took him to the Mayo Clinic at Rochester, Minnesota. There a complete study revealed brain damage, probably the result of encephalitis, measles or chickenpox. The prognosis was indefinite.

In recounting this episode, Roger's mother told Miss Larson: "They said put him in an institution. . . ." But the family refused.

At the clinic, a psychometric test indicated a full scale IQ of 63. This was the first of a series of tests on which Roger's IQ changed. At age five, Roger was tested again on the Binet scale, and exhibited a full scale IQ of 75. Another test—the Minnesota Pre-School—showed a verbal IQ of 93, a nonverbal IQ of 78 and a full scale IQ of 88.

When Roger was six, he underwent another series of tests. They showed that he was impaired in visual perception, ability to organize and in thinking, but could be presumed to have a normal or potentially normal IQ.

Roger was placed in Miss Larson's class for brain-injured children of normal or potentially normal intelligence. The seizures had been brought under control by medication. Then, at age eight, Roger seemed to have a case of scarlet fever. He became aphasic in school. He had a seizure the same day.

He recovered. Since then, he has been free of seizures, although he continued to take a mild medication—just in case.

At age ten years and eight months, Roger was tested again. He had gained 29 IQ points since he was first tested. On the Wechsler Intelligence Scale for Children, his verbal score was 101, his performance, 83, and the full scale, 92.

After five years in the special class, Roger was placed in a regular fifth grade class. He was one year behind his age group. From then on, he made steady academic progress. When he was graduated from high school in June 1967, his academic standing was 186 in a class of 489. He was functioning well within the normal IQ range.

After that, Roger attended Joliet Junior College for two years and received a general certificate in drafting.

Before getting a job with the garage, Roger worked at a filling station where he pumped gas and made minor repairs. He is a capable mechanic, knows cars and recommended "cruise control" as an extra.

"You drive it up to the speed you want it, push a button and it stays there," he said. I wondered if there wasn't danger of falling asleep with so little to do.

"Actually, I think it helps you to stay awake," said Roger. "You don't realize until you use it how much strain there is on that foot."

Besides cars, which he discussed with the enthusiasm of a salesman, Roger indulges in other hobbies: he plays the organ and the stock market. He is also a figure skater. He has taken courses in all three.

> I've been dabbling in stocks and options for the last year and a half. I've got options on Caterpillar and Phillips Petroleum. Options are definitely risky, highly risky, but on the other hand you can come out with a big percentage gain.

Roger then proceeded to explain to me how options work. He is one of the few who has done so in a way I could understand. I knew that he understood this complicated game.

Does he read?

> I've been trying for a number of years to get into one of these speed-reading courses. I just can't stay with it. I pick something up and start reading and in a half hour I'm asleep.
>
> I read the paper—not everything in it. Just a few highlights here and there. Sports. Yeah. I don't seem to have time to read a novel or anything like that, because I read so slow. Just to read something like *Jaws* would take me a year and a half.
>
> The problem I have—they call it "sub-vocalization." You actually say everything. You can't read any faster than you talk. I took a night course to improve reading, but I wasn't able to advance the way some of them did in the class.

What about television?

> I don't need a TV. I remember in junior high. I read something in the paper about the number of hours a kid averaged in front of the

contingent on the health of the market itself. Is it a good market? Is it good in terms of the problems of society, economically, socially . . . these all affect the stock market.

The young lady delivering this lecture regarded me solemnly with brilliant blue eyes, framed by a heart-shaped face and curling blonde hair. She was a little above average height, with a full figure that she feared was a bit too full, and she wore the businesslike pants suit that seemed to have become the career girl's uniform.

Although I had probably seen Jeanette as a child, I did not recognize this energetic, purposeful young woman who came striding toward me at the corner of LaSalle and Adams where we had agreed to meet.

"Hi," she said, holding out her hand. "Your description was perfect."

I had told her to look for a short, bald, middleaged gent in a brown suit.

Like so many others who had to struggle to get a grip on the world as children, Jeanette left nothing to chance. On the day we were to meet for lunch, she called me at home the moment she got off the commuter train in the Loop from Joliet. Like the train, Jeanette ran precisely on time.

"I must say that my real interest lies in the equity market," she said after we had battled our way to a table in a noisy restaurant. "I love it. I participate in it. But the job I do here is in municipal bonds."

I asked Jeanette what she did.

My job is as follows. As the trades are done, through the various brokers and dealers, I put through tickets showing what was bought and sold; account number, so on and so forth; these tickets are then sent to the computer which in turn prints out a confirm to clients showing purchase and the sale of the security, purchase date, settlement date, and, with bonds, I don't know how familiar you are with them, the purchase date and the settlement date determine the price. Okay? So—basically, that's what my job is here.

I asked Jeanette about herself. Did I want the long story or the short story? I suggested she just start talking.

I graduated high school at nineteen. I took a job at Joliet. It turned out to be a totally nothing job, with no challenge, no money, no future, so far as I was concerned. I wanted something more than that. I didn't know what it was. So I said, I'm going to Chicago. It was really only general office work, which I found very dull. No brains required.

So I came to Chicago and worked for a typesetting firm, now a division of Continental Can. I worked there two years. Then I got a job with a security dealer and I loved it. It was just what I wanted. I felt that I could go on for years and years and years.

Jeanette moved from one job to another as better opportunities came into view. One of her bosses was promoted and wanted to take her with him as his secretary, but she wanted to be more directly involved in the securities market. Her main concern was getting stuck in a job she didn't like or one that kept her in a static situation. She felt an overpowering impulse to move on, reach out.

Although independent and capable, Jeanette was living at home with her mother, a widow for five years. She talked about getting her own apartment, but worried about her mother living alone in a changing neighborhood.

This was a pattern I kept seeing in these interviews. Most of the young adults I interviewed who were handicapped as children had strong ties to parents. This was not so much a result of their dependence as it seemed to be a sense of responsibility. Jeanette explained her own situation:

Three weeks after I graduated high school, I went to Chicago with a girlfriend and we moved into a small apartment on Elm Street (the near north side, a habitat of many adventurous singles).

Well, it was very, very swingy, or whatever you want to call it. I learned a lot. Anybody coming from a smaller town would have. We encountered realities, of many people and many things in the world. I was living off my savings—I worked while in high school—I worked practically all my life, I think. But I just loved it on Elm Street. We stayed there until September until I ran out of money and then we went back home.

"But I couldn't stay at home and work there. I would feel like nothing was happening. So I came back to Chicago to get a job and I've been working up here ten years.

I asked Jeanette whether she had considered marriage.

I've thought about it many a time, but it never went beyond that. I've had a couple of bad experiences—unfortunate, unpleasant, whatever. I guess I still have hopes for marriage in the future. Sometimes, things don't work out the way you'd like them to.

If she moves out of her mother's house, Jeanette said she would rather live alone than with a roommate.

I don't necessarily like the idea of living alone, but I'm sure I'd just go home at night, make something to eat and do laundry or what have you. I'd hope to have a couple of places to go; you know, organizations. I've been trying to get into organizations. It's difficult to do so because—I love bowling and I've been trying to join a bowling league; but it's impossible to do it unless you come in with your own league. Okay?

Jeanette said she found people in Joliet to be "clannish." She likes to go out on dates, have a few drinks, socialize, but she doesn't care much for hanging around bars.

I've never met too many people that I would really, uh, consider seriously as far as guys are concerned in that type of environment. A lot of the people I knew are married. And the others, the singles, well, they're out for one thing, and there's a little bit more to life than that. It's got to be a little more of a meaningful relationship. Some of the people I know have different values.

Jeanette said she wanted more than a casual affair and on two occasions she believed she had found a meaningful relationship, only to see it crumble, partly because of the suitor's indecision, partly because of mutual loss of interest. In these situations, her role was passive. She wondered: Should she have been more aggressive?

I asked: Don't you want to keep on with a career? Wouldn't marriage and having a family interfere with that?

"I'd rather be a homemaker. I'm only doing this because I can't find anybody to pay my way," she said with a laugh. "No, really, I'd

always want to pursue the market. If I were married, the main difference would be that I wouldn't have to catch a train and work eight
hours a day. I could pursue it at home."

WHO WAS PHOEBE SNOW?

Joliet is a railroad town. On hot summer mornings when he was not
working at the college, Jack left the house early and rode his bicycle
downhill to the railroad depot. He loved to watch the Amtrak trains
come in, their diesels roaring. He was fascinated by the names
painted on the freight cars: *Santa Fe, Hiawatha, Route of Phoebe
Snow*. Who was Phoebe Snow?* He made a mental note to look it up
in the library of the junior college where he was employed as a
dishwasher for breakfast and lunch when school was in session, but
he always forgot. Jack liked to help with the baggage and in spite of
his limp he could handle the big pieces pretty well. His big hope was
to work for the railroad, but he feared that they wouldn't hire handicapped people.

At the time I interviewed him Jack was twenty-eight years old and
lived at home with his parents. He and his mother had attended the
tea for Miss Larson and he recited the whereabouts of other former
students who had been there. "It was real good to see everybody," he
said.

Jack came to the attention of the school psychologist because of
learning difficulties in kindergarten. He was diagnosed as having mild
cerebral palsy as the result of brain injury. He exhibited some stuttering. When Dr. Strauss saw him during a visit to Miss Larson's class,
he predicted that the stuttering eventually would abate, and it did.

His mother and father recalled that Jack required foot surgery as
an infant to enable him to walk. He did walk, but poorly, at eighteen
months. In early childhood, he had difficulty with stairs. It was a
struggle for him to learn to ride a tricycle.

---

* Phoebe Snow was the name given to a professional model who posed for
Delaware, Lackawanna and Western Railroad advertisements in a white dress
at the turn of the century. She symbolized clean, soot-free passenger trains. Her
real name was Mrs. Marion Murray Gorsch.

Jack's mother recalled that he always exhibited a "fantastic" memory for names, dates, addresses. He talked at twelve months and at eighteen months could recite a whole list of words, including "mommy, "daddy," "cookie," "potty," and he could say the names of relatives and neighbors. Before he started school, he could recite lines from *The Birth of Jesus* that his mother often read to him. He remembered them perfectly.

Even before Jack exhibited difficulties in kindergarten, his parents realized that he was "other" and that his development, aside from his physical difficulties, was not the same as that of their two younger children. One physician counseled them to accept Jack as he was and predicted sadly that the child would not develop beyond a mental age of three years.

Like many parents of the brain-injured children who have been similarly advised, Jack's parents did not accept that prognosis, but made the rounds of specialists. A family physician associated with a church kindergarten that Jack attended recommended a specialist who diagnosed brain damage causing probable cerebral palsy. The parents were urged to "give him a chance and see how he develops."

Jack entered Miss Larson's special class in 1955 and remained in it until June 1959. He entered a regular fifth grade class in September that year at age eleven. Because the family moved to another city, Jack was put back a year, but he completed high school and was graduated in 1967 at the age of nineteen.

"Well, for a while I didn't do anything after I graduated," Jack said. He was a young man of medium size, with strong features, and he spoke with a slight hesitation, the residue of the early speech difficulty.

I just stayed home. There was a training center for disabled kids and I went there for three-and-a-half years. Mostly what I did was pull putty out of a barrel, wrap it in paper and weigh it in pounds. It didn't pay much, but it was supposed to give us experience. There was also some piece work on machines.

Then I went to work at Burger Chef, but business got slow during the summer and I was laid off. They never called me back. I finally got a job at a high-class restaurant as a dishwasher, but quit when we moved back to Joliet.

Jack said his social life is centered at the college where he works and at the church which is connected with it. He worked out with the church softball team, mostly as the bat boy. He played in only one game during the summer. The team lost, 15 to 1.

"In practice, I can hit the ball, but I can't run so good," he said. "They don't allow someone to run for me in the league games. Last year, I joined the church bowling league. I like it; it's fun. But I haven't done much bowling this summer."

Unlike Roger or Jeanette, Jack doesn't drive a car; he never learned. That is usual for many brain-injured adults. They are capable of driving, but those with an additional physical handicap often do not. In Jack's case, his parents were not anxious for him to drive and he did not press the matter. Instead, he rode his five-speed Schwinn bicycle wherever he wanted to go and hoped it would not be stolen as a previous bicycle was.

"I'm really handicapped without wheels," he said.

Jack's main focus is home. He gets up in the morning before 7 A.M. His mother makes breakfast, usually pancakes, eggs, cereal, and then Jack pedals off to the college cafeteria where he operates an array of dishwashing machines in the kitchen five days a week.

"There are eight or nine others in the kitchen," Jack said, "and some students. It's cafeteria style, with hot beef sandwiches for lunch, sloppy joes, creamed beef on toast, coke, pop, or Kool Aid."

He finishes his day at 3 P.M. and comes right home. There is a basement recreation room where he watches television, has his hi-fi and an elaborate HO gauge model railroad that he and his father built.

Jack looks forward to family reunions when his married brother and married sister and their spouses visit the house. Everybody comes home at Christmas. At these get-togethers, Jack entertains by playing the accordion and guitar "a little bit."

"Well, that's a funny story about the accordion," he said. "They drew my name out of a fishbowl. Then they called up my Mom and asked her if her son wanted to take lessons on the accordion. I got to try out and then got free lessons and I picked it up. On the guitar, I had a friend who taught me a little, and later I took lessons."

In the afternoons after work, Jack likes to go downstairs and strum chords on the guitar. He likes country and western music, and has a record collection. For the model railroad, he has recordings of steam and diesel engines, complete with whistles.

"This year, I thought I should get out of the house a bit more," Jack said. "I joined a young singles club and we went to Chicago for Cubs and [White] Sox games. On Sundays I usher in church, not every Sunday, but on certain Sundays each month."

Jack gave up reading comic books. He likes model railroad magazines. Occasionally he goes to the movies alone. He saw *Jaws* and liked it. But he didn't want to see it again.

He does not date. There was a girl he liked at the sheltered workshop. They went out together, but "I broke up with her." Jack's mother did not encourage the relationship.

"I couldn't take on another handicapped person," she said.

KENNETH

The town library was in an ancient building that had once been a church. I didn't have much advance data on Ken; I expected to find him stacking books or doing another of the routine chores of younger library employees. Instead, when I asked for him at the desk, a young woman escorted me to an office on the mezzanine. There was Ken sitting behind a desk. He was the director of the library.

"I didn't attend the reunion," he said. "I'm recently back. I was in the Army for two years, nine months, at Fort Campbell, Kentucky. I was drafted originally and then enlisted, like the day before. Then my father had a stroke and I got out on a hardship discharge, to take care of my mother, which I did until she died."

At the time of the interview, Ken was twenty-seven, a young man with a positive, professional air of purpose and confidence. The small library ticked away like a Swiss watch. I wondered if any of my books were in it.

"Probably not," said Ken. "We're just rebuilding. There was a policy here for many years of saving money by not buying books. That has been changed."

Ken had attended Miss Larson's class only part time for special help in the afternoons. He was in a regular class in grade school. He explained:

> I had a severe speech impediment at the time. I just sort of cut off the ends of words. Well, in the primary grades, I went to a country school situation. The teacher knew me and I had the same teacher for the first two years. Then we moved into the city and I had to go to a different school. Nobody could understand me, you know. If you knew me, you could tell what I was talking about. That affected my whole learning situation. I was a very poor reader because, you know, I just didn't get the basics.

Speech therapy had worked well for Ken. Aside from certain common mannerisms and a slight lisp, there was no sign that he had ever exhibited serious speech problems. He remembered Miss Larson as having just a few other pupils.*

> I think I liked it because I think she was more in tune with—you know, me and my difficulty; there was more toleration; she was more anxious to help, whereas the other teachers didn't seem to care. I think the sad thing is that she was only one person.

Ken liked his Army hitch. He was assigned to the famous 101st Airborne Division "and I sort of enjoyed it." At Fort Campbell, he became involved in a special project to computerize the division's personnel, payroll and supply records.

> What we did was we took IBM computers, installed them in a van, actually a semi-trailer truck, and programmed them to handle everything. And then after we went through the whole thing and set up all the complementary software, the project went under a test and all the biggies from the Department of the Army came down from Washington and looked it over. If we passed the test, which we did, the system would go division wide. So, essentially, every division now has one of our setups. Exactly as we had planned it.

---

* Ken was one of the early "itinerant" program pupils. Speech therapy and reading help were given him in the supplementary program that replaced the contained class for children of average intelligence.

Ken said he would have been content to have completed his three-year-hitch if the family matter hadn't come up. He was promoted to Specialist-5th grade and felt that he was participating in an important innovation for the Army.

Despite his early reading difficulty, Ken had done well educationally. After being graduated from high school in 1968, he received a bachelor's degree from Illinois State University in 1972 in library science and also took graduate courses at Fort Campbell. At the time of my interview, he was working toward a master's degree in communications science.

Possibly as a result of his early speech problem, Ken's schooling has been oriented toward communication. He agreed that his occupation as librarian was an aspect of it. He became interested in library science through a reading teacher who was also a librarian in the junior high school he attended. He worked for her, liked the work and continued it in high school. Later, after receiving his bachelor's degree, he was employed in a small city public library until the opportunity to become the director of a smaller library presented itself.

Through high school and college, he studied foreign languages, Spanish, French and German. While an undergraduate at Illinois State, he joined an exchange program which enabled him to attend the University of Grenoble in France for a full summer. He said,

At first, it was very difficult. You had to get acclimated to the situation. Everything was in French. The teachers there are quite different from here because they actually want to help you. Most of the teachers I've had—well, they tolerated you, especially in the lower grades. They knew if they didn't pass me on, I would stay right there.

Although he expects to continue as a librarian indefinitely, Ken's long-term ambition is to teach library science or audio visual communication at a university. In addition to a master's degree in communication science, he is aiming at a second master's in library science.

I asked him how well he reads now, in view of his childhood reading problems.

"Pretty well," he said. "It all depends on what it is. Journals—yes. Or something I really have to read."

One might theorize that Ken's library vocation and language avocation represented victories that compensated for his early childhood deficits. That does not seem to be an unusual response of persons who have experienced learning disabilities as children.

THE EDUCATION OF PETER

Peter came slowly down the stairs and flopped on the living room couch, fully relaxed. "Hi," he said. "Is your tape recorder on? Okay. I am nineteen years old. Don't ask me about my early education because I don't know anything about it. I don't have very many memories of when I was young, you know, real young. My memory wasn't too good then."

The young man crossed his stocking feet and lay flat on his back on the sofa, with his right arm trailing over the edge.

"My memory is good for some things," he continued, "but it's pretty bad for others. I usually have a good memory for what I think is important; that I find interesting or something like that. I'm going to junior college."

I asked what he was taking.

Development, of course, and some English. It's pretty hard. English. But I guess I need it because I didn't get too much of it in grade school. I never did understand what a verb was or that sort of thing. I frequently got confused with what a pronoun was and that sort of thing. If we ever got into English [grammar] a little bit, I got lost.

What else are you taking?

"Why, that's all," he said, as though surprised that anyone would take more than two courses. "My other course is reading development. Work on speeding up my reading."

Do you like to read? It was a question I asked everyone. The answers were usually revealing. Peter answered:

Oh, yeah. It's just that I get usually frustrated if I haven't covered very much in a while. You know, a book I'm very much interested in, after a while I find I haven't gotten very far. I usually start to lose interest because I read very slow. Or slowly. But I just get frustrated because I want to find out what's happening next. I reread it because I didn't understand what it was, y'know. Or I'm trying to get the right pronunciation, y'know. And sometimes I read so slow I can't get past the first chapters. It has to be pretty simple reading or else I . . . it just takes me forever.

Otherwise, by the time I get to the end I find it dull for sure. I like adventure stories, mysteries. I spend more time in front of the TV than I ever do reading. I'm not really interested in sports.

Peter said he liked science and theater. He took a dramatics course in high school.

"I'm sort of shy. Because I was so shy I didn't get a chance to perform with very many other people, y'know. I did monologues. That sort of stuff."

Peter doesn't remember his early education because he spent little time in school; he was taught much of his reading and arithmetic skills at home by his mother and by his father, a research chemist.

Peter is the youngest of four brothers. Two are physicians and one is a financial analyst. When his mother was pregnant with him, she had German measles in the first trimester. She and his father worried about that. The family doctor said her chances of having a normal child were good. Peter's mother said:

I was very ill with it. Then, in addition to that, I had the flu, not just the twenty-four-hour flu, but the bad flu. So I was really not well throughout most of my pregnancy.

But when he [Peter] was born, he was perfectly all right. I mean his heart was all right, his eyes, his ears, all right. He has three older brothers, and I'm not bragging now but we have very bright children, and he talked before he was a year old.

At age three, Peter had a middle ear infection. His mother said:

He went to bed perfectly all right and then he got sick in the middle of the night. He had a seizure and stopped breathing; he stopped for several seconds. Then he started breathing again. He was not all right after that. He ended up in the hospital with pneumonia. A neurologist looked at him and said he was perfectly all right, nothing wrong with him. But he said that because I had the German measles in the trimester, this child was insulted in the womb, and there was a predisposition to have something happen to him at some stage of development. He said we were lucky it didn't show until he was three. That was the neurologist's theory. We just don't know.

After three, Peter exhibited neurological, learning and behavior problems of the brain-injury syndrome. The Chicago area suburb where the family lived had a fine school system. The director of special education was sympathetic and arranged special kindergarten training for the child. Peter couldn't tolerate half a day, so he was allowed to spend forty-five minutes to an hour a day.

In the first grade, the parents and the director arranged for Peter to have a one-to-one relationship with a special teacher. She was a reading specialist and she worked with him for months alone in a classroom. In the meantime, Peter was under the observation of a physical therapist. He was the first hyperactive child she had ever seen.

At Christmastime, the special teacher concluded that she could do nothing more for Peter. All she could do essentially, said the mother, was hold him and love him.

After the Christmas vacation, the school employed another special teacher for Peter, a woman who previously had been engaged by the family to work with him. She had training in special education from Columbia and Northwestern Universities.

In addition to working with this teacher, Peter received regular physical therapy to improve his motor coordination.

Eventually, Peter was placed in a special class for brain-injured children which the city set up in 1964, but he could not remain there. He began to have seizures. He was unable to walk a straight line. He could not go up or down stairs unassisted.

The trained teacher who had worked with him at school then came to the home to continue Peter's education. Later, he was able to attend a tutoring center for brief periods at the school.

In addition to special teaching, Peter required continuous physical therapy to develop muscular coordination. The family took him to an institute developed at Purdue University by Dr. Kephart. They conferred with psychologists at the Cove School in Evanston, but the school was not equipped to handle Peter's physical problems.

Peter's father suggested that the city director of special education enroll a teacher in a special education course which Charlotte Larson was giving in a nearby community.

"He sort of dragged his feet," said the father. "And then he said, 'Why don't you go?'"

"My husband used to be a teacher a long time ago," explained the mother.

"I took the course," the father continued. "I was the only man in the class and the only non-teacher."

At this time, Peter's father became a member of the city school board. When its meetings conflicted with Miss Larson's course, Peter's mother attended the course in his place.

"So you see, I really shared this experience with Charlotte," she said. "But my husband taught Peter most of what he knows. Grandma used to think he was a slave driver. He worked with Peter furiously, drilling him over and over."

At home, the father applied perceptual training methods developed for brain-injured children to teach Peter to read. These stressed letter identification and phonetics. Peter was taken to the library. He became interested in several books. Now he wanted to read. He reached a speed of 114 words a minute, the father recalled, with full comprehension. It had been a long, uphill climb, but he was reading.

Dr. Kephart had diagnosed part of Peter's handicap as an inability to distinguish rightness from leftness. His thesis held that we are bilaterally symmetrical animals and for basic orientation we must be able to distinguish one side of our bodies from the other. One side has to be dominant, at least in early life; later, both sides can be trained, ambidexterity can be developed.

When laterality (knowing which side is which) is established, the individual is able to perceive his relationship to the outside world in a normal way. Moving objects are perceived as coming toward him until they pass the center line of his body; then they are perceived as going away. The visual system supports this center line reference. As objects approach, they become visually larger; as they recede, they diminish in size. A similar attenuation operates for the senses of hearing and smell. Distance is perceived in this way, in terms of the size of a known object in relation to the individual. Where the size of the object is not known from experience, its distance from the observer is difficult if not impossible to judge. That is one reason why the bright planet Jupiter has, under certain "seeing" conditions, been misconstrued as (1) a UFO or (2) an airplane. Many UFO reports have been found to be misperceptions of such commonplace phenomena.

All of this bears on understanding Peter's basic problem. In terms of perceptual reference, each person is the center of the universe as he perceives it. The base line is his own bilaterally symmetrical body. Being aware of rightness and leftness thus becomes a fundamental requirement in perception of the outer world.

But suppose that one is not aware of which is right or which is left? Or, suppose one is able to perceive phenomena only on the right-hand side of the body and not on the left, or vice versa, either because he has lost vision or the visual image is not being processed properly in the brain?

In that case, he may be able to perceive an object approaching him from one direction, but after it passes the center line of the body, it disappears. It vanishes, just as though it has never been. Imagine the difficulty one would have with such a handicap—especially a child, struggling to organize the real world in terms of what he can actually perceive.

Much of Peter's training was designed to restore or enhance bilateral perception, which evidently was deficient.

"We kept taking him over to Kephart's institute [for perceptual training] at Purdue," the father said. "We worked with him every night to improve muscle coordination and integration. He was incapable of passing the body midline."

The father constructed a pegboard with pegs and holes of different colors. Peter would be coached on matching the pegs with the holes. He would fill the holes from left to right, then from right to left. Then he would be given rings to place over the pegs. He practiced arranging similar patterns with corks and bottle caps.

It was Kephart's observation that motor activity of this sort helped develop spatial perception in brain-injured children; and that space perception was essential in learning mathematics.

Peter was continued intermittently in elementary school with a great deal of teaching at home by his parents and intermittently by teachers sent by the school system or employed by the parents. He was not always able to attend classes on a regular basis, or for a full day. He had about four years of classroom instruction. His father said:

> We made a deal with Peter. If he got through eighth grade math by the time he finished the eighth grade, he would get a color television set. We worked every Saturday and every Sunday at home. He really wanted that TV and he worked his tail off for it. He made it in math and he got the set.

In high school, Peter's attendance capability improved. He took regular art and singing courses, and some subjects in a special class. The way high school worked, as the mother described it, "if you just showed up with your books and didn't do anything else, you'd get a 'D'—you'd pass. Lots of kids would drop out. Peter stayed."

"Well, you can say that," Peter himself interjected, "but I couldn't have quit if I wanted to."

The parents had no hesitation about discussing Peter's problems in his presence. His father said:

> He's attending a junior college. There's no time limit. He's taking only two courses. He's still pretty immature in a lot of ways. This is his first experience in being in classes where there isn't some form of handicap in almost everybody. It's true he's in remedial classes, but other kids are in them for different reasons. Socialization is rubbing off. Next summer, we hope to get him a summer job assisting a veterinarian, because he likes animals.

The mother said: "I don't think he could handle the academic work, but he could work as an aide."

After years of struggle, there was confidence in the family that Peter would "make it." But many times during his childhood, his parents had been assured by experts that he would not.

"Pediatricians told us to stop banging our heads against the wall," his mother said. "That was how they interpreted what we were trying to do."

The father related that some years after Peter began training at Dr. Kephart's institute, the psychologist confessed that Peter was accepted as a challenge; that it had seemed at first there was little the institute could do for him.

"He was turned down by one school after another," the mother said.

But Peter's parents never gave up. Nor did Peter.

In order to appreciate the magnitude of their accomplishment, the reader may find it useful to consider the perceptual problem that children like Peter exhibit from Dr. Kephart's point of view. He told a symposium:[1]

> Let's look for a moment at a very simple activity. You know, when your child goes to kindergarten, the first thing they do is to give him a test called a readiness test. There is a picture on this side of the page and a picture on that side of the page and the teacher reads a sentence describing these two pictures. The child is to draw a line from this picture to that picture. . . . Let's not worry about the thing we are trying to test here. Let's look at the even simpler activity of designating the answer, which is just a matter of drawing a line from one point on the page to another. We take this ability for granted, don't we?
>
> All right. What may be involved? First of all, the child has to have sufficient neuromuscular control throughout his entire organism so that he can maintain a sitting posture, so that he can hold himself erect and can hold his head erect on his shoulders. . . . He must have sufficient control and coordination in the arm and fingers to grasp the pencil and to hold it and to maintain that grasp so that there is a certain pressure on the pencil while it draws the line.
>
> There is something else. The first thing the child must do, assuming he is able to perform these gross muscle activities, is to decide where to start. To do that, he must decide which of these pictures is on the left-hand side and which is on the right-hand side.
>
> We take this for granted. But did you ever think that there is nothing that comes into your eyes that tells you which is left and which is right? The only thing that comes into your eyes is a series of light rays and they only tell you that something out there is darker than something else. They don't tell you where it is or what relationship it has to anything else.
>
> The fundamental problem of rightness and leftness is inside, not

outside the organism. We develop this concept of one side versus the other side within our own body—not outside. . . .

Can you imagine what position you would be in, sitting here right now, if there were no definite and distinct rightness and leftness about this room? Where would you be if you weren't sure which of these corners were which? Where would you be if you weren't sure which of two objects was on which side?

Where would you be if you had no definite concept of right and left, and you looked at a letter *b* and sometimes it would be a *d*? This is not a confusion between *b* and *d*; this is the result of the fact that for this child at this moment there is no difference between a *b* and a *d*—because, in fact, the only difference between a *b* and a *d* is one of laterality, right and left. The letters vary only on this lateral coordinate. And unless he has that lateral coordinate inside himself, how can he project onto things out there in space?

Indirectly, Peter may be considered a beneficiary of Miss Larson's teaching. There were many others who received basic help from the methods used in the program. The Joliet experiment was extraordinarily successful in the period from 1951 to 1959, when the contained classes were superseded by an itinerant program.[2]

In September 1959, Miss Larson found that many of her students in the contained class for brain-injured children with average intelligence were ready for regular classes. In the five years since she had set up the class in 1954, students who had been transferred into the special class from neighborhood schools had been returned to their home schools as they showed the ability to adjust to regular classes.

Some of the children in the special class could tolerate regular class for short periods. She began trying out in regular classes pupils who had made progress in spelling and arithmetic in the contained class. She related:

The first two youngsters sat in a regular class for only fifteen minutes to take a spelling lesson. The rest of the time they were with me. Then we worked them in [to the regular class] for arithmetic. It made their eventual adjustment from the contained to the regular class that much easier.

From these experiences, Miss Larson and school officials worked out what they called an "itinerant" program. It was designed to give special help on a part time basis to students in a regular class who otherwise would have to be placed in the contained class.

She found that many of these youngsters didn't need a full day of self-contained class. But they needed some of the help it gave. The itinerant program seemed to fill this need. "It was a gradual weaning away from the self-contained, protective environment," Miss Larson said.

Eventually, the itinerant program replaced the contained class for brain-injured children of normal intelligence. Miss Larson conducted it for the first six years. Students were sent to the class for as many hours a week as Miss Larson and other teachers thought they needed. For the most part, it was successful, she said, but in one or two cases, the self-contained class would have been more effective.

However, budget limitation at state and local levels did not permit both itinerant and contained classes for the brain-injured or learning-disabled children of average IQ. The contained class for the brain injured with IQ scores below average was continued, however.

This pattern of special education spread generally throughout Northern Illinois and eventually was adopted in most of the state. In many districts, however, the classification of brain injury was abandoned in the 1960s and the term learning disability gradually replaced it. The itinerant program, as it was developed in Joliet, became a widely adopted model. It provided a method of enabling children with learning disabilities to keep up with a regular class. But not all children benefited from it. Some of average IQ still required the special environment of the contained class. But this need remained unmet in school districts which provided a contained class only for the educable mentally handicapped and itinerant or resource teaching for the learning disabled with normal IQs.

Looking back at her experiences as a teacher in both contained and itinerant classroom programs, as a supervisor and as an assistant director of special education in the Joliet school system, Miss Larson has drawn these conclusions:

The needs of the child tell you what type of program he should have. But, of course, in a public school, to get something tailored to the child's needs is not easy to do.

I worked eight years in the self-contained class, six years in the itinerant program and seven years in administration in Joliet, so I've seen it from several points of view.

Youngsters who can get the learning help they need in an itinerant program, who can tolerate a regular program and can adjust to the social requirements should not be removed from the normal stream. Those who cannot do this should have the services of a self contained classroom. Because of its therapeutic environment, behavior problems are not as severe. Nevertheless, adjustment to the normal classroom situation should not be neglected. Integration into the regular classroom should be tried as soon as the pupil can tolerate it.

THE CASE FOR OPTIMISM

In most instances, the children in Miss Larson's classes showed gains in verbal and performance IQ scores. She viewed the gains as nothing magical. Their scores improved because they were learning, she said; they were learning because they were in an environment that made learning possible for them.

Miss Larson remembered one boy who appeared to be so handicapped that a physician advised the parents the child probably could never go to school. She related:

We took him. He progressed to the sixth grade. When it came time to enter junior high school, he was sent back to the [same] doctor for a physical examination. Well, the doctor couldn't believe this boy was going into junior high school. The boy completed junior high school and went back to the doctor for a physical examination preparatory to entering high school. The doctor said that boy really had him fooled; that if the boy ever needed another physical for college—send him to another doctor. He said he couldn't have been that wrong!

After a year in the contained class, a ten-year-old girl showed a verbal IQ gain of 11 points, but a drop of 1 point in performance score. The net full scale gain was 3 points over an earlier test result.

The girl was then transferred to a regular class when the contained class was discontinued. Miss Larson continued to work with her in arithmetic in the itinerant program. She said the girl's ability to enter into conversation improved in the regular class.

A seven-year-old girl exhibited the brain-injury syndrome in the first grade. It was confirmed by a neurological examination. After two years in the contained class, she entered a regular grade. She had gained 11 points on the full scale intelligence test.

At the age of nine, a boy was referred to the contained class after persistent learning difficulties. Tests had shown that lateral dominance in the brain had not been established and that he was socially and emotionally immature.

In the special class, it was discovered that he had a hearing loss. This helped explain why he had failed in the first grade and was failing in the second.

After two years, his full scale IQ gained 6 points. When the contained class was discontinued for the group with average or near-average intelligence, the boy was placed in a regular fifth grade class, a year behind his age group. Subsequently, he did well. Although he dropped out of high school to enter military service, he returned to complete high school, found steady factory employment, married and established a home.

A brain-injured boy was placed in the contained class at the age of eight. In three years, his full scale IQ score rose eight points. When the contained class was discontinued, he was placed in a regular sixth grade class.

He completed junior high school. After two years, however, he dropped out of high school. It is probable that he dropped out for the reason many learning-disabled adolescents do. They feel they are not making progress. But then they find no one wants to employ them.

This boy entered military service. He was lucky to receive specialized training in a technical field. It set him up with a means of earning a good livelihood in civilian life.

One of Miss Larson's pupils who entered the contained class at the age of nine remained in it for five years—until it was discontinued. He had been diagnosed as brain-injured and while his verbal score was in the normal range, his performance was below normal.

At the end of five years, he had gained 27 points on the performance scale. He was placed in the sixth grade and completed junior high school.

One day when he was twenty-one years old, he visited Miss Larson. He brought his wife and little boy. He was working at a steel plant, earning $4.80 an hour. He was attending high school two nights a week to complete his deferred high school education.

"I'm proud of him," said Miss Larson. "I'm really quite proud of them all."

Chapter 7

An EMH Follow-up:
Outcome of a High School Program

So far, I have presented some re-sults of intervention in the primary grades in the development of the neuromentally handicappeed child. What is the effect of intervention in secondary schools?

This appears to depend on the type of intervention. The effect is greatly enhanced if a job orientation and experience program is pro-vided in addition to academic work.

One of the most successful secondary school intervention programs in the United States was directed by Mrs. Margaret West at Evanston Township High School, Evanston, Illinois, during the 1950s and 1960s. She supervised classes for educable mentally handicapped students who did not expect to go to college, as 85 percent of the high school's enrollment did.

These classes contained students with a variety of learning prob-lems. Some had been diagnosed as perceptually handicapped or brain injured. Most of them were simply considered to be "retarded" and therefore unable to do regular high school work.

One of the underlying assumptions of the educable mentally handi-capped (EMH) program was that these students could not compete successfully in the job market after graduation without some training in high school. Essentially, the interventional aspect of this program was job preparation.

I think the results are noteworthy.

Mrs. West made a follow-up study of one hundred Evanston EMH students to determine how they were faring five years after leaving the high school. The subjects had attended the high school between 1953 and 1965. Seventy-four had been graduated, forty boys and thirty-four girls. The other twenty-six, including ten boys and sixteen girls, had dropped out of the program before graduation. Three had been reassigned to regular classes.

Except for a few considered perceptually handicapped, the group fitted the general "slow learner" pattern, with IQs mainly between 70 and 84. Some of the boys were fine athletes, starring on the swimming and basketball teams. A century ago, in a rural setting, few would have been considered mentally handicapped.

Aside from the small number of perceptually handicapped students, it was not possible to determine in high school whether the handicap was the result of so-called familial retardation or of early environmental deprivation.

In the period when this group entered elementary schools, it was generally assumed that slow learners exhibited familial retardation. The assumption was confirmed in some instances by the low income status of the family. School authorities did not undertake further exploration of the pupil's learning disability after he had been classified in the educable mentally handicapped or educable mentally retarded range on intelligence tests.

In general, the EMH program in high school dealt with an array of specific learning disabilities that were exhibited as poor reading, poor math and a poor grasp of the more sophisticated subjects such as history, economics and political science. The main goal of the EMH program was to improve the student's basic academic skills so that he could function independently in an urban environment.

And this was the basis on which the EMH program was judged to be a success or a failure. In these terms, it was phenomenally successful.

The most conspicuous finding of Mrs. West's follow-up study was the fact that seventy of the seventy-four graduates were steadily and gainfully employed at the time she interviewed them. The employment rate, 94.6 percent, was higher than the national average.

Among the four not employed were a boy in military service, a boy who had suffered an emotional breakdown trying to "make it" in a junior college, a girl who received a substantial inheritance and a girl who moved away from the community.

Most of the seventy-four EMH graduates received hourly wages. In 1965, the average was $1.70 an hour or $68 a week. Starting pay for graduates who had some job experience while still in school ranged from $1.20 to $1.45 an hour. After several years' experience, they earned $1.89 to $2.25 an hour. A few received $3 an hour. Although these rates may seem low by 1977 standards, they were nearly average hourly rates in the mid-1960s for unskilled or semi-skilled persons.

On an annual basis, two boys earned $5000 to $6000; four earned $4000 to $5000; thirty earned $3000 to $4000 and two earned $2000 to $3000. Among the girls, thirty earned $3000 to $4000 and two made $2000 to $3000.

One girl participated in the company profit-sharing plan and one boy was buying stock in an employee stock-purchase plan. Since 1970, after Mrs. West's survey was completed, I have located fourteen of her former students. All of them are gainfully employed, eleven in the type of service or clerical jobs they got after graduation and three in industrial employment which was not open to them at the time of high school graduation. Two of the three received training in military service for their current employment.

Anyone who observes these young men and women at work, in a food concern mail room, a hospital service center, or a large department store, would not consider them as mentally handicapped. The EMH term is now irrelevant. It defined an educational program rather than a state of being, for there is nothing except a high school record to distinguish these people from the general population of the community.

In Mrs. West's EMH classes, the students were shown how to fill out job applications. They were counseled how to present themselves for a job interview. Nearly all of them told her that this instruction was a key factor in helping them get jobs.

But there was more to it than that. Mrs. West and teachers in the special education department promoted job opportunities for the students by making personal contact with employment and personnel managers in the community served by the high school.

During this period, organizations for the physically and mentally disabled promoted a campaign to "hire the handicapped" among commercial and industrial concerns. A number of them responded. Experience showed that handicapped people made good workers; they were more inclined to remain on the job than nonhandicapped persons, possibly because jobs were harder for them to get and also because they were apprehensive about changing jobs.

Absenteeism among this group was conspicuously low. Trained personnel managers knew this. They knew also that handicapped workers were less inclined toward militancy than others. While they would join unions, they would not agitate for them. They were not "troublemakers" in the sense of aggressively demanding better wages and working conditions. These characteristics served the interests of employers. Besides, it was good public relations to hire the handicapped. Where the labor force was unionized, the unions went along with the program.

In surveys I have seen on employment of mentally handicapped persons, desirable personality characteristics, such as cheerfulness, patience and cooperation, were more likely to promote job success than IQ. This was demonstrated by Mrs. West's study, by the Cove School report and by a survey conducted at the Pennsylvania State University in 1958.[1]

By obtaining the interest and cooperation of local business and industrial managers, Mrs. West was able to get regular hours of job experience for her students. They worked several afternoons a week. In this way, those who had never held a job before acquired some idea of what it was like. In addition to this, she encouraged her students to become involved in community services for children who were more handicapped than they, for the elderly in convalescent homes, for the blind and at child care centers.

These experiences not only gave the students some insight into community problems other than their own, but aroused interest in service occupations, which many of them entered after graduation.

"These were extrovertive activities to counteract introvertive tendencies observed in most EMH pupils," Mrs. West said.

The experiences were indeed reflected in post-graduate employment. Twenty percent of the group found full-time jobs in hospitals and convalescent homes.

The post-graduate survey showed that 90 percent read Chicago and local newspapers regularly; 75 percent subscribed to one or more magazines and 60 percent used the public library.

As I have noted earlier, handicapped children tend to be loners. This pattern persists in adolescence and adulthood. Mrs. West observed this tendency in her students. Although school records did not provide detailed information into family backgrounds, she and members of her staff gained insight into family situations from conferences with parents or relatives. During the period of her directorship, which ended when she retired in 1970, the EMH classes were relatively small and quite manageable. She knew all of her students and nearly all of their families. Consequently, her observations about the students comprise a record that I believe is at least as valid and probably more useful than individual psychometric studies.

So far as such evaluations are concerned, the only psychological examination for all but a few of the students was a routine psychometric test. The results of it determined whether they would fit into the EMH program or not. Those who scored higher than the legal IQ limit for the program were automatically placed in a regular class. In the three instances where EMH students were transferred to regular classes, they performed poorly, and although they managed to be graduated, their job experiences were unsatisfactory.

During the survey period, community services for mentally handicapped children were undeveloped. The only effective program for most of the high school EMH group was a club created by the Young Women's Christian Association. It provided such activities as folk dancing, bowling, group attendance at theater and concerts, hay rides, picnics and field trips.

For some of the students, this was the only social activity they engaged in while in high school. As they matured, many never found its counterpart for adults. However, 89 percent, Mrs. West found, said they were members of a church. They took part in church activities, such as the choir, and performed tasks such as ushering and collecting.

Looking at the large group of one hundred former students, Mrs.

West noted forty had married, one was divorced and fifty-nine were single at the time of the survey.

Among the seventy-four graduates, ten of the boys were married and thirty were single; one of the girls had been divorced, nineteen were married and fourteen were single.

Mrs. West noticed that of thirteen girl graduates from the classes of 1953 through 1960, all but one married. None of the husbands was an EMH individual.

Among the twenty-six nongraduates, five of the boys were married and five were single at the time of the interview, while six of the girls were married and ten single.

EMH girls tended to marry earlier than other girls in the community, Mrs. West observed. The observation underscored the need of stressing homemaking studies early in the secondary school EMH curriculum. This was necessary, she said, because the girls did not acquire these skills from their environment as readily as other girls.

"With the EMH, homemaking is not incidental learning; it must be taught," she said.

Nine of the EMH graduates, all boys, had done well in military service. More than one-half of the graduates had qualified for drivers' licenses and one-fourth of the group owned their automobiles.

Eighty of the hundred continued to live in Evanston after leaving high school, including fifty boys and thirty girls. Ten lived outside the city but in the Chicago area (eight boys and two girls); nine moved to other states (five boys and four girls) and one girl lived overseas.

Among the graduates, ten boys and eight girls took post-graduate training at a business college, in evening typing classes at the high school, at a barber college, a modeling school, vocational training schools, an art school, a university evening program and in a sheltered workshop.

Most of the graduates (80 percent) said that vocational training and job-experience classes at the high school had been helpful because they had learned what a job was like. The most useful electives they listed were speech correction, homemaking, technical arts, typing, music and horticulture.

Employment data for the twenty-six nongraduates were not presented in the survey. But their employment pattern showed that they changed jobs more frequently than the graduates and many were intermittently unemployed. Not only academic but personality characteristics that led some to drop out of school seemed to account for a less favorable employment experience by the nongraduates than by the graduates.

Among the graduates, job continuity was high. Of sixty-four who were graduated between 1953 and 1964, a total of twenty-three held the same job they got after graduation when interviewed. One, for example, changed jobs only when he was laid off; another was forced to leave a job because of friction with other employees, but found another job in the same type of work. A third was persuaded to leave a job by members of her family who believed the job was too menial for her, but she was not able to find employment at a higher level.

In general, Mrs. West believed that job persistence confirmed a tendency of EMH students toward "failure avoidance." She surmised that they preferred to keep the jobs they knew how to do rather than risk failing in a new job, even though it promised higher pay.

The nongraduates did not seem to display the same work attitudes as the graduates, she noted.

Employers rated EMH graduates high in such job performance criteria, she said, as competence, energy, personal relations and dependability. The head of a hospital dietary department said:

> The EMH worker takes a little longer to train and unfortunately cannot be shifted around to different jobs. However, when the EMH worker understands his work he is dependable and is not always trying to get a better job.

Another manager commented about an EMH graduate who came to work in the firm as a mail boy after graduation. "This boy has a job with us for the rest of his life if he wants it. We have given him two raises."

Mrs. West noted that her study illuminated the importance of identification and placement of pupils with learning difficulties in special classes early in their schooling. Success was less frequent with pupils who were placed in the EMH program only when they entered high school or later. In fact, she said, initial placement in the EMH program when the student reached high school "invariably presented major difficulties in adjustment and was not recommended."

In conclusion, she noted that nearly all of the EMH students had become productive and contributing members of the community.

Of particular importance, she said, was the individualized placement of the students in specific jobs. This was supplemented by continuing post-school vocational guidance and follow-up placement service.

Placement should start while the student was still in school on a part-time basis, with a view, shared by the teacher, the counselor and the employer, of keeping the student on full-time after he was graduated.

Of key importance, too, she said, was "realistic parent involvement from the early stages subsequent to EMH placement."

Speech correction and the ability to communicate were important to the EMH job hunter. They were basic to successful job adjustment and social acceptability.

It was essential during the school program to provide the student with successful experiences, so that he would gain confidence and enhance his image of himself. Many of these young people have strong feelings of inadequacy and defeat. These often are detected by experienced personnel interviewers when the students apply for jobs. Mrs. West stated:

> It was noted, that if the EMH young adult could earn his living, he seemed to lose his identity as a retarded person. This was true also of the EMH female, particularly if she was able to maintain a home.

EARLY INTERVENTION

The question of early intervention that Mrs. West raised in her survey appears to be critical. Not all children who may be classified as educable mentally handicapped are actually neuromentally handicapped; many are environmentally handicapped insofar as they have been deprived of certain experiences that promote learning readiness. In the case of the neuromentally handicapped child, as I have suggested earlier, these experiences may have been sensed, but like faulty photographic film, the perceptual centers of the brain have not developed them.

There are thousands upon thousands of children who are not neuromentally handicapped but who have not been exposed to the experiences that are usual for their age group in our society. Insofar as these experiences they have missed promote learning readiness, they are retarded.

For these children, a preschool program of environmental stimulation was devised and introduced in metropolitan "inner-city" centers in 1965 with federal funding. It was called Head Start. Its purpose was to provide certain types of prelearning experiences for environmentally deprived children, namely, the poor, on the theory that they would then be able to perform better when they went to school. The logical conclusion of such an experiment was that if it worked, many of these children would acquire sufficient schooling to extricate themselves from the web of poverty in adulthood. In this way, poverty could be attacked and living standards of the perpetual poor could be raised.

Head Start was administered by the Office of Economic Opportunity (OEO) as a campaign in the war on poverty. The program was the offspring of a legion of child development specialists who were unqualifiedly "environmental" in their outlook on scholastic achievement.

Head Start was launched as an eight-week summer program in 1965, a year after the OEO called together a panel of child development experts to draft it. The philosophy of the program is expressed in the panel's report, issued by the chairman, Dr. Robert Cooke, Pediatrician-in-Chief, Johns Hopkins University Hospital, Baltimore. The report stated:

> There is considerable evidence that the early years of childhood are a most critical point in the poverty cycle. During these years, the creation of learning patterns, emotional development and the formation of individual expectations and aspirations take place at a very rapid pace. For the child of poverty, there are clearly observable deficiencies in these processes which lay the foundation for a pattern of failure and thus a pattern of poverty throughout the child's entire life.

Not long after the summer program was started, funding was provided by the OEO to extend the preschool program. The age group it served was from three to the start of school, either in kindergarten or the first grade.

Head Start was designed to provide preschool education, social activity and training and administer to the health, nutritional and psychological needs of the underprivileged. In 1969, it was transferred to the Department of Health, Education and Welfare (HEW). And in 1974, it was extended to 1978 by the Head Start Economic Opportunity and Community Partnership Act (Public Law 93-644).

The program actually is administered by 1350 grantees in local communities. They are citizens' groups, other recognized community agencies or public school systems. Parents are invited to participate in the planning of the programs.

Because of local direction, the educational design of Head Start programs has been variable. Parental "involvement" has not always been a positive factor.

Quality of the programs varies considerably. But quality is not taken into account specifically in the numerous evaluations of Head Start. These rely mainly on the performance of Head Start children after they are in grade school.

In general, evaluations have not illuminated the effectiveness of individual programs per se, but addressed only the value of the concept of a compensatory preschool program. Even so, there has been wide disagreement on the value of the program from several viewpoints.

Starting from an appropriation base of $96.4 million in the 1965 fiscal year, Head Start has grown to a $454 million program in ten years. It has served nearly six million children.

In 1968, after Head Start was in operation three years, the OEO commissioned the Westinghouse Learning Corporation, a subsidiary of the Westinghouse Electric Company, to make a study of its effect.

The study reported two conclusions: first, that a summer Head Start program was "totally ineffective" and second, that the full-year program was only "marginally effective."

The report became a subject of heated controversy. The Secretary of Health, Education and Welfare, Robert Finch, denounced the Westinghouse study as containing "insufficient facts" and "sloppy data."[2] Dr. William Madow, of Stanford University, the chief statistical consultant to the study, withdrew his name from the report. He wrote OEO stating:

> Far from accepting payment for my work, I would appreciate your removing my name as a statistical consultant, since I would not want anyone to think I had any responsibility for the design; and the analyses and conclusions based on it seem to me to be incorrect.[3]

The Westinghouse report set off a hurricane of papers and surveys, all evaluating Head Start from several points of view.

The views of social and behavioral scientists toward intervention as a means of counteracting adverse family and neighborhood effects on scholastic achievement were by no means harmonious.

One group contended that intervention does not work because it cannot. As a result of generations of selective mating, they argued, the poor have become genetically inferior to the higher economic classes. They are not capable of responding to public education as effectively as their middle-class and upper-class peers do. This view regards intelligence as a hereditary trait, like red hair.

There is another, a middle-of-the-road group. It does not espouse the hereditary view of learning capability. But its adherents argue that intervention has not worked because the few hours a week children may spend in preschool training programs are not enough to overcome the negative aspects of a ghetto environment.

A third group contends that there is evidence of positive impact of Head Start, Follow Through and similar intervention efforts in subsequent school performance—if the children are studied long enough. Further, this group contends that some of the negative evaluations are faulty and fail to present a true picture.

However, the Office of Child Development of HEW issued a monograph in 1974 that confirmed the Westinghouse study. It was entitled, *Is Early Intervention Effective?* and as John H. Meier, former director of the Office of Child Development, observed, "it offered some rather pessimistic answers."[4]

The study asserted that even when early intervention does produce substantial cognitive gains, Meier said, the gains erode away, "wash out" after the child leaves the program. It found that the most environmentally deprived children seem to benefit the least. The greatest "erosion" of gains came after the children entered the regular school system.

Intervention was attacked from the genetic point of view by Professor Arthur R. Jensen, the University of California psychologist, who contends that intelligence varies by race. In his 1969 article in the Harvard Educational Review, "How Much Can We Boost IQ and Scholastic Achievement?" Jensen announced that, "Compensatory education has been tried and apparently it has failed."

Jensen, as I have related earlier, considered intelligence as a unitary, heritable characteristic. Much of the evidence he adduced was based on Cyril Burt's twin studies in England. It was Jensen's conclusion that some populations, especially blacks, were genetically inferior to whites in their ability to manipulate abstract symbols and solve certain types of problems.

Although the heritability concept of "Jensenism" has been vigorously assailed by other scientists, the vast amount of publicity that the controversy has received tended to tar and feather Head Start as a controversial if not ineffective effort.

A number of critics of Jensen have argued that when he arrived at the conclusion that compensatory education had failed, not enough time had passed to make a thorough assessment of it.

The attack upon intervention involved the whole concept of remedial education insofar as it was based on equalizing environmental deficiencies. It provided a scientific base for the old argument that children from the ghettos and barrios of America are genetically unable to achieve much academically no matter how much is done for them.

Such compensatory programs as Head Start and Follow Through had been launched on the theory that there is no difference in innate learning ability among classes or races. But the initial failures, or alleged failures, of the program tended to disprove that thesis.

At the outset, in the mid-1960s, the predominant view among psychologists and educators held that effective intervention would prevent mental retardation in children from deprived environments. For a time, it had seemed as though it might triumph. But then, the

Westinghouse study and other data that indicated the gains from intervention were temporary at best raised new doubts.

The stakes were very high. For on the shifting sands of opinion about compensatory education rested the probable future of federal funding of the programs.

At a time when teenage crime and delinquency had reached the highest levels in the nation's history, and when reading levels in cities like Chicago were falling, especially among the poor, the only national remedy that had ever been implemented by federal funding seemed to be going up in smoke.

It seemed likely that the fate of special education across the board was tied to the fate of the early compensatory programs. For that reason, it was important to take a second look at them.

A number of analyses of the Westinghouse data presented a different picture of Head Start, particularly of the summer program. Burt S. Barnow in a doctoral dissertation presented at the University of Wisconsin reanalyzed the data in terms of Head Start's effect on different ethnic groups: blacks, Mexican Americans and whites. He concluded that the summer program helped blacks and Mexican Americans, but not whites.[5]

A review of Head Start research was prepared by the Social Research Group of the George Washington University, Washington, D.C., for the Office of Child Development, HEW.

It reported that the majority of Head Start evaluation studies showed that youngsters participating in the program improved in performance on standard intelligence tests or in general ability; that they performed as well or better than their peers when they began regular school and fewer were held back or placed in special classes compared with children who did not take part in Head Start.

One study examined the results of the participation by 248 children in Head Start programs in Hartford, Connecticut. It found that the participants started out with an eighteen-month deficit in language development for their age norm. However, they improved on an average of thirteen months after eight months in Head Start. They also did better than their peers (from the same neighborhood) when they began regular school.

A study in Warren, Ohio, compared 80 Head Start children and 240 children who did not take part in the program. Results of the

Stanford Early School Achievement Test showed that the economically disadvantaged children who took part in Head Start demonstrated achievement equal to that of their "more affluent counterparts from the same neighborhoods," the Social Research Group's review reported.

FOLLOW THROUGH

Critics of Head Start questioned whether its effects would be lasting. The long-term effect was investigated by a research group at Yale University consisting of Victoria Seitz, Nancy H. Apfel and Carole Efron.[6]

They followed the academic progress of 130 children from "economically disadvantaged" families in inner-city neighborhoods. About half, or sixty-six, attended Project Follow Through, a four-year program that supplemented Head Start, for children in kindergarten through third grade. The remainder, 64, attended their own neighborhood schools for the period of the study.

The two groups of children were again divided into two subgroups: those who entered kindergarten in 1967 and those who entered in 1968. For reasons not exhaustively analyzed, Dr. Seitz reported, the effects on boys were different than those on girls. Developmental differences were conjectured.

By the end of the third grade, boys in the first age group attending Follow Through scored significantly higher than non-Follow Through boys in mathematics, vocabulary and general information. But Follow Through Girls did not differ significantly from non-Follow Through girls in any of six measures. These included reading comprehension, reading recognition and spelling.

For the second age group, the Follow Through program showed the same results—but for girls rather than for boys. At the end of the third grade, Follow Through girls scored significantly higher than non-Follow Through girls in mathematics, vocabulary and general information. No program effects were found in reading comprehension, reading recognition and spelling in either the first or the second groups.

Subsequent testing of 93 percent of both age groups showed that the effects persisted, the researchers said. When the first age group was retested in the eighth grade, Follow Through boys continued to score higher than non-Follow Through boys on the same three tests. The Follow Through girls showed a delayed gain, a "sleeper effect," as Dr. Seitz described it. In the eighth grade, they scored significantly higher than non-Follow Through girls on mathematics achievement. That had not been evident in the third grade.

A similar pattern appeared when children in the second age group were retested in seventh grade, the report said. "The Follow Through girls continued to score significantly higher than non-Follow Through girls on the same three tests. The boys in the second age group did not differ significantly either in third grade or in the later testing.

The experimenters noted that the test scores of Follow Through children were generally "somewhat below" national norms with two exceptions. Follow Through boys in the first age group performed at the national average in general information and vocabulary in the eighth grade. Follow Through girls in the second age group scored half a year above national norms in mathematics achievement in the seventh grade.

Dr. Seitz presented the report for her research team February 23, 1977, at the annual meeting of the American Association for the Advancement of Science in Denver. Her paper was part of a morning-long discussion arranged by the Office of Child Development, Department of Health, Education and Welfare on the topic: "Found: Long Term Gains from Early Intervention."

Aside from the material, which attracted press attention, the program was significant in the context of the long-term battle over the effects of early intervention. It seemed to indicate that the forces of early intervention are beginning to shoot back at the critics who have been trying to sink such programs since Head Start began.

It looked to me like a counterattack. A member of the audience arose during the question period and asked where the opposition was. He turned out to be a geologist. What he was doing in a meeting of behavioral scientists was not clear. He wanted to hear rebuttal, but none had been arranged.

Dr. Seitz apparently had not expected to find sex differences in program effects. They might be accounted for by different rates of maturation of boys and girls of elementary school age. The "sleeper effect" was a new development. Future testers will be looking for it.

Essentially, the investigation contradicted claims by other researchers that early gains from intervention, if any, tend to fade out, that children who did not take part in Head Start caught up rather soon to those who did.

The work of Dr. Seitz and her colleagues suggested that such results might be due to evaluation bias or error instead of any instrinsic failure in the intervention program itself.

"Our study is unusual," Dr. Seitz said, "as the children were followed for a prolonged period of time. For those children who responded positively to the program there was no fade-out of the intervention effects. Benefits evident at the end of the third grade when the intervention program ended were still found four to five years later.

"These findings suggest that a cautious optimism is appropriate regarding the effects of early intervention programs."

It remains to be determined, she added, why some groups of children showed effects and others did not and why the effects were limited to mathematics, general information and vocabulary.

A second salvo was fired from the prestigious AAAS podium by Francis H. Palmer, Professor of Psychology at the State University of New York at Stony Brook. Dr. Palmer warned that Americans "seem ready to default on the promissory note of universal education."

"The average poor child is not deriving the benefit from schools that his middle-class peer is," he said.

In 1974, he said, there were two high schools in Manhattan where 100 percent of the students were reading at grade level or better, but there were seven other schools in Manhattan with 6500 students where only 7 percent were reading at grade level or better.

Dr. Palmer reported the results of a "longitudinal" study of 310 central Harlem children in New York. In the patois of the psychometric community, a longitudinal study is one that follows up children for a number of years. Because intervention programs are relatively recent, longitudinal studies of their effects are just now coming into view. And they are reversing the findings of the early negative reports of these programs.

The children were selected from 1500 birth records between

August and December 1964. They were all black males. Developmental differences between boys and girls represented a variable that would have required more staff and more facilities than the funding of the study allowed. They were all blacks, Dr. Palmer said, because the research design called for children from a broad range of social class in a manageable geographic area. It included middle-class as well as ghetto children.

Each child had weighed over five pounds at birth. All the parents spoke English. None had a history of narcotics. Half were families whose heads of household were unemployed; half had jobs ranging from menial to the professions.

The 310 participants were divided into three groups. One group of 120 was exposed to a special program at twenty-four months of age. Another group of 120 was exposed to the program starting at thirty-six months of age. There were 70 control group children who were not exposed.

The 240 "experimental" children were exposed to two different intervention programs. In one, half of each age group was given special training in basic concepts that the psychologist believed had to be acquired before more complex ones could be learned. Some of these were *up, down, hard, soft, long, short, over* and *under*. Dr. Palmer noted that the environmental stimuli for acquiring these concepts are present universally, regardless of culture or language, "but we felt that the earlier the child learned them the earlier he could acquire more complex ones."

The twenty-four-months age group started the experiment in modest circumstances. The learning center was in a loft that had once been a machine shop on 126th Street "between Charlie's Bar and the 24th Precinct Station," the psychologist related. Most of the two-year-olds knew the concept *on top of*, whereas those such as *next to* or *far away* were difficult for them.

Thus, half of the two-year-olds were given this form of concept training in addition to other more conventional preschool activity twice each week in one hour sessions for eight months. The teaching was on a one to one basis—one teacher, one child. The children who were not given concept training but who took part in conventional preschool activity also received training on a one to one basis. Both groups outperformed the control group when they were tested at the end of the training period.

A year later, when the second group of participants reached thirty-six months of age, the 120 children in this group entered the program. They were divided into a concept training group and a non-concept training group as the two-year-olds had been.

A year after the second group completed its training, its members were tested. As in the case of the two-year-olds the year before, the three-year-olds in both sections of the training program outperformed the control children who had not received any training.

The group that had started at twenty-four months of age was re-tested at this time. They retained their gains.

When the two participating age groups were retested at four years, eight months of age, only minor differences were found between the participating children and the controls. At that point, he said, the funds ran out and "we lost track of the children."

Five years later, the New York State Education Commission made a grant to locate the Harlem children and see how they were doing. During the years of the study, 15 of the 310 children who started dropped out before the training was completed. That left 295 to be found. It wasn't easy, Dr. Palmer related. It required an elaborate "private eye" operation in Harlem. Investigators canvassed groceries and shops asking whatever became of people like Mrs. Blank and her son, John.

Eventually, 233 of the 295 were found. Information was obtained on 183 of the children in the experimental groups and on 50 of the controls. The boys were eleven years old and most were in the fifth grade.

The IQ scores on the Wechsler Intelligence Test for Children were higher for the four experimental groups (average 99) than for the controls (average 93). Individually, three of the experimental groups were "significantly higher than the controls," Dr. Palmer reported.

In reading achievement, all four experiment groups had higher scores than the controls. In arithmetic achievement, the average child in the experimental group was still below the national norm, but was more than six months advanced over the controls.

Dr. Palmer regarded it most significant of all that while 45 percent of the controls were one year or more behind in grade, only 22 percent of the experimentals were one year or more behind in grade.

"In the population we're dealing with," he said, "some 40 percent of those kids are set back within the first six years of school. For this particular study, there's absolutely no question but what we've made an effect. The sample of 233 we found was 12 percent of all the children in central Harlem in the fifth grade in 1975.

He characterized the training given the two-year-olds and three-year-olds as "Minimal."

THE SOCIAL POLICY CONNECTION

As I have indicated earlier, the question of whether intervention reduces learning disability or increases intelligence and academic performance is not merely academic. Few so-called academic questions are. It affects the future welfare and the future structure of American society. In view of these high stakes, parents are entitled to wonder about the validity of the research on this question and the logic of the hereditarian and environmental schools of thought.

Historically, as I have taken some pains to point out, the hereditarian position has been socially destructive. It tends to treat the handicapped as slightly subhuman. It perpetuates an intellectual caste system, based on race, color and IQ. It is essentially a pseudoscientific rationale for social stasis.

Except for the learning-disabilities movement, which I will review in some detail later, the system of special education in most American school districts reflects the hereditarian view of intelligence. Even the best programs for the educable mentally handicapped assume an innate *lack* of intelligence. Pupils are classified accordingly. But that is not the direction pioneering intervention programs are pointing. They show us that a child's intellectual capability is plastic enough to be molded one way or the other by his early experiences. How long will it take before special education catches up with this development and overturns the nineteenth century dictum that you can't pour a quart of knowledge into a pint bottle?

One of the main pillars of hereditarian theory has begun to sag in recent years under the erosion of critical analysis. It is the research of the British psychologist, Cyril Burt, who claimed that separated twins showed a high correlation in intelligence in spite of being reared in different environments.

American and British psychologists who have been perusing Burt's data have found a number of inconsistencies in it. On October 24, 1976, the medical correspondent of the *London Sunday Times* reported that he could find no trace of two women researchers whom Burt listed as having assisted him in gathering the twin studies data.

Burt, who died in 1971 at the age of eighty-eight, has been described as a "towering figure" in educational psychology in England. He was a major influence in the adoption of the British national education system in which children may be assigned to one of three educational levels on the basis of a test at the age of eleven.* Probably no more effective way of perpetuating a caste system has been devised by a modern nation.

The *Sunday Times* report was significant as a piece of negative evidence concerning Burt's twin studies. These formed the research basis of his thesis that intelligence is genetically determined. The studies, as I have indicated earlier, consisted of three reports in 1955, 1958 and 1966 covering more than a hundred pairs of twins that had been separated at birth and reared in different home environments. Burt claimed to have found incontrovertible evidence of high correlation in the intelligence of all pairs.

At Harvard, Professor Leon Kamin has branded Burt's twin studies as a fraud.[7] He was one of the first to claim inconsistencies and gaps in Burt's data. These were later noticed by others.

Burt formulated his theory about the heritability of intelligence in the first quarter of the century. "I suspect that everything the man did from 1909 on is wholly fraudulent," Kamin was quoted as saying in a report in the journal *Science*.[8] The report noted that Jensen, who used Burt's twin studies to support his racial intelligence claims, was a postgraduate student of one of Burt's disciples, H. J. Eysenck.

What can the parent of a handicapped child infer from all this? I suggest the obvious inference is that theories about the immutability

---

* It has been a long standing practice in British education to place children in separate college preparatory, vocational or general education high schools on the basis of an "ll-Plus" examination. However, in recent years, many local school authorities have dropped the examination. All three curricula have been housed in the newer, educationally desegregated, comprehensive high schools. These changes have largely resulted from parental demands for equal educational opportunity.

or plasticity of intelligence are as much a matter of opinion and of emotional bias as they were a century ago.

From this point of view, the only data that can make sense to parents are the life experiences—or "longitudinal studies"—of children who exhibited learning disabilities and behavior problems early in life. They indicate what parents can expect.

I have related some of these in the context of special settings.

But what are the consequences when learning-disabled children are pushed into institutions or are allowed to struggle as best they can in overcrowded, inner-city grade schools where the classes are too large and the teachers too harassed for any kind of special program to be effective?

PART III

EMANCIPATION

Chapter 8

Normalization: The De-Institutionalization Trend

Evidence that early intervention enhances the development of the neuromentally handicapped child is so strong that it seems to be indisputable. It provides parents with a powerful case to bring before school boards or courts in districts where the needs of the mentally handicapped are not being met.

But what about the child with learning disabilities for whom no program of intervention or remedial teaching has been available? Can some form of intervention in adolescence or early adulthood help him?

Evidence exists that it can. Like early intervention, the later remedy is effective only if it is carefully designed and carried out to enable the subject to overcome behavioral difficulties and deficits in learning and experience.

An important feature of late intervention is to alter the environment. This means pulling the subject out of a life situation where the prevailing behavior model is one of institutionalized, retarded persons and thrusting him into a community life situation where he experiences a normal behavior model. With supervision and counseling, there is a good chance that he can adapt to it.

If he is an inmate of an institution, it means breaking him out of its behavior pattern and helping him establish the prevailing life-style of the community. It means enabling him, by training and coaching, to find a job and a place to live. It means providing social service backup when he needs it.

Such a program requires a social service operation of considerable magnitude and sophistication. It is costly, but much cheaper than allowing a potentially useful adult to vegetate in an institution.

The social service concept behind such a program is called "normalization." Although the idea of normalizing retarded persons was an institutional goal in America before the Civil War, it faded after the war when the treatment of that era failed to "cure" retardation. In the latter part of the nineteenth century, as I related earlier, mental deficiency came to be regarded as a social evil. The retarded were viewed as a social menace.

As a result of this attitude, retarded persons were segregated. For most of them, it meant lifelong custody in a large, generally overcrowded institution.

This pattern of dealing with retarded persons is essentially custodial. It does not educate; it does not rehabilitate; it simply warehouses human beings from the cradle to the grave.

After a century, this process is slowly giving way to a more optimistic social policy. This policy, normalization, restores the old belief that retarded persons can be trained to live and work in normal society. But it has some new techniques, new ideas.

As Wolf Wolfensberger has described it, the term "normalization has since 1969 become the watchword for a whole new ideology of human management."[1]

In 1969, the normalization principle was written into the social welfare laws of Denmark governing services to the mentally retarded. Its chief advocate was N. E. Bank-Mikkelsen, head of the Danish Mental Retardation Service. The principle was recognized in Sweden where Bengt Nirje, executive director of the Swedish Association for Retarded Children, defined it as "making available to the mentally retarded patterns and conditions of every day life which are as close as possible to the norms and patterns of the mainstream of society."[2]

The theory behind normalization is quite straightforward. Since the "Wild Boy of Aveyron," it has been known that human beings are sufficiently plastic in infancy and early childhood to be molded by their environment. The Wild Boy, reared among animals, behaved like an animal and, indeed, did not develop the human capacity of speech.

The degree to which the environment shapes the individual and determines his abilities is the subject of a great debate in psychology. But there is a wide consensus that environment makes the difference between a Lord Fauntleroy and a Tarzan of the Apes, heredity being similar.

Retarded children are not immune to this shaping. As Skeels found (Chapter 4), retarded orphans in Iowa who were adopted after an intervention program of environmental stimulation grew up to be normally capable adults, whereas orphans of higher IQ who remained in the orphanage fared poorly.

Advocates of normalizing retarded persons by moving them out of institutions and placing them in supervised habitats and work facilities in normal communities contend that the big state institutions for the retarded simply promote retardation.

The child placed in an institution acquires "inmate" behavior. Since he is among other children and also adults who are retarded, he develops the behavior pattern of the environment. It is abnormal in terms of normal behavior outside. Consequently, when the inmate goes outside, his behavior appears to be exceptional or inappropriate so long as he follows the institution model. And what other model is there for him?

An effective normalization program provides another model, a real-life model. In the Chicago area, for example, several large private social service agencies operate state-funded normalization programs.

The goal of the agencies is to set up the subject, usually called the "client," in a job and a residence. This requires planned programs of job training, supervised living arrangements and, often, the modification of the client's behavior so that he can get along with fellow workers and neighbors.

As social reformers believed a century and a half ago, normalization theory predicts that retarded persons, even severely retarded ones, are capable of adapting to new environments and of acquiring new skills as adults.

In modern terms, this is a revolutionary idea, even though it goes back a long way, as many "revolutionary" ideas do. Between 1860 and 1960, institutional practice assumed a cutoff point in the learning capacity of retarded persons. Beyond a certain "mental age" such a person could not learn much of anything. The belief provided a convenient rationale for allowing the patient to linger in an institution.

So long as this frame of mind persisted among institution superintendents, there was little hope that inmates would be trained beyond basket weaving and pottery skills. The idea that even the severely retarded could be taught to operate lathes, drill presses and perform a myriad of production-line tasks seemed much too farfetched to take seriously. That they could be shown how to live a normal community life seemed unimaginable.

These are the prejudices which normalization theory has sought to overcome.

THE WORKSHOPS

From a bureaucratic point of view, the trend toward normalization has had the practical effect of removing inmates from institutions and thus relieving overcrowding. It has been accelerated by studies showing successful vocational and social adjustment of persons classed as retarded.

The transfer from institutional to community living has been engineered by public and private agencies in a number of ways. In many instances, the clients are moved into "sheltered care" facilities. These provide communal living for a number of men and women clients under the supervision of social workers. They are operated in some states like Illinois by both *nonprofit* and *for-profit* organizations. The for-profit operators conduct the communes as businesses, much as private nursing homes are operated. The operators are reimbursed by the state on a per client basis. The nonprofit shelters are operated usually by social service agencies or community trusts, some of which started out as parent organizations.

Although the purpose of the shelters is to deinstitutionalize the "clients" and thus set them on the road to normality, the communal facility itself tends to become a miniature institution. It tends to perpetuate an exceptional behavior model, even while training clients to adapt to independent living. In the Chicago area, where several old-line social service agencies are involved in the normalization process, there is growing concern about the institutional aspect and inadequacies of the shelters generally.

Some social workers and agency directors are critical of sheltered living arrangements and workshops. They perceive the pseudo-institutional aspects of the shelters as debilitating. They try to get the clients out of the shelters and into independent quarters as soon as possible, even if the state has to continue to subsidize the client in rent, food and clothing. In theory, the sooner the client can stand on his own feet, the sooner he is likely to be able to support himself.

In Kalamazoo, Michigan, a private social service agency took the challenge of habilitating former inmates of a state institution that was closed down. The project was an alternative to transferring many of them to another institution. One technique that was tried was to recruit roommates to share quarters with clients. In one instance I encountered, the roommate was a university student majoring in social psychology. He helped a neurologically handicapped young man adjust to independent apartment life. It seemed to work. Both young men liked the arrangement and regarded it as successful.

I found that social workers were critical of some for-profit shelters on the grounds that operators tended to encourage clients to remain as a stable population and steady source of income. Such a practice would defeat the object of normalization efforts, the critics complained.

In theory, the shelters were designed to be "halfway" houses, or buffers between institutional and independent living. But their critics charged that some were being run as junior asylums.

A similar objection was raised by the critics of sheltered workshops. These were operated by both for-profit and nonprofit organizations. In some cases, they were connected to the sheltered living facilities, so that the client might reside and work under the auspices of the same organization.

Critics of the sheltered workshops contended they denied a moderately retarded client the experience of working in a normal environment, since all of his fellow workers were retarded, too. Although he might acquire some industrial skills in the sheltered workshop, the behavior models to which he was exposed were similar to those in the institutions. He therefore was not learning how to get along with a normal mix of average employees.

TRANSITIONAL EMPLOYMENT

What was the alternative to the sheltered workshop? The answer was a facility that would train the client for a job in private industry where he would rub shoulders with normal employees. Although this was also the goal of most sheltered workshops, it was not being realized on the scale that critics thought possible.

Such a facility was developed by one of Chicago's oldest, private social service agencies, the Levy Center, a former Jewish orphanage. It organized the Chicago School and Workshop, a nonprofit agency with the goal of training clients to get and to keep jobs in private industry.

The Chicago School and Workshop took part in a state-financed program called transitional employment. It was designed to prepare retarded adolescents and young adults for jobs in private industry.

But that was only half the problem. The other half was to persuade employers that young men and women who bore the label retarded could be trained as productive workers.

The burden of training was on the social service agency. Clients were first placed in sample work programs. At the Chicago School and Workshop, the training was carried out in the agency's sheltered workshop, but with the understanding it was only temporary.

Clients were given a battery of intelligence and performance tests. They were given training in tasks that would be useful in general industrial employment, sometimes involving the operation of power tools and machinery.

When they had progressed to a level of competence that their workshop coaches believed made them employable, the agency lined up jobs for them in private enterprise.

I observed and interviewed a group of clients who were employed in two types of occupations: factory work and food service. In each case, the employer had agreed to cooperate with the Transitional

Employment Program. And in each case, the employer was pleased with the result.

Not all the clients had been transferred from state or sectarian institutions. Several of the young men and women I talked to had histories of chronic employment failure. On-the-job training was not enough for them; they had to have special assistance until they acquired appropriate work and social habits.

The assistance was provided by young social workers, several fresh out of college, who served as employment coaches.

Their job was to counsel the client both on and off the job. They acted as surrogate big brothers or sisters, advising the clients about dress, about handling their finances, about arranging transportation between the job and the residence, about social activities outside the job and about interpersonal relations inside, with other employees.

In the two employment groups I observed, each client was given a six-month probationary period. The employer then had the option of hiring him as a regular employee. After that, the monitoring by the agency coaches was reduced, but since a relationship existed between the coaches and the clients, there was help available if the client needed it.

Essentially, it was the responsibility of the agency coaches to "shape up" the clients so that they could fit into the work situation. Sometimes, the coaches had to serve as umpires in disputes between clients and as peacemakers in disputes between clients and fellow workers.

One of the employers that had agreed to take as many as thirty clients into its labor force was a manufacturer of pinball and slot machines. To the uninitiated, the "innards" of these devices are unbelievably complicated. There are thousands of parts and hundreds of assemblies and subassemblies.

Much of the manufacturing operation consists of making and assembling parts. The personnel director of the plant told me there were eighteen clients working in the manufacturing operation. Twelve were in training and on probation; six had been placed in permanent jobs. The personnel chief said:

> We've always had a commitment to hire the handicapped. We've had such success with Chicago School and Workshop that I think

we should have one trainee in each department. We have thirty-five departments here. We will put on more trainees where there is funding for more job coaches. The job coach is the key to the success of of the program. It wouldn't work if that feature isn't present.

In some cases, the productivity of clients the plant has hired is 15 percent above the plant standard, the director said. Pegging the standard at 100, the permissible minimum productivity is 90, he said. Trainees usually do better than that.

The director said that the plantwide average for absenteeism is 10 percent, but among those in the training program, it is 0.75 to 1.5 percent.

After the trainee is formally hired and put on the regular payroll, there is a structured follow-up training plan. It serves to confirm the client in the job. There is a closed shop at the plant. The union, the International Brotherhood of Electrical Workers, goes along with hiring the handicapped. Clients are required to observe the work rules like everyone else. That is an important aspect of their training. Those who succeed in staying on the job join the union.

Handicapped employees are paid at the same rate and get the same raises as all the others.

I observed a production room where two clients were at work. One had been there only a few months, the other more than a year. Until they were pointed out to me, I could not distinguish them from the nonhandicapped workers.

At this plant, the clients were doing assembly, soldering, electrical connections, silk screening and stockroom and maintenance work.

Skills were not the big problem, the coaches explained. The big problem was behavior. In most cases, it had to be modified. This was done by patient explanation of "dos and don'ts" in a normal job situation.

The Chicago School and Workshop coaches opposed the reward-and-punishment method used in state institutions to modify behavior. At one state institution where severely retarded and mentally ill patients were warehoused, tokens were awarded for performing certain tasks or simply for periods of good behavior. Inmates wishing to attend church services on Sunday could do so only by depositing tokens at the door.

Most of the agency's clients were highly motivated to achieve some form of independence. Getting and holding a real job seemed to be the pinnacle of achievement. It was frequently enough to convince them that inappropriate behavior would defeat their efforts and cause them to fail. And then it was necessary to show them what appropriate behavior was.

"When you take a person and stick him in a special environment," one of the women coaches explained, "he acts special; in a nonspecialized situation, he acts nonspecialized. The people in a subculture tend to reinforce each other."

One of the young women clients gave this version of her behavior modification: "On the bus, I can't act funny when all different kinds of people are on it."

At the factory, young women clients soon began to change their appearance. They switched to "smarter" clothes and more sophisticated make-up. They observed how the other women dressed and behaved. Friendships were formed.

Of 600 clients served by the Chicago School and Workshop and the Levy Center, only about 100 live with their families. Most do not have families and have been in institutions much of their lives.

Some are placed in sheltered care quarters in apartment hotels. Several shelters are large, with more than 400 beds. The coaching staff prefers smaller shelters of no more than twenty. One of the women coaches said:

> The shelter houses tend to encourage people to stay, and supervision is generally poor. One of the big operators has a staff turnover of 105 percent a year because of low pay. Services are poor. Except for us, the people living in these places have no advocate; no one looks out for them; no one gives a damn about them. They are the disenfranchised in our society.

The main thrust of the social service teams in the Transitional Employment Program is to move the clients into independent living quarters about three months after they settle into a job. When they are working, state support ends.

The majority of clients in these programs are young adults, from eighteen to twenty-five years old. There are a few middle-aged men and women who have spent most of their lives in institutions, and are severely limited as a result. I was told of a blind boy who remained in an institution for the mentally retarded until he was twenty-five years old. When he was tested from the Transitional Employment Program, he was found to have normal intelligence.

Not all the Transitional Employment Program clients make the grade. During a fifteen-month period after the program started, the Chicago School and Workshop reported that 29 percent of its clients succeeded in holding onto private industry jobs after the training period.[3]

The percentage appears unimpressive until it is compared with the 6 percent placement record of the sheltered workshops. Jacob Ginsburg, director of the Chicago School and Workshop, has observed:[4]

> It is clear that industry and rehabilitation have much to offer one another on a pragmatic level as well as on a humane level. The normalizing features of the environment, such as structure, salary, companionship, recognition, improved family estimate, seem to operate in a sustaining fashion for the retarded graduate of a transitional employment experience.
>
> The job coach systematically and judiciously retracts his presence and his guidance as the placement candidate begins to develop greater experience and autonomy in his own problem-solving abilities.

By contrast, Ginsburg regarded the sheltered workshop as a "dead end" that tended to "reinforce dysfunction and separation from total society." Their populations can be given nonsheltered work experiences that may enable them ultimately to achieve private employment, he said.

Ginsburg and other social service experts in this field see the sheltered workshop as a resort for a much smaller and more severely handicapped population than these facilities support at present. Many of those now in sheltered workshops can be trained to work outside, Ginsburg contended.

> If the graduates of the Transitional Employment Program have given us one dramatic learning it is that the ceiling level of perform-

ance capacities of the retarded worker are higher than many employers realize and also, to our regret, higher than many rehabilitation professionals realize.

SAM

One of the graduates of the program is a young man I will call Sam, age twenty-three. He lives at home with his mother and his grandmother. His father died suddenly, but the mother was able to support the household until Sam completed the training program and got on the regular factory payroll. He was found to be capable, efficient and responsible. Soon, Sam was promoted to the job of inspector.

"It's a nice job," he said, speaking slowly to master a speech impediment. "I find it interesting. Every day, it's something different."

Sam attended a Chicago public school for the physically handicapped. He was placed in classes for the educable mentally handicapped as well. His handicaps were multiple: loss of hearing, serious speech difficulties and neuromotor problems that made it difficult for him to walk.

He was born with yellow jaundice, his mother recalled. She said:

The doctor told me: there's something wrong with this little boy. When he got to be a few months old, I noticed it; the way he reacted; the way he moved. He didn't sit up in time.

He was premature. He weighed three pounds two ounces at birth, a seven-months baby. I had him in the hospital until he reached five pounds. He progressed very late in everything.

After completing school in a program for the educable mentally handicapped, Sam went to work, but none of his jobs lasted long. He started with a printing company. It failed. He got another job in photo offset. Again, the firm "folded up." Sam said:

It got to be tough. Today to get a good job, you've got to have connections. Or relatives. I just didn't know the right people. I went to another printing company because it was the only experience I had.

I worked there in the bindery. But it was kind of far from home, hard to get to and back, and I quit on my own.

Sam then got a job with Amtrak through an employment service. He worked on the "docks" doing heavy manual labor, although a spinal problem has made walking difficult for him all his life. After a while, Amtrak laid him off.

I worked in the warehouse where we stored the canned goods and frozen foods, you know. We supplied the trains. I worked there six months and then was laid off. At that time, you know, the economy was a little shaky. That was my problem. When I was laid off from Amtrak, I was out of work for about a month. I worked for an optical company for a while; then I got sick.

Sam had serious spinal complications, resulting in partial paralysis of the legs. He underwent surgery for spinal fusion and made a reasonably good recovery. He applied to Amtrak for his old job, but the company physician disqualified him.

"He said I couldn't speak good enough and I had one leg that was shorter than the other."

What now? No one would give Sam a job after his surgery. He tried to collect disability pay. Social Security told him: "If you can walk, you can work," he said. Sam could walk, but he did so with a rolling gait, "like a drunk," as his mother said.

"I do walk with a slight limp," Sam admitted.

The Social Security office put him in touch with Chicago School and Workshop. There he was trained for factory work. He completed the probationary period at the game machine factory, got a regular job and was promoted first to general inspector and then to precision inspector.

Sam blamed his disabilities for his difficulty in finding and holding jobs. The inspectorship is the best break he's ever had. He drives his own car and arrives at the plant at 6:30 A.M. "to get parking." Work starts at 7 A.M. and the day ends at 3 P.M.

He maintains a savings and checking account at the bank. "A guy I know in the neighborhood—he prepares my income tax." His recreation is limited; he doesn't date. But he learned to play the guitar in high school. He took a few lessons but learned by ear. He plays with a group that includes another guitar, drum and organ at social functions, especially weddings. On some occasions, he makes $75 an evening.

When you talk to Sam for a while, you no longer notice his inconspicuous hearing aid, his speech impediment or the fact that he walks with a rolling gait. I found him to be a practical young man who now believes that his handicaps are not seriously disabling—now that he has a job that commands the respect of his peers and family. He said:

> I consider myself normal. I try to do the things everybody else does. But there are people out there who look down on you if you aren't exactly like them. You have to live with that, but here, after they get to know you, and you get to know them, it don't matter.

An early physical examination of Sam found that he had suffered mild cerebral palsy, hearing loss resulting from neurosensory dysfunction and speech difficulty. In public school, he was classified as educable mentally retarded.

However, Sam was not retarded by any measure as a young adult. On the Wechsler Adult Intelligence Scale, his verbal score was 89, his performance, 104, and his full range IQ, 95—in the normal range.

At the end of his training period, it was reported that he "shows high aptitude for learning and performing inspection tasks. He picks up new routines easily and retains what he has learned with good carryover between similar jobs."

TONY

Unlike Sam, who was broad, blocky and exuded determination, Tony was lean, hunched over a bit, unsure of himself and frantically talkative. Sometimes he would talk himself into a panic. He had just turned thirty-one. He had qualified after training as a factory maintenance man.

Tony was an only child. His parents were alcoholics and neglected him. At the age of five, he was placed in a state school for the mentally retarded. After six months, school authorities decided he did not belong there. He was too advanced. He was returned to his family and the jurisdiction of the Family Court.

The court then placed him in a foster home. His recollections of early schooling were confused. His records show that he attended kindergarten and first grade. At age nine, he was placed in an ungraded class. His adjustment was good.

At age ten, he was placed in a residential school for educable mentally retarded boys. On the Stanford-Binet test, he exhibited an IQ that vacillated between 58 and 62.

Tony remained in the residential school until he was seventeen. On weekends and holidays he visited his parents. Usually, he found them quarreling and drunk. Neither father nor mother was anxious to see him.

In early adulthood, Tony continued living at charitable institutions associated with the school. He attended a sheltered workshop. He worked at Goodwill Industries and then took an evening course at a high school to learn offset printing.

In succession, he worked for a tannery, as a janitor, in a nursing home laundry and as a day laborer. When he was referred to the Chicago School and Workshop, his reading level was fifth grade, his arithmetic skill fourth grade and his spelling, third grade level.

Yet, his potential was higher than it seemed. On the Wechsler Adult Intelligence Scale, he exhibited a full scale IQ of 72. Significantly, so far as job placement was concerned, he showed a performance IQ of 86, which was 12 points higher than his verbal score of 64.

Had Tony not been picked up by an alert and concerned social service agency he might have kept on drifting. In Chicago, the end of the road for drifters is Skid Row. The population of West Madison Street has been largely composed for generations not simply of chronic alcoholics but of handicapped human beings nobody bothered to rescue at a time when their rehabilitation was possible. Tony said:

> I remember my first job. I was a messenger boy. My trouble at that time—I didn't know where anything was. I got over that. It's so hard to explain. I got $1.60 an hour and they gave me bus fare. Well, like I said, I worked there four years.

Tony got tired of being a messenger. It was dull work, and didn't pay much.

> It was always rainin' and snowin' . . . kind of hard to explain. I helped my parents out. Bought food for them. My father kept callin' me at work, for money. Finally, it got so I had to quit. I ran all the way to Las Vegas.

What did you do at Las Vegas?

"I don't want to talk about that. Kind of to get away from it all. I returned by Greyhound bus and I moved back to this hotel I stayed at."

Tony said there was something else he wanted to talk about:

> Here's the story. My mother was drinkin' beer and whiskey and my father came home. She started hollerin' and screamin'. This had been goin' on for a long time. My father was kept up all night and he had to go to work.
>
> That had gone on as long as I can remember, even before I was sent away to school, when I was a kid. Then she had to go to the [state mental] hospital.

Tony recalled that when he visited the hospital to see her, he opened the wrong door while looking for the toilet. A group of black youths attacked him, he said, and beat him up.

Tony's mother later ran away from the hospital. She came home but neither Tony nor his father could put up with her. He said:

> I went with my father to a hotel, so's we could get some sleep in peace. This fighting had been goin' on and on. She would hit my father; my father would hit her. This drinkin' and hollerin' would go on all night. My father pushed my mother; my mother beat my father.

These episodes were intermittent as Tony recalls them. There were reconciliations when the family was reunited, but they didn't last long. More drinking, more fighting, more fleeing by Tony, usually to cheap hotel rooms or flop houses. That was his life in later adolescence and young adulthood.

During the interview, Tony kept referring to something that was bothering him. He thought it might have been the cause of all his trouble. The only way he could pin it down was to tell it narratively as part of the sequence of events. The story:

> While I was workin' as a messenger boy, my father wanted my mother to go to work. She was too nervous to work. Maybe he wasn't workin' or was laid off, I forget. She was just a housewife. I think she used to work as a waitress.
>
> My father kept trying to force my mother to go to work. Now she wanted to commit suicide. So what happened was she took a spoon of Drano with acid and put it in her mouth. Then after that, she was screamin'. It must have happened in the morning. I was workin' messenger at the time.
>
> My father said to my mother: "What happened?" My mother said, "I took some Drano." My father says, "What!" So right away my father had to call the police. The cops sent my mother to Cook County hospital. When my father told me the next day, I said to him, "Did you say she took Drano?" It was so hard to believe. "You're not putting me on?" He said, "She did take Drano." I said, "Are you sure about that?" He said, "Yes." My father and I went to see her. She was spittin' white spit. She cried, "Oh, I'm sorry. I took Drano." She had to go on the operating table.

Tony's father was fatally burned in a fire.

> The landlord told me the whole house got burned. Inside was all burned. All black. Walls were black. See. What happened was he smokin' cigarettes and he was sittin' there on the couch and he was sleepin' with the lighted cigarette in his hand. The couch caught on fire and it was blazin' up in the air. Then the whole kitchen went. The front room was on fire. Lucky, the ceiling didn't fall apart. They put out the fire.
>
> What happened was my father was burned. His face was all red. His clothes were on fire. He couldn't get out, you know. He was trapped in there. The fire ambulance rushed him to County Hospital. He was there a couple of days and he passed away.
>
> Thank God I still have my mother still living.

Does he take care of his mother now?

Well, see, I just go an' visit her. She takes care of herself. She's
okay now. I just live by myself. She doesn't drink much any more.
My aunt is watching over her. She's turned all gray.

I visited her last Mother's Day. I took her to a show. Called a
taxi. So we had a nice day.

But she still don't care.

DANNY

Danny, twenty-four, was a factory maintenance man. The agency
coaching staff had high hopes for him to achieve regular employee
status during the training period. He didn't disappoint them.

The youngest of a family of four, including three girls, Danny was
cast adrift at the age of five when his parents were divorced. He
said:

I didn't know about it until I was about eight or nine years old. I
didn't even know who my mother was until I got to a certain age.
Later on, my sister told me. My mother and father had problems,
y'know.

Well, everybody has problems today. You don't expect a man to
know everything in the world, y'know.

Danny spent his childhood in church-supported institutions. He
completed about two years of high school. He believed that he failed
to complete four years because, "I was a kind of slow learner at the
time."

At age eighteen, he was given a series of jobs in the church institutional group, first in the laundry of an old peoples' home and later in
the kitchen of another care center as a dishwasher. At that age, he
lived outside the institution, in a rooming house.

Working in private institutions was the only experience he had. He
said he had not been trained to do any skilled or semi-skilled work,
and he was convinced he could not "go out and get a job." This
attitude persisted until a religious order referred Danny to the Chi-

cago School and Workshop, where he was given training and then placed in the factory on six-months' probation.

Did he have any desire to complete high school?

Well, maybe in previous years. I think I'm pretty well caught up the way things are now. As far as I know, I don't think I need any more education. I think I'm capable.

I read the paper every day. The *Chicago Tribune*, which is one of the best papers in the city of Chicago. In the last couple of weeks, I was reading an article discussing Mr. Kissinger on Arabia and Egypt. Mr. Nixon arranged a conference on it about four months ago. I been reading about peace talks with China and the Soviet government. I'm very much interested in international politics, y'know. It's very important today to know how the economy is going. We have to get more oil and gas, y'know, for our machines, our automobiles, things like that.

Danny does not drive a car. He thought he might learn in a few years, "if I get the experience."

I like to watch sports, Cubs and Sox games, and like that, but I'm not much for doin' them, y'know. I used to play sandlot baseball at the residential school, y'know, but had a little difficulty batting. I didn't learn how to ride a bike because my legs aren't steady enough for that, y'know, but as a kid, I could roller skate a little bit."

Like Tony and Sam, Danny had a limited social life. He lived at a YMCA where he found casual companionship. He had one male friend, but no girlfriends, and was always pleased to be invited to his friend's house to watch television with the family.

His life, as he related it, seemed particularly uneventful, dull, gray, institutional. His father died when he was in grade school.

I had to get out of school to come for the funeral. "I didn't want to come home, y'know. I figured if I go home I would lose my schooling. It would put me behind. I wanted to improve myself through my education, y'know. Then I figured if this is what they want me to do, then this is what I must do.

Danny scarcely knew his father. But he did know his mother.

My mother is living, but she don't care for me. I don't know why. I've asked why she don't care for me, she don't say. My mother is an alcohol drinker and she gets very dangerous when she drinks very much. So she has a problem. She also smokes. Her problem is that she gets nervous, very nervous, y'know. Every time when some-one comes to see her, she gets nervous. So we don't see her any more. I don't even know exactly where she lives.

TWO WOMEN

Zoe was twenty-eight years old, a quiet, stoutish young woman, with placid features and a small voice. In childhood, she had been diag-nosed as mildly mentally retarded. Intervention in the primary grades might have changed that picture, as it well might have for Danny and Tony.

She recalled that she had been told that her mother died of cancer. Zoe was six or seven years old at the time. She had only a dim recollection of her mother's death. She continued to live with her father until the age of ten when she was placed in a foster home. Her father had become an alcoholic and then remarried after her mother died.

The foster home placement did not last long. Zoe was transferred to a children's home maintained by a religious order. She remained there into adulthood.

For a short time, she was placed in a sheltered workshop, but was dismissed when she was found to be too advanced for its program. The facility dealt mainly with trainable retarded persons. Zoe was classified as educable.

At the Chicago School and Workshop, Zoe was found to possess well-developed visual motor abilities. She read at a fifth grade level but her arithmetic ability was hardly third grade.

Her pronounced quietness and efficiency, however, enabled her to fit nicely into food service. She was employed in a cafeteria and had started there at $2.20 an hour.

Zoe lived in an eighteen-bed home maintained by an organization for retarded persons. She said she was able to stretch her average $70 a week take-home pay to cover living expenses.

"Before I got this job," she said, "I was working at the home, taking care of girls in one of the cottages. Two or three summers ago I worked in a nursing home and took care of old people."

Did she like that kind of work?

"It was sort of hard to do. So I wanted to quit."

What then?

"I was in the workshop for a while, but they did not keep me."

Does she like this job?

It's okay. I like cafeteria work. After work, I go off at three o'clock, I go home. I start early here and I'm tired. I rest. You can do anything you want where I live now. Sometimes I take a ride on my bike.

Zoe's social life is limited to acquaintances in the residence shelter. Occasionally, she likes to visit a brother and his family in another city. They live in a trailer and it is a bit crowded, she said, so she can't stay there long. But they plan to get a farm and then she believes that she will be able to live with them.

Television is not for Zoe. She reads young people's classics* occasionally and believes reading is getting easier for her. She reads the *Chicago Tribune*, but is primarily interested in the advertisements and clothing prices.

"I watch for sales," she said. "But I haven't hit any real good ones."

What about your father?

"He's still living," she said. "But I haven't seen him in some time. I think he's planning to move south."

Milly is thirty-three, a taciturn, calm woman who lives with her retired father and keeps house for him. She was trained by the Chicago School and Workshop in factory work and achieved a full time job in fabrication of plastic parts for electronic equipment.

* The classics Zoe referred to are standard literary works reproduced in simplified form and in large type for students with reading problems.

As a result of a speech impediment, Milly began public school in a special class for retarded children. Because of family difficulties which she did not recall clearly, Milly was placed in a charity home when she was eleven years old. She remained there until she was nineteen.

For six years, she worked in a laundry. After her mother died, Milly returned home to live with her father. He needed somebody in the house, she said.

> I didn't like the laundry. I was okay on pressing, but then they put me downstairs to sort dirty clothes. I asked my boss to change me. He wouldn't change me. So I quit. So I went to see Mr. G. [a social worker] and he told me about this. I was on a trial basis six months and now I'm on my own, so I've been here a total of eleven months. I like it.

Milly has made some friends at the factory, but does not date. Occasionally, she likes to see a "good" movie. Like Zoe, she reads. She likes children's books because they are easy to read, the type is large and the stories are easy to follow.

Her pay is sufficient to support herself and part of the upkeep of the apartment. Milly confessed she is not a good cook; her father does most of the cooking. They both do the cleaning.

Milly said it was her ambition to travel, but she never was able to do so. She had a vacation in prospect and looked forward to spending it with an aunt.

CHARLIE

Most of Charlie's twenty-five years were spent in a state school for the retarded and a mental hospital, although he is regarded as "developmentally disabled" rather than mentally ill. He worked in a private sheltered workshop and lived in a sheltered residence. Every morning, a bus called for him and took him to the workshop. Every evening, the bus took him back to the residence.

As nearly as Charlie could recall, he had never had more than a few years of formal schooling. His education was confined to classes at the school for the retarded. These left him with large gaps in grammar and arithmetic.

Charlie said he had been "appointed" to the shelter care residence and workshop from the state hospital where he had spent the previous four years. Before that, he had been living at the state school.

"I was committed there by the court," he said. "I run away from home. I broke into other peoples' houses. I run down the street carrying a handful of rocks and busting out car windows."

Charlie did not recall why he did it. He was mad about something. Most of his life, he thought, had been spent running away from something, or wishing to run away.

His parents were living, but he did not see them often.

> I have three brothers and no sisters. My older brother used to go to high school and now he has been promoted to college, and later placed in the Army, in the state of Alaska. That is one of the coldest states, near the north pole.

Charlie showed considerable difficulty in language. He was confused about tenses. Meanings of some fairly common words were not clear to him. Whatever degree of learning deficiency he exhibited as a school child, it was deeply confirmed in adulthood.

"I haven't been to any grade school, any high school or any school in the community," Charlie said. He was able occasionally to get a sentence out straight. Then he faltered:

> The only schools I ever go to be in kindergarten when I was put in . . . state school and then afterward they promoted me to a lower room for being good education. I stayed at that state school for about fifteen or sixteen years. I was been put there when I was five years old.
>
> I got along pretty well there. My father is living. My mother is almost living.

Was she ill?

> Not that ill. My father was a very sick person. Well, where I live now it's a lot nicer than keeping me stuck in a mental institution.

That state hospital where I was. It had ugly red brick buildings, sort of like a penitentiary, with chain link fences all around it.

Why was he sent to the state hospital?

I had trouble, sort of [at the school for retarded children]. I run away a lot of times. Then the security had to handcuff me and take me to [the state mental] hospital. Me and another resident, he was a black resident.

Were you unhappy at the state hospital?

Yeah. I was locked up in a maximum security ward, with these big, heavy-duty screens. You know what we did to those screens? I took a piece of a coat hanger and unlocked one of those sonofa-guns. And we got out the window—and out you go! And we went all the way down to the main gate and then Security brought us back just in time and they locked me up. They leave me stuck down in A-3 [a detention cell] for a day or two afterwards. That's what happens to everybody that gets sent to the [state mental] hos-pital.

I run away from there three times. I tried to make it all the way to Chicago. I got scared. I didn't want them state troopers to grab me and throw me in the slammer.

Charlie said his life was better since he was released from the state hospital and placed in the sheltered care situation. At the sheltered workshop, the clients were working on lathes, presses and other in-dustrial equipment. They made plastic and metal items under con-tract for jobbers of variety and notion stores. Although their hourly wages are low, their living expenses are subsidized.

Charlie shared a room with an older man. He enjoyed the relative freedom he had at the shelter.

I get to go shopping on Saturday mornings, at 10 o'clock. We got to go with an aide in that van you see parked outside. That's our bus. We go to the Treasury and K-Mart stores and buy what we want. In the evening, they [the shelter staff] get films from the library, but they're old-time movies, like Laurel and Hardy, Little

Rascals, kid stuff, like they show in the state institutions. I have my own television in my room. My parents brought it out. I have AM and FM radio.

What do I do now? I don't know what. I been run away so much but it never got me nowhere. I don't run away any more. There is no place to go. You can say that again. Not without an education.

OUTCOME

In the Chicago area where these clients reside, normalization efforts are too recent for a prognosis. In cases where the clients had completed the transitional employment program, I found the young men and women proud of their accomplishments and free of anxiety about their ability to hold a job.

So-called longitudinal studies may forecast the future for some of these people, but there are not many that cover the long term. One of the best known was a study made in 1960–61 by Dr. Robert B. Edgerton of the Department of Psychiatry, School of Medicine, University of California at Los Angeles.[5]

Edgerton followed the life experiences of twenty men and twenty-eight women who were discharged from the Pacific State Hospital at Pomona, California, between 1949 and 1958 after a period of vocational training in nearby communities. All forty-eight were diagnosed as retarded. All seemed to have made a successful adjustment to community life after their discharge.

In 1972, some twelve years later, Edgerton made a follow-up study with Sylvia M. Bercovici. He noted that the most consistent finding in follow-up studies of mentally retarded persons was the high proportion of adults who achieved satisfactory adjustment.

In their 1972 study, Edgerton and Bercovici were able to locate thirty of the forty-eight they surveyed in 1960–61. The group consisted of fifteen men and fifteen women.

The questions to which they sought answers were: Had the individual's adaptation to community life improved in twelve years? Had it remained much the same? Or had it worsened?

The investigators reported:

We rated the life circumstances of eight individuals (three men and five women) as better; twelve individuals (five men and seven women) as the same; and ten others (seven men and three women) as worse.

One man with an IQ of 66, who was judged to have bettered his life circumstances, had earlier been dependent on his wife and mother. Since the 1960–61 study, he had divorced his wife and had become largely independent of his mother. The investigators noted:

He was recently awarded a twenty-year pin at the factory where he worked (he was now a punch-press operator), had accumulated some stocks and real estate and was generally regarded by himself and others as a normal, even successful, forty-one-year-old man.

In another case of improved circumstances, a thirty-five-year-old woman with an IQ of 66 had been divorced when the initial survey was made. She had been supporting herself by appearing as a "headless lady" in an amusement park. She had drifted from one man to another. Now and then she had collected welfare checks. In the 1972 survey, the investigators found that she had been married for nine years and was rearing three children. She and her husband worked in the same factory, seemed to have sufficient income and presented a picture of a "stable, pleasant home life."

In other cases, predictions of success in the earlier study were found to be wrong in the later one. So were forecasts of failure to cope with life. The investigators said:

. . . there may be special circumstances that make the prediction of future adaptation for persons released from institutions for the mentally retarded an even more perilous undertaking than it would be for persons never so labeled or institutionalized.

Edgerton and Bercovici observed that the lives of most of the thirty subjects had been marked by major fluctuations. While these might be viewed as an aspect of the human condition, such fluctuations may be more extreme in retarded persons than in normal ones, they said.

This may be so because persons who have been institutionalized as these were have so few reliable resources that can stabilize them in times of crisis. Most of these retarded persons would seem to have only a tenuous control over their life circumstances. As a result, their lives are probably more unpredictable than those of persons who control some essential aspects of their lives through savings, job security, retirement plans, health insurance and networks of friends and kin who share an interest in their welfare.

Chapter 9

Mainstreaming: The New Integration

When they apply it to the school room, educators refer to the principle of normalization as *mainstreaming*. The term is virtually self-explanatory. It describes a policy of integrating neuromentally or learning-disabled children with non-handicapped children in regular classes.

In theory, integration benefits the handicapped child by enabling him to receive more stimulation and acquire a more normal behavior model in the normal class than in the segregated special class.

Special help is provided through a reading specialist, a remedial math teacher or even a physical education therapist as an auxiliary service. High quality tutorial resources are critical to mainstreaming. The classroom in which exceptional children are seated with normal children also requires an exceptional general education teacher.

Unless all of this expertise is available, mainstreaming is a delusion. For the hyperactive, distractible child the practice sets up an intolerable situation. More stimulation is precisely what he does not need. It merely exacerbates his problem of hyperattentiveness, otherwise known as "limited attention span." There are so many things for him to attend to he cannot attend to anything very long.

A second grade teacher in a Pittsburgh public school explained why she opposed mainstreaming:

First of all, it is a gimmick cooked up by theoreticians who have
never tried to handle a classroom of thirty to forty kids with the
inevitable slow learners, perceptually handicapped and behavior
problems. Second, we simply don't have enough resource people to
handle the L.D. [learning disability] kids. Third, the ones we have
are bright-eyed, bushy-tailed moppets out of teacher training institutes, special summer institutes, or maybe a master's program in
special ed., who have no experience and don't know anything except
theory—the same stuff the mainstreamers are pushing.

Even the most ardent advocates of mainstreaming agree that its
implementation requires highly trained personnel and small class size.
In an inflationary period, when taxpayer resistance to rising costs of
public education often persuades school boards to cut corners, the
tendency is to increase class size rather than reduce it; to enlarge
teacher load rather than ease it; to lay off specialists rather than add
them. When "cut out the frills" becomes the watchword of a board of
education, special education is a prime target. Administrative bodies
regard educating the "mass" as their first priority. The minority of
learning-disabled students must then struggle as best they can without
the "frills."

Under adverse economic conditions, a mainstreaming program is
unlikely to provide much remedial service. Yet, its advocates consider
its effective implementation as a social challenge. But whether it is
desirable even under optimum conditions is controversial.

Wolf Wolfensberger, one of the most widely published advocates
of normalization in services for retarded persons, has expressed firm
opinions about the value of mainstreaming in education. He contended that it is:

a well-documented fact that retarded children who are placed into
special classes underachieve grossly when compared to their retarded
peers who are carried along in regular classes even without any
special attention.[1]

The principle, Wolfensberger maintains, is to:

encourage deviant persons to imitate nondeviant ones. Deviants
should have maximum exposure to the nondeviant and minimal

exposure to institution workers, volunteers or others who appear deviant. Often the deviant is dehabilitated by being deprived of normalizing social contacts. By placing a deviant client among other deviant clients we reduced his social contacts with nondeviant persons.[2]

Wolfensberger, a psychologist in special education, has worked as a clinician, researcher, teacher and administrator in mental retardation. He was a mental retardation researcher at the Nebraska Psychiatric Institute, Omaha, and later a visting scholar with the National Institute on Mental Retardation in Toronto, Canada. He said:

Segregation is particularly self-defeating in any context that is claimed to be habilitational, which includes special education. . . . Too often, training takes place in one context, an artificial, segregated, nonnormative one, and at the end of the training period, there comes a precipitous transfer into realistic, normative social settings. Handicapped children should be integrated into generic developmental day care and as much as possible into regular classes.

Wolfensberger contended that most of the mildly retarded can function in regular grades if special additional services, such as resource rooms, resource teachers and specialists, are provided. So can many severely handicapped children, such as the deaf or the blind and others who may have some very severe and rare handicaps. Other severely impaired children, he said, can learn in special classes that are integrated into regular schools, rather than in special classes grouped together or located in separate wings or buildings.

Laird Heal, a research psychologist at the University of Illinois, commented:[3]

For mainstreaming, you need small classes. Society should invest enough resources in education so that you hold the pupil–teacher ratio at 15 or 20 to 1. You can have a lot of teacher aids—50 percent. It's necessary to invest more in individualized education; we're failing in that. Parents and society in general have failed. It scares me. You can't afford to let education slide in a democracy.

AN "UNHOLY TREND"

Like its mainstreaming corollary, normalization theory is by no means accepted as a universal truth. Some critics believe that state and county mental health services have espoused it because it offers a defensible way to reduce institutional overcrowding without increasing long-term debt. It also shifts part of the burden of caring for and attempting to habilitate retarded persons to the private sector. This does not reduce the overall cost because the state or county must subsidize the private agencies, but it provides an illusion of savings and it diffuses responsibility.

One of the pioneers in modern special education, William M. Cruickshank, director of the Institute for the Study of Mental Retardation and Related Disabilities at the University of Michigan, had this comment:[4]

> It's fine to empty out the institutions if something is done in the community. If nothing is done in the community, then the situation gets worse. We're very much concerned here in the state in Michigan about normalization. It's a national or an international philosophy at the present time.
>
> To my way of thinking, it's a travesty the way it's being handled where communities are not ready or are reluctant to receive these people from institutions. This institute is trying to work with a number of agencies in this state to develop community readiness programs, but we've just scratched the surface—to say nothing of the training of community living personnel who may be serving these people.

Dr. Cruickshank said his concern carried over to "the so-called mainstreaming process in the public schools where it's just a different age level you're dealing with."

> The backlash against this philosophy is just beginning to pick up steam among parents. Parents whose kids are getting a raw deal. Because general classroom teachers have never been sensitized to the nature and needs of these children and they have some of the most complex kinds of child-development problems dumped on

them. They don't have the proper attitude, they don't have the background, they don't have materials, they don't have enough hands to make the thing work. It's an absolute travesty.

Cruickshank's criticism of mainstreaming did not imply an endorsement of the adequacy of special education. Historically, he said, special education classes have been poor in the United States because there hasn't been an adequate selection of teachers. There hasn't been an adequate preparation of programs in the colleges and universities, he said, and, "We haven't had decent attitudes on the part of administrators toward special classes; they were the dumping grounds of the public schools."

Administrators, he said, did not go out of their way to find out what the problem was. Still, he added, there are examples of excellent programs in special education where there have been good administrative orientation and good teacher education. And there have been successful special classes where reasonable curriculums have been developed for them.

As early as 1930, there was an outstanding special occupational education program in New York City, Cruickshank said. But it was shot down by politics. There have been splendid special programs in Oakland County, Michigan; Arlington County, Virginia, and Montgomery County, Maryland. Cruickshank said:

These are good spots, but not the mine run. So when the concept of mainstreaming came, everybody started moving in that direction, as though it was the answer of everything, which it isn't.

My feeling about the matter is that the nature and needs of mentally retarded children are sufficiently different that in terms of their adult requirements—that is, in order to live—they very definitely need to have self-contained facilities. But not in a special school. I would prefer to have two or three units in a good, regular elementary school.

So far as resource teaching was concerned, Cruickshank said "an hour or two a week won't solve these kids' problems." There is a place for the resource teacher, he said, but more than an hour or two a week of such help is essential.

If a child needs a resource teacher, he needs her constantly, not merely from time to time. Resource rooms are not a substitute for poor mainstreaming or for poor teaching.

Cruickshank criticized the quality of special education teacher training. It seemed to him to be "extraordinarily poor" in many places.

We have produced too many college professors too quickly without giving them time to grow up. I would want the classroom teacher to have a minimum of a couple of years of general experience. Special education is a graduate program. Every five years or so, the special education teacher should have a year's experience with normal children in order to keep in focus normal developmental processes.

While he is not entirely negative toward mainstreaming, Cruickshank said, it has appeared in some districts without adequate planning. Parents were lulled into a belief that their children would have a better chance in the regular grades; they would not be labeled or singled out.

Theoretically, mainstreaming or integration of the learning-disabled with normal children appears to follow the rule of "least restrictive placement." But the manner in which some mainstreaming efforts have been carried out has made it the most restrictive placement for handicapped children, Cruickshank contended.

Parents now are getting wise. They see that their kids are unhappy. They see that they're not being helped. One told me that his child comes home and cries at night because he can't do the reading; can't do the arithmetic. The teacher gives him the same books and materials the other kids use. The child has an attention span of three or four minutes. He's not progressing. He's getting his report card and it shows "Fs" because the teacher sees him at the lowest end of his capability. All of these things are unfair to the child, unfair to the family and I suspect to the teacher, too, since she doesn't know what she's doing. One teacher told me, "but I don't know how to individualize."

We're in an unholy trend toward normalization . . . which I

would approve of if we could see time and money and effort being spent to make normalization a possibility.

It appeared to me that mainstreaming, which began to influence special education at the end of the 1950s, had sidetracked the body of special education theory as developed by the neurophysiology school of Goldstein, Werner, Head, Strauss, Lehtinen, Kephart, Orton and others. As a result, remedial practice was moving away from treating disabilities in terms of their underlying pathology.

Consequently, special programs for the perceptually handicapped that had evolved from a firm base of neurological research were supplanted by a theoretical approach whose research base was essentially sociological rather than medical. Further, its effects were only hypothetical.

In many communities, special classes for the brain injured and/or emotionally disturbed were discontinued. Resource or "itinerant" teaching programs were substituted. But they were only supplements to aid handicapped children who were integrated into a regular class.

A generation of teachers was influenced by a new emphasis on noncategorical (specialized) programs of remediation. Cruickshank said:

In colleges and universities, we have gone to such extremes about noncategorical training that students are being exposed only to vacuum. They're not given content. They don't know what these children are; the children they're supposed to be integrating. I see the curriculum that the kids [student teachers] have. There's nothing there to give content.

I would like the university student to know first what a learning disability is. It can be defined, despite a general impression that it can't be. He should understand the relationship of learning disabilities to perceptual processing deficits. That is what learning disabilities are the result of. He should realize that perceptual processing deficits have a neurological base.

That doesn't mean that the classroom teacher has to be a specialist in neurology. But at least she should be aware that the disability has a neurological origin, whether diagnosable or undiagnosable.

From that point on, I would like the teachers of these children to understand the details of the characteristics of these children. That they have figure-ground problems; that they have problems of association; that they have short attention spans; that they are hyperresponsive to stimuli; that they often perseverate and how perseveration in these children differs from perseveration of the psychotic; also that the problems of the learning-disabled are also found in the mentally retarded. And I would like them to understand many other psychological characteristics of perceptual deficits: visual, auditory, kinesthetic and so on. I'd like them to know also what the educational implications of these things are. How one develops an educational program for a child that has a dissociative problem; what dissociation means in terms of handwriting, lacing one's shoes, in terms of writing one's name on a top line; in terms of being able to conceptualize a three-digit arithmetic problem as a unity. And, of course, what these problems mean in terms of teaching.

We haven't produced college professors in this area since Strauss and Werner died. In 1963, when the term learning disabilities came into vogue, a whole Pandora's Box was opened. Before that time you could count the qualified college professors in that field in the United States and Canada on two hands.

Now you go to meetings and there are crowds of persons calling themselves chairmen of departments of learning disabilities. They're instant specialists. They've gone away for six-week programs or they have, as in this state, almost literally changed their title, as one man who was known in the area of the emotionally disturbed changed his to one concerned with learning disabilities.

There are some outstanding young professors coming along, a small cadre of well-prepared, well-oriented professors in the second generation after me and Sam Kirk. We were working on the training of teachers forty years ago. Then there is a vacuum in the first generation after us. Only now do I see a growing number of well-qualified young people, but not enough to solve the problem in the universities of turning out well-qualified specialists.

I have quoted Dr. Cruickshank at length because he not only expresses what many other experts in the field believe but does so from a perspective of personal experience that covers the origin and evolution of the learning-disabilities movement.

I believe that these views are useful for the orientation of parents who face the challenge of educating children with learning problems. Mainstreaming today appears to be a case of caveat emptor. Parents who buy it ought to look into the qualifications of the general education teacher in whose custody the handicapped child will be placed and of the resource teachers. Parents have a right to know. They have an obligation to protect the child's legal right to an adequate education, whether he is handicapped or not.

RALPH'S PROBLEM

Like other spin-offs of social reform, mainstreaming is an extension of racial desegregation policy and projects the same values. Its proponents challenge the self-contained classroom as a segregative device. One might with the same logic regard the hospital ward as a segregative device. Both are treatment facilities.

Although some learning-disabled children can function in a regular class, many cannot; for them, mainstreaming is an educational and emotional disaster.

Consider the case of Ralph, a twelve-year-old, perceptually handicapped boy whose parents balked at the public school's decision to move him out of a learning-disabilities program into a regular junior high school. This was not so much a matter of mainstreaming Ralph, although that was implicit in the decision, as it was a matter of passing him on. He had reached the limit of the special program and there was nothing more it could do for him. At twelve, he "belonged" in junior high school, in the judgment of school authorities.

Ralph had not been performing as well academically as his parents thought he could. He was emotionally immature, but not a behavior problem. He was mostly passive, shy, and tried to be cooperative. His parents feared the rough and tumble, unstructured experience of a junior high school would overwhelm him. A psychologist who examined Ralph agreed. Ralph was not ready for junior high school, but ready or not, the school district's decision was he had to go.

Ralph's parents exercised their option to take him out of the public school and send him to a private school which provided the type of program and structured environment he needed. Of course, they did so at their own expense, which represented double taxation.

State law provided that if the special education program of a school district was unable to meet the needs of a handicapped child, the school district "shall pay tuition or $2000 whichever is less and shall provide him with necessary transportation."* The district would then be eligible for reimbursement by the state for payments in excess of $600 per student—provided that the district certified to the State Superintendent of Public Instruction that "the special education program of the district is unable to meet the needs of the child."

Although the private school met all the requirements of the state, the school district declined to pay tuition. Its officials took the position that the special education program it provided had been adequate for Ralph's needs.

A QUESTION OF MANAGEMENT

The question frequently asked of mainstreamers is how the general education teacher can manage the hyperactive, distractible, disinhibited child in a classroom with twenty or thirty others. Can she quiet him down by isolating him from distracting surroundings? When that method was tried in a central Florida grade school, the parents protested that the child was a victim of discrimination.

Critics of mainstreaming contend that it fails to consider the therapeutic benefits of the self-contained classroom for the hyperactive, distractible, learning-disabled child. These have been established by research into the neuropathology of learning disabilities over the last century, especially the last sixty years. I am aware that some professionals today regard the pathology or etiology of learning difficulties as irrelevant to their treatment, so long as the specific disability can be identified by tests and some standard remedy exists. The trouble with this outlook is that the "specific" learning disability is not so specific; it is not like a broken arm; it is part of a general syndrome

* Illinois School Code. Chapter 122, Article 14, Section 7.02, Illinois Revised Statutes, 1973.

that may involve the functioning of the entire central nervous system. The learning-disabled child may require a program that takes this into account and provides a broader base of perceptual training than remedial reading or math.

Even the term learning disability itself tends to provide a convenient category for a child's learning problems without reference to the pathology behind it. In fact, many of the younger generation of parents of learning-disabled children today are hardly aware that the condition often expresses some form of neuromental pathology.

THE RESEARCH CONNECTION

In an earlier chapter, I related the experiences of Billy, a dyslexic child who could not learn to read in a regular class. He did not learn until he was placed in a program where dyslexia was understood as the expression of a pathological condition.

What is the background of this understanding? Dyslexia or word blindness is a disability peculiar to civilization, especially one with a high rate of literacy. In an illiterate society, or one in which most people can neither read nor write, the dyslexic passes unnoticed; he has no handicap. The disability is distinct from intelligence.

One of the pioneer investigators of this condition was a Scottish physician, James Hinshelwood, at the turn of the century. He defined it as an inability to interpret letters and words that the individual can see perfectly well.[5]

Hinshelwood described a middle-aged teacher who had become word-blinded overnight, probably as the result of a stroke. He had lost the ability to hold a visual memory of printed and written characters. Although he could still write, he could not read what he had written. He had no other memory deficits.

When the patient died, an autopsy showed that brain tissue on the left side had become atrophied as the result of the destruction of fibers connecting the two brain hemispheres. Hinshelwood concluded that this trauma had caused the loss of reading ability; that this mental process was concentrated in the left hemisphere.

Although Hinshelwood's ideas about the nature of dyslexia have been greatly modified by later investigators, his main contribution seems to have been the suggestion that word blindness in children was the result of similar pathology.

A generation later, Samuel T. Orton, a neurologist, also developed a theory about word blindness. Like Hinshelwood, he studied the effects of brain injury in adults and from them deduced the existence of a similar condition in children with dyslexia. As I have related earlier, Orton contended that the dominant (usually the left) side of the brain was the seat of language. He believed that a lesion there would result in disorders of spoken or written language.

He proposed that strephosymbolia (failure to recognize a symbol or word) could be corrected by teaching the phonetic equivalents of printed letters and by blending them rather than by the visual-perceptual or "sight" method that took in the whole word as a unit. Phonetics or phonics provided auditory reinforcement.

Other sensory modes were brought into play to reinforce the visual-auditory ones. The dyslexic child was shown how to trace over a letter, group of letters or a word. This procedure lent kinesthetic reinforcement to the percept of the word. At the same time, the child was persuaded to give the sound of the letter or word he was tracing.

Largely as a result of the research of Hinshelwood and Orton, it became clear that specific areas of brain damage could lead to disorders of written and spoken language. Their work provided guidelines, as Wiederholt has expressed it, for the remediation of reading disability. And both warned that no single method or combination of methods applied to all cases.[6]

In a similar way, the work of Henry Head in England and of Kurt Goldstein, Heinz Werner and Alfred A. Strauss in Germany and the United States and of Newell C. Kephart in the United States have set up guidelines for the special teaching of children who exhibit the brain-injury syndrome. One focus of the guidelines was a specialized environment that would reduce the counter-learning irritants of hyperactivity and distractibility.

In failing to provide such an environment, which must be a self-contained situation, advocates of mainstreaming have turned away from a century of neuropathological research.

What have they substituted? Essentially, they have brought back the one-room schoolhouse with the teacher for all seasons. There was the paradigm for the mainstreaming goal of individualized teaching for each child; the goal of making all education "special." Average and exceptional pupils were taught together.

Cruickshank exposed a conspicuous flaw in the mainstreaming model. He pointed out that the readiness age for children to begin school is a mental age of six. But a child with an IQ of 75 at a chronological age of six will theoretically have a mental age of four-and-a-half years. He said:

> While normal six-year-old children are experiencing success with a new tool, the retarded child is having a failure experience. The lower the IQ the greater the disparity between the retarded child and normal children with whom he is integrated.[7]

What about the child with learning disabilities who may or may not be retarded? Cruickshank observed that while parents of such children very often know what the child needs, "general educators as a group have not reached a similar level of professional sophistication."

"In this field," he commented, "parents too often have read more than the teachers who teach their children. But the issue is integration!"

He questioned whether untrained regular teachers can adequately meet the unique perceptual and education needs of these children,

> perhaps the most complex of any of those in child development, without specialized training and when thirty other children simultaneously command attention and different types of teaching materials![8]

RETARDED VS. DISABLED

What are the distinctions, if any, between retarded children and children with learning disabilities? Semantically, the distinction seems spurious. Retarded children are disabled in learning compared to the normal child; the learning-disabled child often appears to be retarded in some areas, although not in others.

When educators talk of a retarded child, they usually refer to a condition called "familial retardation." What they mean is that the retardation is a genetic characteristic of the child's family or a result of environmental factors. The so-called retarded child seems to exhibit a generalized slowness across the spectrum of learning-behavior development. The so-called learning-disabled child seems to exhibit an unevenness in development and often a higher IQ. He may come from a privileged environment as well as an underprivileged one and often from a family of average intelligence or above.

Now we have three classifications of children who are educable but who have difficulty learning: the "retarded" child, the child with learning disabilities and the brain-injured child.

What is the difference? In terms of the pathology, either diagnosed or assumed, there may be no difference in kind between the labels *brain injury* and *learning disability*. The difference is in degree. The disability itself may be evidence of some deficit within the central nervous system. Whether it is a product of trauma or disease or some failure of cell development is not at all clear, but the fact remains that the brain-injured child and the learning-disabled child exhibit evidence of "minimal cerebral dysfunction." That means the brain is not functioning in the normal way.

Many years ago, Dr. Samuel A. Kirk sought to unify an approach to teaching learning-disabled children by basing remediation techniques on behavioral symptoms rather than neurological zones.

He pointed out that minimal brain damage cannot always be diagnosed with precision even by neurological techniques. Further, he said that not all children with retarded development in reading, writing, spelling and arithmetic have a learning disability per se. Trainable mentally retarded children, for example, are delayed and retarded in all aspects of communication, not because of a specific learning disability, but "because of a generalized mental retardation."[9]

In addition, deaf and blind children may be retarded by their physical handicap and others may be retarded by lack of opportunity for environmental stimulation or by poor instruction. The so-called retarded, the blind, the deaf and environmentally deprived should not be considered to have a specific learning disability.

Kirk then defined learning disability as referring :

to a retardation, disorder or delayed development in one or more of the processes of speech, language, reading, spelling, writing or arithmetic resulting from a possible cerebral dysfunction and/or emotional and behavioral disturbance and not from generalized mental retardation, sensory deprivation or cultural or instructional factors.

The separation of learning-disabled children from retarded children precipitated a whole new category in special education. It was pleasing to many parents because it removed the onus of familial retardation without substituting the horrendous term brain injury with its implication of mental defectiveness.

If some sort of diagnostic label was necessary, learning disability was the easiest to live with. It implied some act of God rather than a failing in the parental line. And it made it unnecessary for parents and educators to think about the child's problems in terms of brain dysfunction. So long as the disability could be identified behaviorally from tests and observation, there was no need to go any further.

The term learning disability referred to the effect rather than the cause of neuromental dysfunction. In the fifteen years since Kirk proposed it, the term has become a major category in special education. It has so widely replaced "brain injury" or "minimal cerebral dysfunction" that many younger parents and teachers may not be aware of its derivation from the older nomenclature.

Kirk and others held that it was feasible to treat the effect without knowing precisely the nature of the cause, since the cause often was ambiguous. Over a decade or more, the relevance of the neurological aspects of learning disabilities seemed to fade. So did the specific treatment and environment they suggested.

The optimal educational setting for the brain-injured child has not changed in the thirty years since it was defined by Strauss, Lehtinen and Kephart. They explained why it was optimal:

During the course of time, the perceptions of the normal child become firmly established. Variations in the environment which modify the sensory stimulus patterns do not affect the stability of the perceptions. Even extraneous perceptual patterns may cross over the psychological field of the moment without distorting or destroying its character. This is not the case with the brain-injured child.[10]

The implication of this condition is that the brain-injured child's perceptual patterning is more readily disturbed by external influences than that of the normal child. The authors explained:

> The child is thus handicapped in two ways. First, he has succeeded in achieving a loose and fragile organization of the task he is engaged in, but because of its unstable structure, it is easily disturbed or displaced by other percepts. Second, any extraneous stimulus brings about a condition of momentary disequilibrium until it is satisfactorily identified and related to the total situation. For the brain-injured child, this may be a longer process, and one in which he may even require assistance. . . .

Because his perceptual field is so easily disturbed, the brain-injured child requires a learning environment where such disturbances are kept to a minimum. The normal child does not. That is a simple, basic reason for not putting the brain-injured child in a regular class until he is old enough to handle it. Maturity does reduce his distractibility in most instances, but until this takes place, he requires a special classroom environment. This basic, physiological requirement does not appear to have influenced the theory of mainstreaming.

Moreover, Strauss, Lehtinen and Kephart noted that the brain-injured child achieves the best relationship to his environment when he is in a small group, "with explicit and orderly procedures."

> He relaxes under routine because with it he can predict the day's events. He is quieter when there are no distracting displays or pictures to attract his attention. He is more comfortable and functions better if his desk is turned toward the wall so he is not distracted by the sight of the other children. He may even be at his best if he is off entirely by himself in another room or working behind a screen or large piece of furniture. . . . for the brain-injured child, the classroom is a hygienic environment, arranged to permit his optimum functioning despite deviations. . . .[11]

BRAIN REPAIR

Although some educators believe that there is a genetic component in learning disability, accounting perhaps for about 20 percent of it, most do not question the role of the environment in the remedy. Jeanne McRae McCarthy, Professor of Education at the University of Arizona, Tucson, believes there is evidence that environment can effect changes in brain functioning despite damage. She told a conference on learning disabilities:

> I come from a generation where we knew specifically that if the brain was damaged, there wasn't anything you could do but work around it and exercise alternative parts of the brain. New evidence suggests that effects of birth trauma can be diminished by the postnatal experience of the child. Such mediating processes are improved nursery procedures, bringing the mother into contact with the child, enriched sensory environment, increased vestibular stimulation. . . . The earlier we can program stimulating environmental influences, the more chance we have of impacting a damaged brain.[12]

Dr. McCarthy referred particularly to premature infants who are allowed to remain in incubators for periods of time without any contact with the mother. Recent data, she said, indicate that handicaps attributed to prenatal brain damage in infants of low birth weight actually were postnatally acquired and were preventable. Lack of fondling, warmth, human relationship may have been the cause of the later learning problems—not the prematurity itself, she said.

> We are also beginning to provide for extra handling or mothering. Mother-child contact is being increased and handling of the baby [referring to prematures] is also being increased. These kinds of experiences have been shown to influence later physiological and behavioral functioning in children.

There appears to be some functional recovery of damaged brain tissue, she said.

> We see this in adult stroke victims. We don't know what happens, but they get better, some of them. There may be a functional take-

over by adjacent structures. A third possibility is reorganization of neural function in the system, so that there may be a whole reorganization around the damaged area. Another explanation is the postnatal formation of new neurons [nerve cells]. There is evidence that new connections are formed within the central nervous systems. Maybe you can make a real change in the child's brain functioning with environmental stimulation.

McCarthy suggested that environmental encounters may also reduce genetic variations in nervous system functioning. And they may increase the rate of development of certain functions.

Increasing the number of times a mother picks up her baby significantly increases visual attentiveness and arousal levels, she said. This may prevent later attention defects in learning-disabled children.

> The mother needs to be encouraged to pick up that baby more and more. Intervention then is far from futile, even in genetically determined behaviors. . . . What can we do? If we subscribe to a philosophy that heredity has set fixed limits to a child's potential, that class and race differences are due only to heredity, the answer is nothing.

However, there is a "viable alternative," she suggested. It accepts the reality of hereditary transmission and of genetic variation, but it adds the fact that real changes take place in the brain when it is effectively stimulated by the environment.

McCarthy quoted the American geneticist, Theodosius Dobzhansky, on the relationship of hereditary and environmental determinants. What the child inherits is a mode of response to the environment. For each child, there is a range of functioning within hereditary limits. The range is variable and the level the individual achieves within it is environmentally determined. From this point of view, a child's level of functioning is the result of any of an unknown number of environments to which he is exposed.

"Our job as teachers is to provide for each handicapped child that rare environment which would occur by chance only in a hundred possible environments," said McCarthy. For example, she said, a child may be born with an IQ range of 75 to 140. Given most of the environments he would encounter by chance, he might achieve an IQ of 100 or 110.

"However, if you provide that rare environment for him, he may be able to function way up at the upper edge of his range. To me, that's the challenge of teaching."

It is also the challenge of remedial education.

RECOVERY

Anyone who has observed the development of a brain-injured child from infancy to adulthood can testify that changes occur that indicate some process of repair. In some instances, the changes are dramatic, so that the individual is not the same as he was, and may lose the aspect of a handicapped person.

What has happened is only a guess. Once more returning to the adult as a model, it appears that some aspects of normal neuromental functioning have been recovered. This is not solely the result of maturation, although Strauss and his colleagues believed that dramatic changes could take place in adolescence with the hormonal stimulation of rapid growth. Recovery of damaged function may be a biochemical response of the organism to environmental stimulation.

Which environment is better for the learning-disabled child? There may be no general answer. The experienced teacher may find that the learning-disabled child without a crippling perceptual handicap can function in the mainstream, with some support of a remedial reading or math teacher.

But if he cannot, it is a tragedy to keep him there. The perceptive teacher knows it. Perceptive parents know it.

The self-contained special class remains a requirement for some learning-disabled children. It does not seem likely that an integrated classroom experience can substitute for it, no matter how utopian the services become.

It is difficult to disagree with the mainstream contention that all education should be considered special, that each child should be considered as a special case.

But any program that tries to implement this concept must deal with the reality that some cases are more special than others.

Chapter 10

The Learning-Disabilities Movement

The delineation of a neurophysiological basis for learning and behavior problems had a revolutionary impact on the whole field of mental deficiency. It revived the optimistic outlook that had prevailed in the first part of the nineteenth century and established it on a foundation of clinical observation and theory.

Instead of being cast into an indiscriminate mold of mental retardation, children exhibiting such disabilities as poor auditory and visual discrimination and memory, confusion in laterality, that is, between left and right, lack of fine motor coordination, perceptual aberration, distractibility and hyperactivity could now be diagnosed as suffering from specific disorders that accounted for their deficits.

These disorders were treatable, as Strauss, Lehtinen, Kephart, Cruickshank and others had shown, if they were addressed specifically. That approach introduced a new category into special education.

Largely as a result of the influence of Strauss and Lehtinen's *The Brain-Injured Child*, the category was generally identified with the brain-injury syndrome between 1947, when the first volume of the *The Brain-Injured Child* was published, and the early 1960s. My own

240

book, *The Other Child*, written in 1951 for parents in collaboration with Strauss and Lehtinen, probably contributed to the dissemination of the term brain-injured or brain-damaged as a label for this group of children.

Neither Strauss nor Lehtinen were entirely sold on the term. They applied it as a clinical description. It was never intended as a general label. But since there was no other that defined the children exhibiting this constellation of disabilities, it was widely though in many cases reluctantly adopted by parents' organizations that formed to seek help for their children.

The rapid rise of parents' organizations to promote special education for the brain-injured was a spectacular phenomenon. Social historians have largely overlooked it. The size and extent of this movement were unprecedented in education. Hundreds of local parents' groups formed, virtually overnight, energized by the belief that now that the syndrome was identified, special education could do something about it.

They were responding not merely to the new optimism the brain-injury approach engendered but to the relief of the pressure of guilt and anxiety that had been implanted in social attitudes toward mental deficiency by the eugenics movement of the early twentieth century.

It was as though a new cure had been found for an old affliction. Of course, nothing of the kind had happened; but a new point of view toward handicapped children had emerged and it offered hope of habilitation. Uninhibited by professional or by academic reserve, parents' groups now made the rafters ring with demands for action from New York to California. Politically, the educational establishment was forced to respond, but pedagogically it was in a poor position to do so.

Among physicians, especially pediatricians, there was a reluctance to accept the brain-injury label, especially if it could not be established by conventional diagnostic procedures, including an electroencephalogram. In many instances, it could not.

Pediatricians also noticed that the label was frightening to parents. Writing in the *Dallas Medical Journal*, Dr. Meyer A. Perlstein, Associate Professor of Pediatrics, Northwestern University Medical School, expressed his concern:

Actually, the term "brain-injured" is an unfortunate one for parents to hear. It frequently means to the parent that there is some sort of hole in the brain caused by some type of instrument and this creates a type of mental vacuum that cannot be filled.[1]

Dr. Perlstein noted that some of the characteristics of the brain-injury syndrome had been given other technical names, such as short attention span, perseveration, perceptual disturbances, distractibility. He said:

However, many of these phenomena may be observed in individuals who have no other evidence of injury to the brain. Many of these so-called aberrations in mental processes are thus seen in normal individuals under certain conditions and under some conditions at all times.

It is only when these changes become so great that they cannot be compensated for that they become abnormal. The fact that an individual evinces some of the characteristics commonly seen in the brain-injured does not necessarily mean that such organic involvement of the brain exists.

Other terms that might be less frightening to parents and arouse less medical argument from physicians were proposed. Dr. Sylvia O. Richardson, Assistant Clinical Professor of Pediatrics, University of Cincinnati College of Medicine, told a learning-disabilities conference that "many dislike using the term "brain damage."[2]

Dr. Richardson noted that in 1962 the Oxford International Study Group on Child Neurology voted to discard the concept of "damage" in this context. She said:

Since the diagnosis of learning disabilities is made on the basis of symptoms of disordered function rather than on evidence of anatomical damage, the term "minimal cerebral dysfunction" is currently and justifiably more popular.

I have no doubt that this term was more comforting to parents and eased professional objections to the etiological assumption of damage. Semantically, however, it suggested a mild retreat back into the unknown. Perhaps, that was appropriate. The Greco-Latin version gave the term a more impressive medical ring than the common English equivalent of "slight brain impairment." It struck me as an acceptable compromise in cause-versus-effect nomenclature. But the medical textbook aspect of the term should not fool anyone into believing that it signifies an understanding of the underlying pathology.

KIRK'S SOLUTION

However, "cerebral dysfunction" was not entirely satisfactory. Only its effects could be observed by educators, the largest group of professionals who had to deal with it. As I mentioned earlier, Kirk had objected that cerebral dysfunction could not always be diagnosed even by modern neurological techniques.

At a landmark conference on Children with Minimal Brain Impairment at the University of Illinois January 13–15, 1963, Kirk used the term learning disability as one describing the effect of cerebral dysfunction or brain damage. The meeting, sponsored by the Easter Seal Research Foundation of the National Society for Crippled Children and Adults, Inc., had assembled a distinguished group of experts in medicine, psychology and education. The term learning disability seemed to be acceptable to them.

The following April 6, Kirk proposed the term at a conference of parents and teachers in Chicago, sponsored by the Fund for Perceptually Handicapped Children. This organization, formed by a group of Evanston women under the leadership of Mrs. Gordon ("Dolly") Hallstrom, a dedicated civic leader, had preferred the term perceptual handicap in lieu of brain-injured as a more sympathetic way of describing the problem of the child.

Kirk, then director of the Institute for Research on Exceptional Children at the University of Illinois, was one of the Fund's principal mentors. The participants in the conference included a number of educators and psychologists who were emerging then or who have emerged since as leaders in the new movement. Among them, some of whom I have mentioned, were the late Hester Burbridge, director of special services for the Evanston public schools; Lenore Hartman, psychologist; Doris Johnson, a member of the Institute for Language Disorders at the Northwestern University School of Speech; Newell C. Kephart, director of the Achievement Center for Children at Purdue University; Charlotte Larson, who developed the program for brain-injured children in Joliet, Illinois; Laura Lehtinen Rogan, director of the Cove School; Jeanne McCarthy, then a psychologist in Lincolnwood, Illinois; Helmer Myklebust, director of the Institute for Language Disorders, Northwestern University; Miriam Tannhauser, director of special education for the Montgomery County, Maryland, Board of Education, and Mrs. Aaron Mesirow of Tulsa, Oklahoma, a parent who was to become a key organizer of a new national association.

Kirk addressed members of this group and parents:

> I have felt for some time that labels we give children are satisfying to us but of little help to the child himself. We seem to be satisfied if we can give a technical name to a condition. This gives us the satisfaction of closure.
>
> We think we know the answer if we can give the child a name, or a label: brain-injured, schizophrenic, autistic, mentally retarded, aphasic, etc.
>
> As indicated before, the term brain-injured has little meaning to me from a management or training point of view. It does not tell me whether the child is smart or dull, hyperactive or underactive. It does not give me any clues to management or training.
>
> Recently, I have used the term learning disabilities to describe a group of children who have disorders in development in language, speech, reading and associated communication skills needed for social interaction.
>
> In this group I do not include children who have sensory handicaps such as blindness or deafness, because we have methods of managing and training the deaf and the blind. I also exclude from this group children who have generalized mental retardation.

According to J. Lee Wiederholt of the University of Arizona Department of Special Education, "the effects of this speech were staggering."[3]

The conference spontaneously formed a new national organization called the Association for Children with Learning Disabilities.

Kirk was more or less drafted as chairman of the ACLD professional advisory committee. Members included Raymond Barsch, Office of Special Education, University of Wisconsin; Cruickshank, then Director of Special Education and Rehabilitation at Syracuse University; Marianne Frostig, Director of the Marianne Frostig School for Educational Therapy, Los Angeles; Kephart, Lehtinen and Myklebust. Later, the committee was "internationalized" with the addition of Keith S. Armstrong, National Executive Director of the Canadian Rehabilitation Council for the Disabled.

On May 6–8, 1965, the ACLD held its second national conference, this time in Baltimore. The meeting was sponsored by the Maryland Association for Brain Injured Children and groups from New York, Pennsylvania, Illinois and the Midwest and the Southwest were represented by enthusiastic parents demanding a new deal in special education.

In proposing the term learning disability, Kirk had triggered a national response that I doubt he, or anyone else, could have anticipated. A bandwagon started rolling across the United States, into Canada and, indeed, around the world.

Letters asking for information about learning disabilities began pouring into ACLD headquarters which for the time being were housed in Mrs. Mesirow's home in Tulsa.

The Ontario (Canada) Association for Children with Learning Disabilities sent a copy of a brief its executive committee had prepared for the Provincial Select Committee on Youth asking better special educational facilities. It said:

> This association was formed in 1963 by parents frustrated by lack of diagnostic treatment and educational facilities for their children in Ontario. . . . At least 600 are in Ontario's various school systems struggling to achieve adequacy but failing in their classes, or are in special classes in which the teaching methods are totally unsuited to their needs. They represent a waste of time and money in the schools, a sure source of dropouts and a lack of productive ability in the future. The economic cost of their disability is huge; the personal tragedies extremely painful. Much of both cost and pain can be reduced and even eliminated.

This theme was to be repeated time and again. Parents now believed there was light at the end of the tunnel and wanted the schools to turn it on. There was a new attitude in North America, one that had not existed before. The term learning disability had achieved what brain-injury could not—a full measure of parental understanding and approval. It was now a great cause and everyone clamored to join up.

From Brisbane, Australia, Mrs. Judith Garvey wrote for help and inspiration. "We are a small band," she explained, but "determined."

Brisbane parents had formed the Queensland Association for Children with Learning Disabilities. The group met at St. Peters Church of England Hall which, its announcement informed nonchurchgoers was "tram stop 13." Subjects the group proposed to discuss were:

1. Are Parents to Blame?
2. What Can We Do?
3. Your Moment of Truth: You Discover *You* Have a Special Child.
4. How Can We Promote General Awareness Regarding the Slow Learner?

Requests for information, pamphlets on the subject, rules of procedure to start a local association, speakers who might be available and applications to join the international association flowed into Tulsa in a steady stream.

The President of the Edmonton, Alberta, Aphasic Association wrote for a receipt for her registration fee at the 1966 international conference of the ACLD so that she could turn in her expense account. The director of the learning laboratory at the Pocatello, Idaho, School District wanted a preview of the 1967 convention program so that a representative could be prepared to attend it.

The psychology consultant to the Iowa Department of Public Instruction asked for a membership application. "At the present time, we in Iowa are beginning to program for children with learning disabilities," he advised.

"I am interested in joining your association as well as attending your (next) national convention," wrote the Polk County, Iowa, school psychologist.

"Your organization sounds like one to which I would like to belong," said the district school psychologist of the Coffeyville, Kansas, public schools.

"We would like to hear of the work you are doing," wrote the research coordinator of the Coral Gables, Florida, Academy, Institute of Reading.

The educational program director of the Miami Crippled Children's Society asked for published material. "We are establishing a class for children with learning disabilities," the director advised.

A project officer in the Georgia State Department of Education asked for additional copies of an ACLD Special Report on Legislation and Learning Disabilities. The principal of the Robert Morris School at South Bound Brook, New Jersey, asked to be placed on the ACLD mailing list "since we are starting a learning disabilities class this fall [1967]."

A school principal at Las Vegas, Nevada, advised that the Clark County School District "is extremely interested in providing an educational program for its children with severe learning disabilities." The county already had established classes for the brain-injured.

The New Jersey Association for Brain Injured Children sent copies of a monograph it had published on *A Program of Special Classes for Children with Learning Disability.*

A psychologist in the Missoula, Montana, public schools asked for pamphlets. A mother in Springfield, Missouri, asked for help in preparing a legislative proposal to provide special help for the learning disabled. The Minnesota Association for the Brain Injured inquired about joining the ACLD.

The Michigan Association for Children with Learning Disabilities sent an outline of its goals for 1967.

"Please send me a copy of the 1966 ACLD Conference Program and information about registration," asked the director of the Massachusetts Department of Education.

In addition to the international conferences the ACLD was arranging, large state meetings were held by the Louisiana and Texas Associations for Children with Learning Disabilities.

One model for the local associations was the New York Association for Brain Injured Children which was formed by parents in 1958. By the end of 1965, its Nassau Chapter newsletter reported, after it had helped establish the first special class for brain-injured children in the New York City public school system, there were fifty-four such classes in the city, about forty in Nassau County and more than one hundred in the state.

LEGISLATION

How many learning-disabled children were there in the general school-age population? Obviously, the number would be much greater than the number of those considered brain-injured since identification could be made from mass testing programs.

In 1968, the National Advisory Committee on Handicapped Children estimated that at least one million and probably two million children could be considered learning-disabled. The estimate appeared to be conservative. Significantly, the Advisory Committee noted, relatively few of the estimated number were receiving adequate special education.

In a remarkably short time, learning disabilities had become a matter of congressional concern. U.S. Senator Ralph Yarborough (D., Texas) introduced into the Senate the Learning Disabilities Act of 1969. It authorized the U.S. Office of Education to establish programs for learning-disabled pupils by amending Title VI (the 1967 Education of the Handicapped Act) of the Elementary and Secondary Education Act. A companion bill was introduced into the House of Representatives by U.S. Representative Roman Pucinski (D., Illinois).

Other legislation followed, so that learning disability has become legally established as a special category in education at the federal and state levels. In November 1975, Congress passed a new and comprehensive Education of the Handicapped Act (Public Law 94-142). It was the most ambitious effort to assure education to children with all forms of physical and mental handicaps, including learning disabilities, in the history of education. By early 1977, however, the new law's requirement that the U.S. Commissioner of Education set up criteria for defining learning disabilities and for diagnosing children as learning-disabled threatened to open a Pandora's box of controversy among educators, psychologists, psychiatrists and parents.

Early in 1977, U.S. Representatives Claude Pepper (D., Florida), Augustus F. Hawkins (D., California) and Tom Railsback (R., Illinois) sponsored a bill (House Resolution 1137) to provide for a national conference on Learning Disabilities and Juvenile Delinquency. Congressman Pepper asserted:

> It is well established that a learning disability is the greatest single reason children drop out of school—700,000 each year. And 75 percent of these children find themselves in juvenile detention centers.[4]

Pepper said it was scarcely any wonder that youths with learning disabilities "are at greater risk with respect to custom and law than youngsters not handicapped with learning disabilities."

Fourteen years after the ACLD sprouted from Sam Kirk's speech on learning disabilities in the spring of 1963, the organization has become a giant. It has 713 chapters in 48 states, the two exceptions being Wyoming and Alaska. About 40,000 members pay one dollar a year dues to national headquarters at 5225 Grace Street, Pittsburgh, Pennsylvania.

ACLD's fourteenth international conference in Washington March 9–12, 1977, drew more than 4000 registrants. There were 575 participants in 162 sessions, including 15 workshops.

Kirk, now Professor of Special Education at the University of Arizona, was a principal speaker. He appraised the progress of the learning-disabilities movement from the critical stance of a founding father. He warned:

> We have grown too fast. We have learning-disabilities experts coming out of the walls by the hundreds, making speeches, writing books and articles.

Learning-disability programs were becoming "dumping grounds" for slow children who were not actually disabled. There were many in these programs who could be classified more appropriately as slow readers or simply as lazy.

A great deal of research now going on in the field, he said, was irrelevant. It was asking the wrong questions.

Kirk was trying to put the brakes on what he seemed to consider a runaway crusade. It was going too far, too soon; young people were pushing too hard, in too many directions at once.

It was time, he said, for the regular classroom teacher to take greater responsibility for the underachiever; to leave the "hard-core" problems to the specialist.

He hoped the regular elementary teachers would assume responsibility for slow learners. Underachievers should be mainstreamed.

Special education was partly responsible for "ruining primary education," he said. It left the primary teacher without problems.

It appeared that the learning-disabilities movement had become so surcharged with energy that its own leaders were trying to restrain it.

WHERE DO WE GO FROM HERE?

Other "old timers" were also concerned that the movement had gotten away from its founders; that the new gospel was spreading so that it threatened to inundate general education with special requirements. If that was so, it was merely a reflection of what parents had sought for so many years. If the professionals were overreacting, as Kirk feared they were, they were responding to parental frustration, long pent-up.

Learning disabilities had now evolved as a mass movement. It had reached that stage because of a promise, implicit in its outlook, that learning disabilities can be cured. The time is coming when the practitioners of the movement will have to prove it.

In some respects, the situation in the whole field of remedial education is similar to that period of optimism, between 1830 and 1860, when social reformers believed mental retardation could be cured with sympathetic help, training and care. Their belief failed to be realized, as we know, and the result was a social policy of rejecting and isolating the neuromentally handicapped that bordered on barbarism.

Is the new era of optimism likely to collapse in the same way? Do we foresee a repetition of the old cycle at the next turn of the century?

We do not require a crystal ball to see the answer, if we ask the right question.

The right question is not, "can learning disabilities be cured?" but "can a person with learning disabilities be taught to overcome them and acquire sufficient education to function normally in society?"

Can he?

Of course he can. That is what this book is about. I believe the evidence presented here should convince any reasonable person that, given an educational program that takes into account his specific disabilities, the neuromentally learning-disabled child who is educable can become a useful, independent, self-supporting adult—and have a good life.

So I do not believe there will ever be a return to the gothic horror of the "feebleminded" era of mental deficiency.

There are, of course, no guarantees. But the near future, at least, has been mapped by Public Law 94-142 which, if it is allowed to work, might go down in history as the emancipation of the handicapped act. It should free all disabled children from shackles of penny-pinching, money clenching, miserly school boards; from taxpayers' "leagues" that sacrifice human values for property values; and from a collection of administrators who passively go along with the pruning of special programs as job insurance.

Curiously, the only major opponent of PL 94-142 was former President Gerald R. Ford. He contended that the education of the handicapped was primarily a responsibility of the states. He also balked at the funding levels. They were much too high, he argued. Mr. Ford signed the bill after it was passed so overwhelmingly in both houses that it was plain he would be overridden by Congress if he vetoed it. But White House pressure succeeded in persuading the sponsors to cut back part of the funding the House of Representatives and the Senate were willing to provide.

Senator Harrison A. Williams, Jr. (D., New Jersey), the bill's chief sponsor, hailed its passage as the most important legislative event in education since the Elementary and Secondary Education Act of

1965. Representative John Brademas (D., Indiana) was the bill's chief sponsor in the House.

Starting with an authorization for $100 million in the 1976 fiscal year, the act would increase federal support of special education to $3.1 billion a year in fiscal 1982.

The situation it addresses has been defined by the U.S. Office of Education as follows:

> Of 7.9 million handicapped school children in the United States, only half are receiving an adequate education. About 2.5 million are receiving some education, but it is inadequate. And about 1.45 million are not receiving any education.

As I have noted in an earlier chapter, state and federal courts have ruled repeatedly that handicapped children are entitled to receive a free, public school education. A limited number of public school systems can and do comply with that mandate in an effective way, but many are unable financially to do so—although the federal courts have said that lack of funds is no excuse for not complying.

The National Educational Finance Project has estimated that the average cost of educating a handicapped child is 1.9 times that of educating a nonhandicapped child.[5]

Federal funds under the act would be paid to school districts to make up about 20 percent of the excess cost of educating the handicapped.

Of the 7.9 million handicapped children, the largest category is speech-impaired, an estimated 2.3 million children, 81 percent of whom are being served in some program.[6] The next largest is the learning-disabilities category, estimated at 1.9 million children, only 12 percent of whom are being served. Third largest is the mentally retarded classification numbering 1.5 million, 83 percent of whom are being served. In smaller proportion are the physically crippled, 328,000; the hard-of-hearing, about the same number; the deaf, 49,000; the visually handicapped, 66,000; the multiply handicapped, 40,000. Next to the learning-disabilities group, the hard-of-hearing receive the least attention; only 18 percent are being served. Some of them may also be classified as learning-disabled or retarded by the local school system.

Drafted as Senate Bill 6, the new act amended the 1967 Education of the Handicapped Act. It required each state to provide a free and appropriate education to all its handicapped children between the ages of three and eighteen by September 1, 1978, and to those eighteen to twenty-one by September 1, 1980. It encouraged the states to provide special education to handicapped, preschool children between the ages of three and five. The expectation behind this encouragement is that early intervention may make a special program later on unnecessary. The act authorized incentive grants of $300 a child for those receiving special services before school age.

The reimbursement or grant formula was to become effective in 1978. Until then, the act retained the 1975 formula ($8.75 for each child in the state to be used for educating handicapped children).

In 1978 and after, grants were to be based on the number of children between the ages of three and twenty-one who are receiving special education. That number would be multiplied by 5 percent of the national average expenditure per pupil in the 1978 fiscal year.

The multiplier then was to rise to 10 percent of the national expenditure in 1979; to 20 percent in 1980; to 30 percent in 1981 and to 40 percent in 1982. In some poorly financed school districts, federal funds would virtually support special education.

The number of handicapped children each state can count for grants is limited to 12 percent of the state's child population ages five to seventeen. Until criteria were published for determining learning disabilities and for diagnostic procedure, only one-sixth of those counted as handicapped were eligible for grants as children with specific learning disabilities.

Pending the development of criteria, the act limited grants for the learning-disabled to 16 percent of the total counted as handicapped. The U.S. Commissioner of Education estimated the learning-disabled as 24 percent of the handicapped child population. The discrepancy made some experts uneasy—as did the assumption which was implicit in the grant formula that learning-disabled children constituted only 2 percent of the child population. Many experts believe that the percentage is higher.

However, the limitation on learning-disabled children was to be dropped from the grant formula after the U.S. Commissioner of Education published criteria for defining learning disabilities and for diagnosing a learning-disabled child.

Other provisions of the act required the school district to establish an individualized educational program for each handicapped child where this is required.

If such a program is deemed necessary for the child's welfare, it must be prepared in writing, with long-range and short-term goals clearly spelled out. Specific services the child will receive must be described.

The act required that before such a program is started, there will be an initial conference of parents, teachers and any others involved in the child's welfare. During the first year, there will be a formal review of progress and annual reviews after that.

The act also required that where it is appropriate, handicapped children will be educated with the nonhandicapped.

The act authorized the following scale of appropriations: $100 million for fiscal 1976; $200 million for 1977; $378 million for 1978; $775 million for 1979; $120 billion for 1980; $232 billion for 1981 and $316 billion for 1982 and each year thereafter.

The probability that these funding levels not only will survive future efforts to trim the federal budget but will be increased is very high. Senate Bill 6 is one of the clearest expressions of social policy by Congress since the early days of the New Deal. The House of Representatives adopted the conference report on the bill November 18, 1975, by a vote of 404 to 7 and the Senate approved it the next day, 87 to 7.

Insofar as the social and educational philosophy has been encapsulated in the act, it has now become public policy in education. There is now no excuse for local school districts to drag their feet in providing learning-disability programs. Indeed, the act has mandated them to do so, and parents have a clear road to seek enforcement in court if that is necessary.

Public Law 94-142 is not the end of the battle; it is the beginning of an enormous social experiment. Neither psychology nor education has enough evidence to prove that special programs for learning disabilities can be effective on a large scale. The data will be accumulating in the next two decades. By the turn of the century, we should have a pretty good idea of what special education for learning disabilities can deliver.

The prognosis is good. In the Department of Health, Education and Welfare, the Office of Child Development has collected scattered evidence, as I have related earlier, showing that such early intervention programs as Head Start and Follow Through improve the young child's level of functioning. Although the data are not conclusive and some critics claim there is fadeout a year or two later, the studies so far are encouraging.

The present trend, however, points to expansion of these programs. If that is fulfilled, it will help teachers identify and commence treating learning disabilities before the child enters the first grade. There is a firm conviction in the Office of Child Development that early intervention will reduce the future load in special education.

Although the prospects for effective remedial education in America are better now than ever before, the basic questions persist. The "how" and "why" of neuromental handicaps are still with us.

They remain to challenge the basic disciplines: biochemistry, genetics, neurophysiology, anatomy. In the last three decades, we have seen social progress in the field, but not a great deal of scientific development since the 1940s.

The whole area of mental deficiency remains chaotic. We have the mentally retarded, the educable mentally handicapped, the trainable, the perceptually handicapped, the learning-disabled, the autistic, the dyslexic, to mention a few. Just as physics seeks to unify the forces of nature, biology must seek to unify the pathology of these conditions.

I have raised the question earlier of what are the differences between mental retardation and learning disability. Although they are often distinguished as different species of handicaps by state codes, and by current federal regulations, I have yet to hear a scientific definition that will convince me that a retarded child is one thing and a learning-disabled child another.

Is there an IQ distinction? An etiological one? Or is it simply that we call those children who are less seriously impaired "learning-disabled" and those more seriously impaired, "retarded"? Or can it be that the distinction is social? It has happened. Rich kids are "dyslexic." Poor kids can't read.

I do not believe we will see the answer until fundamental research with the verve and style of that which elucidated the brain-injury syndrome and the neuropathology of perceptual handicaps finds it.

I suspect that answers offered by testing, statistical analysis and speculation that constitute so much of the research today will remain vague, ambiguous and unsatisfactory.

The longitudinal studies have given us clues. They show that effective intervention often makes the difference between a full, independent life and an empty, dependent one.

They do not show why, however. And we can only assume that somehow nature has been persuaded by environment to mend its mistakes.

All we do know is that given a program of education and training that deals with his supposed neuromental disabilities and enables him to learn, the Other Child has a very good chance of becoming a competent adult. We did not know that thirty years ago.

NOTES

Chapter 1   FROM RESTORATION TO REJECTION

1. Kugel, R. B., and Wolfensberger, W., ed. *Patterns in Residential Services for the Mentally Retarded.* Washington, D.C.: President's Commission on Mental Retardation, 1969.

2. *Survey of Historical Attitudes Toward Mental Retardation* by the Institute of Research and Development, Inc., Harrisburg, Pa., 1975.

3. *Ibid.*

4. *Ibid.*

5. *Ibid.*

6. Watson, R. J. *The Great Psychologists.* New York: J. B. Lippincott, 1962.

7. Force, G., compiler. *The Jefferson Drafts for the Declaration of Independence.* Washington, D.C.: Acropolis Books, 1963.

8. Karier, C. J. "Testing for Order and Control in the Corporate Liberal State," in Block, N.J., and Dworkin, G., eds. *The IQ Controversy.* New York: Pantheon Books, 1976.

9. Terman, L. M. *The Measurement of Intelligence.* Boston: Houghton Mifflin Co., 1916.

10. Boyd, W. *Genetics and the Races of Man.* Boston: Little, Brown & Co., 1952.

11. Goddard, H. H. *The Kallikak Family.* New York: Macmillan Co., 1912.

12. *Ibid.*

13. Montagu, A. *Race and IQ.* New York: Oxford University Press, 1975.

14. Karier, *op. cit.*

15. Wechsler, D. *Measurement and Appraisal of Adult Intelligence.* Baltimore: Williams and Wilkins, 1939.

16. Karier, *op. cit.*

17. *Ibid.*

18. Kamin, L. J. "Heredity, Intelligence, Politics and Psychology II," in Block & Dworkin, *op. cit.*

19. Karier, *op. cit.*

Chapter 2   THE ENDLESS CONTROVERSY

1. Piaget, J. *Origins of Intelligence in Children*, translated from French by Margaret Cook. New York: International Universities Press, Inc., 1952.

2. *Ibid.*

3. Dybwad, G. *New Neighbors.* Report of the President's Committee on Mental Retardation, Washington, D.C., 1974.

4. *Ibid.*

5. Bane, M. J., and Jencks, C. "Five Myths About Your IQ," in Block, N. J., and Dworkin, G. *The IQ Controversy.* New York: Pantheon Books, 1976.

6. Montagu, A., ed. *Race and IQ.* New York: Oxford University Press, 1975.

7. The studies were made by Newman, et al., 1937; Shields, 1962; Juel-Nielsen, 1965, and Burt, 1966.

8. Kamin, L. J. "Heredity, Intelligence, Politics and Psychology II," in Block and Dworkin, *op. cit.*

9. Montagu, A., *op. cit.*

10. Newman, H. H., Freeman, F. N., and Holzinger, K. J. *Twins, A Study of Heredity and Environment.* Chicago: University of Chicago Press, 1937.

11. Layzer, D. "Science of Superstitions," in Block and Dworkin, *op. cit.*

12. *Ibid.*

13. Hirsch, J. "Behavior-Genetic Analysis and Its Biosocial Consequences," in Block and Dworkin, *op. cit.*

14. *Ibid.*

15. Anastasi, A. *Psychological Testing*, 3d ed. New York: Macmillan Co., 1968.

16. Backhouse, E. T., and Bland, J. *Annals and Memoirs of the Court at Peking.* Boston: Houghton Mifflin Co., 1914, quoted in Boyd, W. C. *Genetics and the Races of Man.* Boston: Little, Brown & Co., 1952.

17. *Science and Public Affairs, The Bulletin of the Atomic Scientists,* vol. 25, March 1970.

18. *Science and Public Affairs,* vol. 25 May 1970.

19. *Ibid.*

20. McGuire, T. R. and Hirsch, J. "General Intelligence and Heritability," in Weizmann, F., and Uzgiris, I. C., eds. *The Structuring of Experience.* New York: Plenum Press, 1977.

21. Beadle, G. and M. *The Language of Life.* Garden City, N.Y.: Doubleday & Co., 1966.

22. Handler, P. *Biology and the Future of Man.* New York: Oxford University Press, 1970.

Chapter 3   THE BRAIN-INJURY SYNDROME

1. Gardner, H. *The Shattered Mind.* New York: Alfred A. Knopf, 1975.

2. Murphy, G. *Historical Introduction to Modern Psychology.* New York: Harcourt Brace, 1949.

3. Strauss, A. A., and Lehtinen, L. E. *Psychopathology and Education of the Brain-Injured Child.* New York: Grune & Stratton, 1947.

4. *Ibid.*

5. Goldstein, K. *The Organism.* New York: American Book Co., 1939.

6. Strauss, A. A., and Kephart, N. C. *Psychopathology and Education of the Brain-Injured Child, Vol. II.* New York: Grune & Stratton, 1955.

7. Murphy, G., *op. cit.*

8. Goldstein, K., *op. cit.*

9. Strauss, A. A., and Lehtinen, L. E., *op. cit.*

10. *Ibid.*

11. *Ibid.*

12. *Ibid.*

13. *Ibid.*

14. *Ibid.*

15. *Ibid.*

16. *Ibid.*

17. *Ibid.*

18. Lewis, R. S. *The Other Child.* New York: Grune & Stratton, 1960.

19. McGuire, T. R., and Hirsch, J. "General Intelligence and Heritability" in Weizmann, F., and Uzgiris, I. C., eds., *The Structuring of Experience.* New York: Plenum Press, 1977.

20. Strauss, A. A., and Lehtinen, L. E., *op. cit.*

21. Strauss, A. A., personal communication, 1956.

22. *Ibid.*

23. Cannon, W. B. *Bodily Change in Pain, Hunger, Fear and Rage.* New York: D. Appleton Co., 1929.

24. Strauss, A. A., and Lehtinen, L. E., *op. cit.*

Chapter 4   THE DISABILITIES SYNDROME

1. Shashoua, V. E. Harvard Medical School. "Identification of Specific Changes in the Pattern of Brain Protein Synthesis After Training." *Science*, vol. 193, Sept. 24, 1976.

2. Aiello, B. "Teaching Exceptional Children." *New York Times*, Apr. 25, 1975.

3. Havighurst, R. J. *The Public Schools of Chicago.* Chicago: Board of Education, 1964.

4. Skeels, H. M. "Adult Status of Children with Contrasting Early Life Experiences." Monographs of the Society for Research in Child Development. Chicago: University of Chicago Press. Serial 105, vol. 31, no. 3, 1966.

5. Heal, L. W. "Developmental Differences Between Institutionalized and Non-Institutionalized Mentally Retarded." Dept. of Special Education, 490-V. University of Illinois, 1974.

6. Kirk, S. A. *Early Education of the Mentally Retarded Child.* Urbana: University of Illinois Press, 1958.

7. Strauss, A. A., and Lehtinen, L. E. *Psychopathology and Education of the Brain-Injured Child.* New York: Grune and Stratton, 1947.

8. Strauss, A. A., and Kephart, N. C. *Psychopathology and Education of the Brain-Injured Child, Vol. II.* Progress in Theory and Clinic. New York: Grune and Stratton, 1955.

9. Goldberg, H. K., and Schiffman, G. B. *Problems of Reading Disabilities.* New York: Grune & Stratton, 1972.

10. Gardner, H. *The Shattered Mind.* New York: Alfred A. Knopf, 1975.

11. Strauss, A. A., and Kephart, N. C., *op. cit.*

12. Strother, C. C. "Psychological Aspects of Learning Disabilities." Second Western Regional Conference, California Association for Neurologically Handicapped Children and Association for Children with Learning Disabilities. Los Angeles, Feb. 3, 1973.

Chapter 5   THE ALUMNI

1. The study was funded by the Bureau of Education for the Handicapped, Office of Education, U.S. Dept. of Health, Education and Welfare, as Project No. 443CH60010, Grant No. OEG 0-74-7453.

2. Speech problems refer to difficulties in articulation such as lisping or stuttering. Language problems are more basic defects in communicative ability. They are related to understanding as well as expressing ideas and wants in oral and written form. Lack of language development in children (as in the Wild Boy of Aveyron) is called *oligophasia*. The more common term, *aphasia*, refers to loss of language after it has developed, usually in adults.

3. Fifteen alumni declined to be interviewed giving various reasons. Some said recollections of their childhood might be painful for them.

4. Lewis, R. S. *The Other Child.* New York: Grune & Stratton, 1960.

5. *Ibid.*

6. *Ibid.*

Chapter 6   REUNION

1. Symposium on the Brain-Injured Child, Marquette University, Milwaukee, Wis. Apr. 26, 1958.

2. In 1956, Illinois Office of Public Instruction issued a report on the progress of ten children in the special class for brain-injured children at Joliet, Illinois. Four made one year of academic progress in each of the three years they were in the class. One made two years of progress in two years; four made two-and-a-half years of progress in three years; one made one year of progress in two years.

Chapter 7   AN EMH FOLLOW-UP

1. Jack C. Dinger. "Post School Adjustment of Special Education Pupils with Implications for Curriculum Revision." An unpublished doctoral dissertation. Pennsylvania State University, 1958.

2. *New York Times*, Apr. 24, 1969.

3. *New York Times*, Apr. 18, 1969.

4. John H. Meier comments in panel discussion of long-term gains from early intervention. American Assn. for the Advancement of Science annual meeting, Denver. Feb. 23, 1977.

5. Jay Magidson, Abt Associates, Inc., research paper, 1974.

6. Seitz, V., Apfel, N., and Efron, C. "Long-term Effects of Early In-

tervention: The New Haven Project." AAAS Denver, Feb. 23, 1977.

7. Kamin, L. *Science and Politics of IQ.* Potomac, Md.: Erlbaum Assoc., 1974.

8. Wade, N. "IQ and Heredity," *Science,* vol. 194, no. 4268, Nov. 26, 1976.

Chapter 8   NORMALIZATION

1. Wolfensberger, W. *Principles of Normalization in Human Services.* National Institute on Mental Retardation, through Leonard Crainford. Toronto, Canada, 1972.

2. *Ibid.*

3. Ginsberg, J. "The Workshop as a Reinforcer of Dysfunction." Paper presented at the 13th International Rehabilitation Congress, Tel Aviv, Israel, June 1976.

4. *Ibid.*

5. Edgerton, R. B., and Bercovici, S. M. "The Cloak of Competence: Years Later." *American Journal of Mental Deficiency,* vol. 80, no. 5, 1976.

Chapter 9   MAINSTREAMING

1. Wolfensberger, W. *Principles of Normalization in Human Services.* National Institute on Mental Retardation, through Leonard Crainford. Toronto, Canada, 1972.

2. *Ibid.*

3. Interview with Prof. Laird Heal, Urbana, Ill., July 26, 1976.

4. Interview with Dr. William M. Cruickshank, Ann Arbor, Mich., Oct. 4, 1976.

5. Wiederholt, J. L. "Historical Perspectives on the Education of the Learning Disabled," in Mann, L., and Sabation, D. A., eds. *Second Review of Special Education.* Philadelphia: JSE Press, 1974.

6. *Ibid.*

7. Cruickshank, W. M. "The Slow Learning Child." *Australian Journal on the Education of Backward Children,* vol. 21, no. 2, July 1974.

8. *Ibid.*

9. Kirk, S. A., "A Behavioral Approach to Learning Disabilities." Conference on Children with Minimal Brain Impairment. Urbana: University of Illinois, Jan. 13–15, 1963.

10. Lehtinen, L. E. "Preliminary Conclusions Affecting Education,"

in Strauss, A. A., Kephart, N. C. *The Brain-Injured Child*, Vol. II. New York: Grune & Stratton, 1955.

11. *Ibid.*

12. McCarthy, J. McR. "The Nature-Nurture Controversy Revisited." Paper given at the 14th International Conference of the Association for Children with Learning Disabilities. Washington, D.C., March 11, 1977.

Chapter 10   THE LEARNING-DISABILITIES MOVEMENT

1. Perlstein, M. A. "The Brain-Damaged Child: What Are His Physical Needs?" *Dallas Medical Journal,* special edition on "The Brain Damaged Child." March, 1956.

2. Richardson, S. O. "Learning Disabilities: An Introduction." Third Annual International Conference, ACLD. Tulsa Okla. March 3–5, 1966.

3. Wiederholt, J. L. "Historical Perspectives on the Education of the Learning Disabled." Mann, L., and Sabatino, D. A., eds. *The Second Review of Special Education.* Philadelphia: JSE Press, 1974.

4. Congressional Record, 95th Cong., vol. 123, no. 39, March 7, 1977.

5. Congressional Quarterly, 1975.

6. Report of the U.S. Office of Education, 1975.

INDEX

Age of Discovery, 49–50
"Alpha" tests, 27–28, 46, 47
American Association for the Advancement of Science, 186
American Association on Mental Deficiency, 11, 37
American Cattle Breeders Association, 14
    Committee on Eugenics, 30
American Eugenics Association, 14
Amerindians, 28
Anglo-Saxons, IQ tests' bias toward, 26–28
Apfel, Nancy H., 185
Aphasia, 107, 108, 122, 147
Armed Forces Qualification Test, 41
Armstrong, Keith, 245
Association for Children with Learning Disabilities (ACLD), 100–101, 108, 249
    founding of, 244–248

Automobile accidents, brain injury from, 57, 150
Aveyron, France, 3–4, 44, 196–197

Bane, Mary Jo, 40
Bank-Mikkelsen, N. E., 196
Bardeen, John, 43
Barnow, Burt S., 184
Barsch, Raymond, 245
Behavior problems of brain-injured child, 79–82
Bell, Alexander Graham, 30
Bercovici, Sylvia M., 218–220
"Beta" tests, 27–28
Bicêtre Lycée, Paris, 6
Billy (Cove School alumnus), 133–139, 231
Binet, Alfred, 16, 20, 24–25, 37
Binet-Simon scale, 25, 26, 147
Biochemical changes, 135
    to improve brains functioning, 85, 99, 239

Blacks
  IQ tests and, 27, 41, 51, 183
  in preschool programs, 41, 51n.,
    180–191
Board of Commissioners of Public
    Charities, 1871 annual report
    of, 9
Boston University, 19
Boyd, William C., 19
Brademas, John, 252
Brain, 59–61, 68
  biochemical changes to improve
    functioning of, 85, 99, 239
  dyslexia and, 106, 231–232
  recovery, 239
  repair of damage, 237–239
Brain-Injured Child, The (Strauss
    and Lehtinen), 240–241
Brain-injured children, 59–60, 65–
    82, 108, 109, 169, 234
  case study, 86–88
  labeling of, 106–109, 114, 240–
    242, 243, 244
  special education for, 65, 67–68,
    74, 76–77, 82, 84, 86–88, 101–
    103, 113–114, 232, 235–236,
    241
  see also Cove School study; Joliet
    report; learning disability
Brain-injury syndrome, 58–82, 83–
    84, 85, 99, 106, 107, 115, 116,
    135, 162, 232, 240, 242
Brandeis University, 38
Brattain, Walter H., 43
Brigham, Carl, 29
Broca, Paul, 60
Burbridge, Hester, 243
Burt, Cyril, 42, 183, 190–191

California, 16
Canada, 45, 245

Canadian Rehabilitation Council
    for the Disabled, 245
Candolle, Alphonse de, 44
Cannon, Walter B., 82
Carnegie Corporation, 51
Carnegie Institution of Washington,
    30–31
Catastrophic reaction, 79–80, 81,
    82, 116
  case study, 140–143
Cattell Infant Intelligence Scale,
    94, 95
Cerebral palsy, brain damage from,
    154, 155, 207
Charlie (Chicago School and Work-
    shop graduate), 215–218
Chicago, Illinois, 133–135, 184,
    197, 199, 218
Chicago Board of Education, 86
Chicago School and Workshop,
    200–218
Chien Lung, Emperor of China, 50
China, 50
Churchill, Winston, 105
Clark County School District, Las
    Vegas, 247
College Entrance Examination
    Board, 29
Columbia University, 7, 50–51, 162
Communities for the mentally han-
    dicapped, 7, 96, 195, 197,
    198–200
  see also Workshops
Concept formation, 74–78
Cook County Family Court, 32–33
Cooke, Dr. Robert, 180
Coral Gables, Florida, Academy,
    Institute of Reading, 247
Counting problems, 103
Cove Schools, Wisconsin, 88, 130–
    131, 134, 137, 140, 144, 244
Cove School study, 115–143

case for special education, 130–133

employment, 116, 119–121, 175

etiology, 117

intelligence test results, 117–119

the interviews, 126–128

living arrangements, 121–126

personality inventory, 128–130

Cretinism, 6

Criminality and mental deficiency, 10, 11, 16, 127

Crissey, Marie Skodak, 88–89

Cruickshank, Dr., 228–229, 233, 240, 245

Cunningham Public School, Joliet, Illinois, 144–171, 244

"itinerant" teaching program, 145, 157–158, 167–168, 169

Dallas Medical Journal, 241–242

Danny (Chicago School and Workshop graduate), 211–213

Darwin, Charles, 11, 12, 13, 14, 18, 34

Davenport, Charles B., 29, 30

Denmark, 196

DeVries, Hugo, 18

Disabilities syndrome, 83–109

"Disabled," *see* Learning disabilities

Disraeli, Benjamin, 45

Distraction and disinhibition, 67–70, 80, 82, 102, 103, 116, 145, 232, 236, 240, 242

Dix, Dorothea, 6

Dobzhansky, Theodosius, 238

Down, John Hayden Langdon, 57

Down's syndrome, 57

Driving ability, 126, 156, 177, 212

Drosophila, 18–20

Drugs, mother's use of, 57

Dybwad, Gunnar, 38, 39

Dye, H. B., 88–89, 96

Dyslexia, 104–106, 107, 108, 114, 133–139, 231, 232

Easter Seal Research Foundation of the National Society for Crippled Children and Adults, Inc., 243

Economic status

Chicago School and Workshop study, 213–214

Cove School study, 116, 121

environmental stimulus and, 94

Evanston EMH follow-up study, 174

genetic inheritance and, 40–42

Edgerton, Robert B., 218–220

Edison, Thomas, 105

Edmonton, Alberta, Aphasic Association, 246

Educable mentally handicapped (EMH), Evanston follow-up study, 172–179

Education, continuing, 169

Chicago School and Workshop study, 212

Cove School study results, 131–133, 135, 138–139, 141–142

Evanston EMH follow-up study, 177

Joliet case studies, 147, 152, 155, 159, 160, 165, 169, 170, 171

Education of the Handicapped Act (Public Law 94–142), 108, 248, 251–252

Senate Bill 6 amending, 253–254

Efron, Nancy, 185

Ehrlich, Paul, 105

Einstein, Albert, 105

Electroencephalograph, 66, 106–107, 117, 134

Elementary and Secondary Education Act, Title VI, 248, 251–252
Elwyn School, Pennsylvania, 10, 16
Emotionally disturbed children, 108
Employment
    Chicago School and Workshop case studies, 205–206, 207, 208, 213–214, 215, 217
    Cove School study, 116, 119–121, 175
    Evanston EMH follow-up study, 173–174, 176, 177–179
    Joliet case studies, 147–148, 150–152, 155, 156, 157–158, 159, 170, 171
    see also Economic status; occupational training
Enlightenment, Age of, 3, 34
Environment, 108
    brain repair and, 237–239
    de-institutionalization trends, 195–220
    heredity vs., 12, 18–20, 28, 32–58, 84, 99, 182, 190–191, 237–239
    IQ variability and stimulation from, 88–89, 169, 197
    perception and, 70–73
    preschool programs for children from deprived, 41, 51n., 180–191, 253, 255
Epilepsy, 147
Eugenics movement, 11–16, 18, 20, 21, 30–31, 39, 99, 114, 241
    immigration and, 28, 47
    sterilization and, 14–16, 20, 26, 30
Eugenics Record Office, 30–31
European immigration
    Northern, 28, 29, 47
    Southern and Eastern, 26, 28–29, 45, 46, 47

Evanston, Illinois, 115, 134, 141, 172
Evanston Township High School, Evanston, Illinois, 172–179, 243
Evolution, theory of, 35–36
    see also Darwin, Charles; genetics; heredity
Eysenck, H. J., 191

Federal Register, 108
Fermi, Enrico, 46
Fernald, Walter E., 14–16
Folling, Dr. Ivan, 55–56
Follow Through, 182, 183, 185–191, 255
Ford, Gerald R., 251
Fort Dix, New Jersey, 21–22
Foster homes, 43, 95, 208, 213–214
France, 3–4, 13, 16, 20, 24–25, 35
Franco-Prussian War, 60
Freeman, F. N., 43
Frostig, Marianne, 245
Fund for Perceptually Handicapped Children, 243–244

Galactosemia, 56
Gall, Franz Joseph, 60
Galton, Francis, 11–14, 30, 44–45, 46
Garvey, Judith, 246
Gelb, Adhemar, 63–64
Generalizing, 75–76
Genetics, 17–20, 31, 51–52, 54–58, 84, 99
    economic inequality and, 41–42
    see also Heredity
George III, King of England, 50
George Washington University, Social Research Group, 184, 185
Georgia State Department of Education, 247

German measles during pregnancy, 161, 162
Germantown, Pennsylvania, 7
Germany, 58, 61–64, 232
    Nazi Party in, 31, 61, 65
Ginsburg, Jacob, 204–205
Glenwood State School, 90
Goddard, Henry Herbert, 20–24, 26, 28, 30, 47, 69
Goiter, 19
Goldberg, Herman, 104–105
Goldstein, Dr. Kurt, 61–65, 68, 70, 84, 88, 227
Goodwill Industries, 208
Gorsch, Mrs. Marion Murray, 154n.
Graham, Ray, 144–146
Great Britain, 12–13, 45, 47, 50, 58, 61, 191, 232
Guggenbuchl, Henry, 6

Hallstrom, Mrs. Gordon, 243
Hard-of-hearing children, 252
Hartford, Connecticut, 7, 184
Hartman, Lenore Dumas, 115–133, 243–244
Harvard Educational Review, 50, 183
Harvard University, 7, 24, 27, 43, 51, 191
    Center for Educational Policy Research at, 40–41
    Graduate School of Education, 16
Havighurst, Robert J., 86
Hawkins, Augustus F., 249
Head, Dr. Henry, 61–63, 227, 232
"Head Start," 41, 51n., 180–185, 187, 255
Head Start Economic Opportunity and Community Partnership Act, 181
Heal, Laird, 95, 226–227

Hereditary Genius (Galton), 12, 13
Heredity, 4, 5, 30, 34–35, 114, 234, 235
    chromosome basis of, 56–57
    vs. environment, 12, 18–20, 28, 32–58, 84, 99, 182, 190–191, 237–239
    eugenics movement and, 11–16, 18, 31, 99, 241
    Goddard research on Kallikaks, 20–24
    Gregor Mendel's work and, 17–20, 23–24, 30
    inherited diseases, 55–57, 107–108, 114
    see also Genetics
Hinshelwood, James, 231–232
Hirsch, Jerry, 45–46, 55, 77–78
History of treatment of mentally handicapped, 3–31, 83–86, 99–109, 196, 197–198, 250
Holzinger, K. J., 43
Hospital for Brain Injury, Frankfurt, 63
Howe, Julia Ward, 7
Howe, Samuel Gridley, 7, 38–39
Human Betterment Foundation, 16
Hydrocephalus, 117
Hyperactivity, 78–79, 81, 82, 102, 116, 131, 135, 146, 220, 232, 240

"Idiocy," 5–6, 37
Illinois, 96, 101, 168, 245
    Office of Public Instruction, 145
    School Code, 108, 109, 168, 230
    see also Chicago School and Workshop; Cunningham Public School, Joliet, Illinois; Evanston Township High School
Illinois State University, 159

"Imbecile," 37, 90, 91
Immigration, IQ tests and, 26, 28–29, 45, 46, 47
Immigration Control Act of 1924, 29, 46
India, 50
Indiana, 16
Indiana State Reformatory, 16
Indiana University, 18
Institute of Exceptional Children, University of Illinois, 96–99
Institutions, see State institutions
Intelligence tests, 13, 16, 24–31, 40, 46–49, 51, 84, 91, 94, 95, 109
    bias of, 26–27, 28, 48, 53
    Chicago School and Workshop study, 207, 208
    child's performance vs. score on, 32
    Cove School study and, 117–119
    Head Start studies, 184
    Joliet case studies and, 147, 150, 169, 170
    myths of, 40–42
International Brotherhood of Electrical Workers, 202
Iowa case study on orphanage children, 89–95, 197
Iowa Department of Public Instruction, 246
IQ ("intelligence quotient")
    as changeable, 84, 88–99, 116, 147, 150, 169, 170, 184, 197, 207, 238
    of Chicago School and Workshop members, 207, 208–209, 211–212
    Cove School study, 117–119
    "educable" range, 114–115, 172, 173, 176, 207
    Evanston EMH follow-up study, 173

Joliet case studies and, 147, 150, 169, 170
mythology of, 40–42
occupational implications of, 29–30, 33, 38, 39, 40–41, 53, 93, 175
race and, 27, 41, 49–55, 183, 190
reading readiness and, 233
Terman and, 25–30, 47, 48–49
testing, see intelligence tests
twin studies, 42–46, 183, 190–191
used for discrimination, 25, 26, 28–31, 32–33, 46–47
Is Early Intervention Effective? (OEO), 182–183
Israel, 45
Itard, Jean, 3–4
"Itinerant" teaching program, 145, 157–158, 167–168, 169, 227

Jeanette (alumna of Cunningham Public School), 150–154
Jencks, Christopher, 40
Jensen, Arthur R., 50–54, 55, 183, 191
Jews, 45–46
    IQ tests and, 28, 29
Johns Hopkins University Hospital, 180
Johnson, Alexander, 11
Johnson, Doris, 104, 244
Joliet Junior College, 147
Joliet Report, 144–171

Kalamazoo, Michigan, 199
Kallikaks, 20–24
Kamin, Leon J., 30, 42–43, 191
Karier, Clarence, 16, 26, 30
Kennedy, John F., 99
Kenneth (alumnus of Cunningham Public School), 157–160

Kephart, Newell C., 84, 106–107, 163–164, 166, 227, 232, 235–236, 240, 244, 245
Kerlin, Dr. Isaac, 10
Kirk, Samuel A., 96–99, 101, 228, 234–235, 243–245, 249–250
Kite, Elizabeth S., 22
Kuhlmann Revision test, 91

Lamarck, Chevalier de, Jean Baptiste Pierre Antoine de Monet, 35
Larson, Charlotte E., 144–171, 244
Laughlin, H. H., 29, 31
Layzer, David, 43–44
Lazarus, Emma, 46
Learning Disabilities Act of 1969, 248
Learning disabilities movement, 240–256
Learning disability, 169, 173, 190, 252
    concept of, 106–109, 113–114, 234–235, 243–246
    retarded vs. children with, 233–236, 244, 255
    see also Brain-injured children
Leeuwenhoek, Anton van, 34
Legislation, 108, 248–249, 251–254
Lehtinen, Laura E., 227, 244, 245
    The Brain-Injured Child, 240–241
    concept formation and, 74
    Cove School study, 115–133
    diagnosing brain-injured children, 66–67, 68, 69
    hyperactivity and, 78, 82
    perception and, 73
    program for brain-injured children, 102, 106, 235–236

at Wayne County Training School, 84, 88
Levy Center, 200, 203
Lewontin, Richard C., 51–54
Limnaea stagnolis, 35
Lippmann, Walter, 47–49
Living arrangements
    Chicago School and Workshop study, 203, 205, 212, 213, 215, 216, 217
    Cove School study, 121–126
    Joliet case studies, 149, 152, 156
London Sunday Times, 191
Louisiana Association for Children with Learning Disabilities, 247

McCarthy, Jeanne McRae, 237–239, 244
McGuire, Terry R., 55, 77–78
Madow, Dr. William, 182
"Mainstreaming," 145, 221–239
Marianne Frostig School for Educational Therapy, 245
Marital status
    Cove School study, 121–122, 138
    Evanston EMH follow-up study, 177
    Joliet case studies, 149, 153–154, 157, 171
Maryland Association for Brain-Injured Children, 245
Massachusetts, 7, 8
Massachusetts School for Idiotic and Feeble Minded Youth, 7, 14–16
Mayo Clinic, Rochester, Minnesota, 147
Measurement of Intelligence, The, 51
Meier, John H., 182–183
Mendel, Gregor Johann, and Mendelian law, 17–20, 23–24, 30

"Mental age," 25, 198, 233
"Mental quotient," 25, 37
Mesirow, Mrs. Aaron, 244, 245
Mexicans, 28, 184
Miami Crippled Children's Association, 247
Michigan, 16
Michigan Association for Children with Learning Disabilities, 247
Middle Ages, 3
Military service, 142, 157, 158–159, 170, 174, 177
Milly (Chicago School and Workshop graduate), 214–215
Minnesota Association for the Brain-Injured, The, 247
Minnesota Multiphasic Personality Inventory (MMPI), 128–129
Minnesota Pre-School test, 147
Missoula, Montana, public schools, 247
"Mongolism," 57
Montagu, Ashley, 25, 41–42, 43
Montgomery County, Maryland, 244
"Moron," 37
Muller, Hermann J., 18, 19–20
Murdoch, Dr. J. M., 10
Myklebust, Helmer R., 104, 244, 245

Nassau County, New York, 247–248
National Academy of Sciences, 27, 29
National Advisory Committee for the Handicapped, 107–108, 248
National Association for Retarded Children and Adults, 99
National Conference on Charities and Corrections, 10, 11

National conferences on Learning Disabilities and Juvenile Delinquency, 249
National Educational Finance Project, 252
National Institute on Mental Retardation, Toronto, Canada, 223
National Research Council, 29
National Youth Administration, 33
Nebraska Psychiatric Institute, 223
Neurosurgery, 61
New Jersey, 21
New Jersey Association for Brain-Injured Children, 247
Newman, H. H., 43
New Republic, 47–49
New York Association for Brain-Injured Children, 247–248
New York, 245, 248
    State Education Commissioner, 101, 189
New York City, 247–248
    school study, 187–190
New York World, 47
Nirje, Bengt, 196
Nordic immigration, 29, 47
"Normalization," 196–220
Northwestern University, 104, 162, 241, 244

Occupational training, 38, 39, 53, 100, 141
    in high school, 172–175, 176, 177
    IQ tests and, 29–30, 33, 38, 40–41, 53, 93, 175
    workshops for, 100, 125, 200–205
    see also Economic status; employment

Office of Child Development, HEW, 182, 184, 186, 224–225
Office of Economic Opportunity (OEO), 180, 181, 182–183
Ontario Association for Children with Learning Disabilities, 245
Orton, Samuel T., 105–106, 227, 232
Other Child, The (Lewis), 241
Oxford International Study Group on Child Neurology, 242
Oxygen deprivation, 57

Pacific State Hospital, Pomona, California, 218–220
Palmer, Francis H., 187–190
Paris Anthropological Society, 60
Patton, George, 105
Pearson, Karl, 13, 14, 45, 46
Pennsylvania, 7, 9, 10, 101, 245, 249
Pennsylvania Association of Retarded Children, 101
Pennsylvania State College, 33
Pepper, Claude, 249
Perception problems, 70–74, 101, 102–103, 107, 108, 116, 240, 242
    among Joliet case studies, 147, 163–164, 166–167
    reading and, 104, 105, 167
Perlstein, Dr. Meyer A., 241–242
Perseveration, 73–74, 80–81, 135, 242
Personality profiles
    Cove School study, 128–130
    Evanston EMH follow-up study, 176
Peter (alumnus of Cunningham Public School), 160–168
Phenylketonuria (PKU), 55–56
Phrenology, 60

Piaget, Jean, 33–36
Pocatello, Idaho, School District, 246
Polk State School, Pennsylvania, 10
Preschool education, 96–99, 101, 180–191, 253, 255
    Head Start, 41, 51n., 180–185, 187, 255
Princeton University, 29, 30, 42–43
Proceedings of the Natural History of Brunn, 17
Program of Special Classes for Children with Learning Disability, A, 247
Pucinski, Roman, 248
Purdue University, 163, 166, 244

Queensland Association for Children with Learning Disabilities, 246
Quetelet, Adolphe, 13

Rabinowitch, Eugene, 54–55
Race, intelligence and, 27, 41, 49–55, 183, 190
Racine, Wisconsin, 88, 115, 140
Railsback, Tom, 249
Ralph (perceptually handicapped boy), 229–230
Reading, 118
    age to start, 77, 233
    case study of dyslexic, 133–139, 231
    Chicago School and Workshop study, 212, 214
    dyslexia, 104–106, 107, 108, 114, 133–139, 231–232
    Evanston EMH follow-up study, 176
    Joliet case studies, 148, 157, 158, 159–161, 163

Reasoning, subjects requiring, 77
Renaissance, 3
"Retarded," 37, 39–40, 67*n*, 106,
    108–109, 114, 183, 252
  brain-injured children and, 74, 76
  vs. disabled, 233–236, 244, 255
  hereditary disease and, 55–57,
    107–108, 114
  with learning disabilities, 115
  "normalization" program for,
    196–200
  occupational training for, 172
Retrospection, 74–75
Richardson, Dr. Sylvia O., 242
Robert Morris School, South Bound
    Brook, New Jersey, 247
Rodin, Auguste, 105
Rogan, Laura Lehtinen, *see* Lehti-
    nen, Laura
Roger (alumnus of Cunningham
    Public School), 146–149
Rousseau, Jean-Jacques, 4

Sam (Chicago School and Work-
    shop graduate), 205–207
Schiffman, Gilbert B., 104–105
"Schn." (German soldier), 63–64
Scholastic Aptitude Test (SAT),
    29, 33
Science, 191
*Science and Public Affairs: The
    Bulletin of the Atomic Scien-
    tists*, 54–55
Seguin, Edouard, 5–6, 7
Seguin, Edward C., 7
Seitz, Dr. Victoria, 185, 187
Sensation and perception, 70–73
Shockley, William B., 43
Simon, Theodore, 24–25
Skeels, Harold M., 88–95, 197
Skodak, Marie, 89–90, 96

Snow, Phoebe, 154
South American high civilizations,
    50
Special education
  for brain-injured children, 65,
    67–68, 74, 76–77, 82, 84, 86–
    88, 101–103, 232, 235–236,
    241
  Chicago School and Workshop,
    200–218
  Cove School study, 115–143
  court cases establishing public
    funds for, 101
  deficiencies in, 85–88
  foundations of, 3–4
  funds for, 5, 7, 101, 108, 181,
    184, 251–252, 253, 254
  heredity vs. environment debate
    and, 34–40, 50–53, 55
  Joliet report, 144–171
  labeling of the slow child and,
    40, 108–109, 114, 168, 234–
    235, 240–242, 243–246
  "mainstreaming," 145, 221–239
  occupational training, 38, 39, 53,
    100, 141, 172–175, 176, 177
  parents' demands for, 83–84, 85,
    99–101, 228–229, 241, 245–
    247
  preschool, 41, 51*n*., 101, 180–
    191, 233, 235
  teaching techniques, 103, 168–
    169
Stanford-Binet Intelligence Scale,
    26–27, 28, 33, 48, 91, 94, 208
Stanford Early School Achievement
    Test, 185
Stanford University, 16, 24, 26, 43,
    47, 182
State institutions, 5, 6–11, 38, 39,
    130, 192, 216–217
  case studies indicting, 89–99, 197

de-institutionalization trend, 195–220
  as farm colonies, 8–9
  follow-up study on former patients of, 218–220
State University of Iowa Medical School, 105
State University of New York at Stony Brook, 187
Statistics, psychological measurement and, 13
Sterilization and eugenics, 14–16, 20, 26, 30–31
Stern, William, 25, 37
Strauss, Alfred A., 227, 228
  The Brain-Injured Child, 240–241
  brain-injury syndrome and, 61–70, 73, 74, 78, 82, 106–107, 113, 140, 232
  brain recovery, 239
  Cove Schools and, 88, 115, 140
  program for brain-injured children, 102, 143, 232, 235–236
  at Wayne County Training School, 84
Strauss, Marie, 88
Strephosymbolia, 232
Strokes, 60, 68, 146–147, 231, 237–238
Strothers, Charles R., 107
Study of American Intelligence, A (Brigham), 29
Stuttering, 154, 155
Sweden, 196
Syracuse University, 245

Tannhauser, Miriam, 244
Tennessee Valley Authority, 47
Terman, Lewis M., 16, 24–30, 47, 48–49

Texas Association for Children with Learning Disabilities, 247
Thalamus, 81–82
Thorndike, Edward L., 30, 50–51
Tony (Chicago School and Workshop graduate), 207–211
"Trainable," 90
  see also IQ, "educable" range
Training School for Feeble Minded Girls and Boys, Vineland, New Jersey, 20, 22, 24, 26
Training School for the Idiotic and Feeble Minded Children, Pennsylvania, 9
Transitional Employment Program, 200–205
Trauma, 57, 66, 67, 68, 82, 99, 114, 231
Traumatic dementia, *see* brain-injury syndrome
Twins, studies of, 42–46, 183, 190–191

United States, 24, 45, 61, 64, 65
  history of treatment of mentally handicapped in, 6–11, 13–16, 25–31, 83–86, 99–109, 190, 196, 197–198, 232, 250
  preschool programs in, 41, 51n., 180–191, 253, 255
  special education in, *see* Special education
U.S. Army, 10
  intelligence testing by, 27–28, 46, 47
U.S. Commission on Civil Rights, 53
U.S. Commissioner of Education, 253
U.S. Congress, 84, 248–249, 251–254

U.S. Department of Health, Education and Welfare (HEW), 181–182, 184, 186, 224–225
U.S. Department of Labor, 54
U.S. Office of Education, 54, 248, 252
Bureau for the Handicapped, 101
U.S. Public Health Service, 28
U.S. Supreme Court, 5, 16, 84
University of Arizona, Tucson, 237, 244, 249
University of Barcelona, 65
University of California
at Berkeley, 50
at Los Angeles, 218
University of Chicago, 43, 46, 86
University of Cincinnati College of Medicine, 242
University of the City of New York (New York University), 7
University of Heidelberg, 65
University of Illinois, 16, 45, 55, 77–78, 95, 96, 223
conference on Children with Minimal Brain Impairment, 1963, 243
Institute for Research on Exceptional Children, 243
University of Washington, 107
University of Wisconsin, 184, 245

Vic (Cove School alumnus), 140–143
"Victor" ("Wild Boy of Aveyron"), 3–4, 44, 196–197

Walter E. Fernald School, 7
Warren, Ohio, Head Start Study, 184–185

Washington, 16, 249
Washington, D.C., 101
Wayne County Training School, Northville, Michigan, 65–66, 84, 88
Wechsler, David, 28
Wechsler Intelligence Scale for Adults (WISA), 117–119, 207, 208
Wechsler Intelligence Scale for Children (WISC), 94, 117–119, 147, 150, 189
Weizmann, Chaim, 45
Werner, Heinz, 75, 84, 88, 227, 228, 232
West, Margaret, 172–179
Westinghouse Learning Corporation, 181–182, 184
Wiederholt, Dr. J. Lee, 232, 244
Williams, Harrison A., 251
Wilmarth, A. W., 11
Wilson, Woodrow, 105
Wisconsin, 88, 130–131, 134, 137, 140, 144, 244
Wolfensberger, Wolf, 196, 222–223
Workshops, 198–200
teaching industrial tasks, 100, 125, 200–218
World War I, 58, 61

Yale University, 96, 185–187
Yarborough, Ralph, 248
Yellow jaundice, 205
Yerkes, Robert, 24, 27–30, 31
YWCA, 176

Zigler, Edward, 96
Zoe (Chicago School and Workshop graduate), 213–214